HOWELLS
His Life and World

BY VAN WYCK BROOKS

Published by E. P. DUTTON & Co., INC.

WILLIAM DEAN HOWELLS, 1896

HOWELLS

His Life and World

By Van Wyck Brooks

E. P. DUTTON & CO., INC.
NEW YORK   1959

CONTENTS

PREFATORY NOTE

I AM GREATLY indebted to Miss Mildred Howells and Professor William White Howells as well as to the custodians of two Harvard libraries. To Mr. William A. Jackson and Miss Caroline Jakeman I owe the privilege of examining the letters of Howells and his correspondents that are now kept in the Houghton Library. Mr. Paul H. Buck and Mr. Robert H. Haynes were extremely kind in opening to me the great resources of the Widener Library. I am also obliged to Professors William M. Gibson and George Arms for their bibliography of Howells,—which I have carefully followed,—and to the studies of Professors Edwin H. Cady and Rudolf Kirk. Miss Mildred Howells approved of my project of writing a life of her father, and she has kindly helped me with the illustrations in this book.

When I have been taken to task for my "haphazard documentation," I have remembered William Blake's remark, "Art and science cannot exist save in minutely organized particulars." If I were to document all the particulars that are minutely organized here, I should be obliged to fill another volume, and readers who are disposed to trust me will not, I think, regret this absence of the usual scholarly apparatus. I use footnotes not so much to prove that I am right as to convey additional information, and readers who feel that I have plagiarized Howells himself I refer to his own essay "The Psychology of Plagiarism" in *Literature and Life*. I have not attempted to write a definitive biography, but I have long been interested in the author of whom Rudyard Kipling wrote, in 1921, to the American Academy of Arts and Letters: "The essential power of the man and the craftsman, his equal gentleness, and, above all, his certainty within himself, are as present to my mind now as then, and with these I recall the slow sideways inclination of the head, and the settling of the chin into the collar that accompanied the even, courteous delivery of the assured words."

HOWELLS

His Life and World

STARTING FROM COLUMBUS

BEFORE THE Civil War broke out, William Dean Howells had been living for three or four years in Columbus, Ohio, where, as a reporter attached to the State Legislature, he had his own desk in the capitol building. In 1860, an aspiring poet, this young man of twenty-three had spent much of his youth working at the type-case in one little town or another to which his father, a country editor, was led by "my constant tempter, Hope." For so this benevolent visionary described his dæmon. The son, slight, short, with a winning manner, dark eyes and a black moustache had set up his own compositions in poetry and prose, at twelve or thirteen years old, directly in type; and with a friend he had published a volume of poems. Now, in the capital of the state, dreaming of a wider world,—and "the pleasures which other sages pretend are so vapid," as he was to remark in *Years of My Youth* —he delighted in some of the girls who were waiting and willing to be called upon in their large pleasant houses on the wide shady streets. Like his own character Shelley Ray, he felt that young women were "the elements" not only of love but of literature also.

The elder Howells told one of his friends that William was a continuation of his own efforts and aspirations, and in fact many of the traits of his unfocussed life were to reappear in this one of his eight children. Born in Wales and brought to America when he was a year old, the son of a Methodist apothecary who had once been a Quaker and who led camp-meetings in the woods, he had become a Swedenborgian and looked for the New Jerusalem and "the wonder" of universal harmony "that shall be." A radical abolitionist and one of the backwoods Utopians who expected to see the millennium any morning, he had published a magazine, *The Gleaner*, reprinting selections from the English poets whom he liked to read aloud in the family circle. He preferred those who celebrated the life of simple villagers, for he said rural life appealed to him because it was romantic, poetic and free. He had once published an English grammar, he was known to have written a melodrama, and he had composed and printed two Swedenborgian tracts, *The Science of Correspondences* and *The Free Will of Man and the Origin of Evil*. Moreover, he was a versatile and adventurous craftsman. He made a Welsh harp of his own design, he made a flute for one of his boys, he contrived a barometer and shaped a skiff for the river, and he built single-handed the little brick house in which William had been born in Martin's Ferry. He invented a kind of grape-scissors for which, in later years, his son's friend Mark Twain tried to find a market, and when William was consul in Venice, he suggested sending there oars for the gondoliers to be made in Ohio. Meanwhile, always hopeful, he had edited small-town papers in Hamilton, Dayton, Jefferson and Ashtabula.

A type of the generally radical and idealistic frontier West, informally but deeply religious, ingenious and deft, this embryonic literary man was to become a State senator and the American consul at Quebec and Toronto. Already, as clerk of the Legislature, he had influential political friends, and he had even a protégé in a future President of the United States whom he was advising at present and advancing for Congress. James A. Garfield became an intimate family friend, while William Dean Howells was to see much of Rutherford B. Hayes when he married this other Ohio President's cousin. He had lived in the thick of politics almost from childhood, and, reading law with Senator Wade, he spent many an evening at parties at Salmon P. Chase's, the Governor's, house in Columbus. But he had small interest in politics, for literature filled his horizon, and the life of the little capital left no such traces in his mind as the years he had spent as a boy in rural Ohio. He recalled the smell of the tulip blossoms and the fragrance of the leafy mould under his bare feet near the log cabin where his family had spent a year in a clearing in the forest, close to the mill where his father hoped that his ideal of "a true state of things" might find some such an embodiment as Robert Owen's. He had known the woods, still full of deer, the clouds of pigeons overhead, the swarms of squirrels rushing up the tree-trunks and swishing as they leaped from bough to bough, the pigs running free and battening on the hickory nuts, the turtle-doves nesting in the oaks. He had watched the white covered wagons crawling westward, as he described them in his poem, *The Movers*, perhaps to Oregon where the other boys all seemed eager to follow them and grow up on the plains as trappers and hunters. He had heard stories of the great camp-meetings in the days of the Leatherwood God and later when his own grandfather exhorted the mourners, and he had heard the tin horns of the boatmen sending forth wild music through the fog along the Great Miami River. Two of his uncles were steamboat captains, and once his father took him to Pittsburgh in one of their side-wheelers on the Ohio. When, at his suggestion, Mark Twain wrote *Life on the Mississippi,* Howells remembered the lofty chimneys of the old battlemented boats and the effigies of the Indians after whom they were named. One of his own brothers had taken lessons in piloting. He knew well the steamboat landings, the swarming drays and huckster carts, the pedlars and the lonely cabins on the shore with their blue smoke drifting in the morning air.

All these episodes and scenes were to reappear in time in Howells's *Years of My Youth, New Leaf Mills, A Year in a Log Cabin* and *A Boy's Town,*—one of his best books, this last, about the years in Hamilton where he had spent his childhood from three to eleven. He described there the world of boys and its unwritten usages, the laws that were binding upon them, though they were known to boys alone, and that no boy could violate without losing his standing. Only by accident could fathers and mothers catch glimpses of what went on within this world, the superstitions and ideals that governed the movements of boys, as the minds of savages are governed by their customs. One of these laws concerned the true way of running off, which everyone expected to do some time or other, the only way to right oneself against the wrongs of a boy's life and that gave one the highest distinction among the other fellows. For there were certain things one felt a boy should not stand, to be made to split kindling wood and carry in logs, for example, or not to be allowed sometimes to go in swimming; and when the circus bills appeared one began to hear of certain boys who were going to run off with the circus. That was the correct way, unless one ran off to the Indians, and the morning after the circus left one heard that they had gone, though they always turned up at school just the same. In *The Flight of Pony Baker,* Howells was to dramatize this ritual of boys really to perfection; and he showed that he was a master of the child psychology that was scarcely as yet so called during his lifetime.[1] Here and elsewhere he evoked the forest of buckeye and chestnut, the herds of red cattle, the meadows dotted with stumps, and the odour of ink and dusty types in the country printing-houses where he had learned to set type when he was six. The printers spouted Shakespeare as they swayed before the cases or flung themselves on the bar that made the impression, and Howells remembered his brother one day carting in a pig that had been accepted for a year's subscription. The old-fashioned village paper was the staple of reading on this frontier, and the elder Howells hoped to form the tastes and opinions of his farmer readers.

Setting type as a little boy, the younger Howells,—his brother said,—had altogether scarcely a year of schooling; yet he contrived to teach himself German, French and Spanish, and even a little Latin, before he grew up. In the Western Reserve, where he had lived, the people were mostly New Englanders, abolitionists, radicals often, and always readers; and Howells fell in with sympathetic villagers, old and young, who liked to talk books and writers with him. One was an English organ-builder who had a passion for Dickens and with whom he took rambling walks; one was an eccentric doctor, a lover of Poe;[2] and there was a German bookbinder in Columbus, a devotee of Heine, a sensitive refugee of 1848. With Lindau, so to be renamed in *A Hazard of New For-*

---

[1] "Francis Parkman came to me during my final year in Boston for nothing apparently but to tell me of his liking for a book of mine describing boy-life in Southern Ohio a half-century ago. He wished to talk about many points in this which he found the same as his own boyhood in the neighbourhood of Boston, and we could agree that the life of the Anglo-Saxon boy was pretty much the same everywhere."—Howells, *Literary Friends and Acquaintance.*

[2] Howells noted later how Poe had suffered in his "poor little vainglorious self-distrustful country" of the eighteen-forties.

tunes, Howells studied the German that his grandmother spoke,—his mother's mother, a Pennsylvania German; and he kept for a while a diary in the language of Heine. With a friend of his own age he read Shakespeare in the beech woods, on summer afternoons, lying on the grass, the plays from which he was to take the titles of many of his novels, *The Undiscovered Country*, *The Quality of Mercy*, *The Shadow of a Dream* and various others. Moreover, he haunted the theatre in one little town or another where, besides Shakespeare, he saw Kotzebue and certain melodramas, among them *Bombastes Furioso*. Before he was thirteen, he had written five plays himself, along with poetical imitations of Goldsmith, Pope and Scott whom, with the *Heavenly Arcana*, his father read aloud. His father often spoke of *Don Quixote* also, and this had been Howells's favourite book from the time when he was ten and was to remain his favourite at eighty-three.[3] He had studied the language in a Spanish grammar his father had bought from a soldier who had just returned from the Mexican war, and Howells was soon planning to write a life of Cervantes. His mind was full of *Don Quixote* when, barefoot, he drove a cow from Dayton, twelve miles away, to the log cabin where, in the loft he slept in, with snow drifting through chinks in the roof, he found a barrel of paper-covered books. Among these were *The Conquest of Granada* and Longfellow's poems with Spanish themes, the *Coplas de Manrique* and *The Spanish Student*; and presently he and his friends were playing Moors fighting Spaniards instead of the usual Indians fighting settlers. Far across the snows through which he trudged with his father to the printing-

---

[3] During the last months of Howells's life, 1919–1920, he went through *Don Quixote* twice and read it to his daughter. Using Jarvis's translation of 1742, he made an abridgement of the book,—"perhaps the greatest work of human wit,"—that was presently published.

office, Spain shone with an allure that made *Don Quixote* the common theme of his and his father's talk.[4]

This passion of Howells's boyhood was largely to shape his point of view,—though he never visited Spain until he was old,—for he was convinced that what he called Cervantes' "free and simple design" was the best for expressing American life in fiction. In this "event follows event without the fettering control of intrigue" and all "grows naturally out of character and conditions," as he was to remark in *My Literary Passions*; and he believed that this "loose, free and variable form" was peculiarly adapted to the picturing of the world he lived in. He thought the intending author of American fiction should study,—along with *Don Quixote*,—*Lazarillo de Tormes* and other examples of the Spanish picaresque;[5] and meanwhile, looking back, he recalled that, as a boy, he had lived in an atmosphere of ghosts and terrors. Attacked by brain fever and ague, neurotic, hypochondriacal, he was pursued by nightmares, recurrent dreams of which he remembered the horrors many years later, suddenly encountering again and again at the turning of long corridors a tall white-clothed figure half lost in shadows. Then a vast impalpable something would roll towards him with enormous airy billows to swallow

---

[4] "When I read *Don Quixote* and read it and read it again, I put La Mancha first into the map of southern Ohio, and then into that, after an interval of seven or eight years, of northern Ohio; and the scenes I arranged for his adventures were landscapes composed from those about me in my earlier and later boyhood. There was then always something soft and mild in the Don Quixote country, with a blue river and gentle uplands, and woods where one could rest in the shade. . . . Now, instead, in Spain, a treeless plain unrolled itself from sky to sky, clear, dull, empty . . . naked levels."—Howells, *Familiar Spanish Travels*.

[5] Certainly, *Huckleberry Finn* was to be a case in point, and so was Howells's *A Hazard of New Fortunes*. It was quite irrelevant to apply to Howells the fictional standard, for instance, of the later Henry James, who regarded as "mere fluid puddings" the novels of Tolstoy, the literary idol of Howells's own later years.

him up, while the shapes of armed men tormented his repose; they were heralded by alarming martial noises. With awful silent tread, they passed in procession to the house where he lay concealed, crouched in a corner, in a frenzied endeavour to keep out of sight of the windows through which he believed the death shot was to strike him. No doubt there was much in the village life to induce in a small boy the kind of dreams he was presently to find in De Quincey. For instance, he had to ride, bareback, through the woods to buy linen for shrouds for a neighbour's dead children. They had been carried off by a mysterious flux.

Naturally, Howells hated the poor little village life. He felt frozen there, he said, finding it narrow and dull as well as "very grim and at times intolerably sad" (his phrase for the scene of *The Story of a Country Town*). He pined for a larger world and prouder pleasures than the sleigh-rides and dances at taverns and the young people giggling and whispering, looking at photograph albums and coaxing one of the girls to play on the piano. The pleasures of Columbus were at least a little prouder, if only because State capitals were more important in the day of States' Rights before the Civil War, and there, as a political reporter, he was meeting some of the most interesting men in the country. Horace Greeley came there, with his white duster and child's face, bespectacled and framed in long white hair; and so did Whitelaw Reid, his successor on *The Tribune*. Then Artemus Ward appeared, the humorist from Cleveland, on some newspaper mission for *The Plain Dealer*, and, with his profile of a drooping eagle, spent the whole time he was there with Howells.[6] Bayard Taylor also appeared one day there, the first professional au-

[6] Howells wrote an introduction in 1912 for a volume of selections from Artemus Ward.

thor whom Howells had met. He heard Abraham Lincoln speaking in Columbus, a dark figure outlined against pale stone, as well as the black-bearded, black-eyed Louis Kossuth, standing on the steps of the unfinished State House. Kossuth's hat with an ostrich plume over his braided Magyar coat set a fashion for the young men and boys, and Howells wore a Kossuth hat with a plume for a while. He saw and heard Emerson lecturing there, and the sculptor John Quincy Adams Ward, who hoped for a commission to model a statue of the pioneer Simon Kenton, stayed in the same boarding-house with him. Howells went over to Cincinnati to see Moncure D. Conway, who had published some of his poems in *The Dial* of the West.[7] Howells had reviewed the first number of this in the *Ohio State Journal*, making there certain comments on New England that explained why he himself soon wished to live there. Boston, he remarked, was the only city in the country where men were able to "say what they think."[8]

Howells was at that time a poet, "with no wish to be anything else," and, "when no good thing was expected to come

[7] "There was about Howells a sincerity and simplicity, a repose of manner along with a maturity of strength, surprising in a countenance so young,—and, I must add, beautiful,—that I knew perfectly well my new friend had a great career before him."—Moncure D. Conway, *Autobiography*.

[8] "That men should say what they think, outside of Boston, is of course astonishing. . . . It is *not* true that men's minds are expanded in proportion as there is a good deal of land to the acre, or that a generous climate and fertile soil grow rich, warm hearts. We all know that the frozen hills of New England have sheltered in their bleakest ravines the spirit of free thought and open speech, after it has been banished from the South, the West, and the mercenary cities of the Middle States. Until now Boston has been the only place in the land where the inalienable right to think what you please has been practised and upheld. If Cincinnati can place herself beside Boston on this serene eminence, she will accomplish a thing nobler than pork, sublimer than Catawba, more magnificent than Pike's Opera House."—Howells's review, quoted in Conway's *Autobiography*.

out of our Nazareth," he had published poems in *The Atlantic* and *The Saturday Press* (Walt Whitman's organ at the moment in New York). John Hay, who had come from Indiana and read Howells's book in Springfield, where he was Lincoln's private secretary, eager to support Western writers, enquired for him at Columbus, hoping to greet the young poet who happened to be absent. The two were to see one another soon after in the White House. So few were the poets in their vast country that they all knew about one another, and even contrived to meet, virtually as boys; yet Howells's earliest poems were really quite feeble, with too little of the old cabin, and the pioneer chimney and well, that readers expected in poems which came from this region. In the West there could be "no question of origins, only of derivations," Howells was to write many years later; and, save occasionally in subject-matter, these poems were derivative, all Tennyson, or all Longfellow or Heine. Although he hoped to make his poetry speak for its time and place, the only poem of interest was *The Pilot's Story*, about a young planter gambling away the slave-girl who was the mother of his child and who leaped from a Mississippi steamboat and was drowned in the river.[9]

Later, Howells spoke of "the thinness of the social life in the Middle West," which led him to seek his fortune in the Eastern centres; and, no more than Henry James, did he care for the low life that he might have found in saloons and with ward politicians. He was to regret that he had missed this school of reality and the lessons in human nature it might have taught him; and he tried to make up for it in after years by visiting the police courts, several times in Boston and once in Florence. But in Columbus he was able to study, some-

[9] *The Pilot's Story* became popular as a school declamation that was often recited at "exhibitions."

times by falling in love with them, the Lilys and the Julias, the Sallys and Fannys, the vivid and self-reliant girls, whether of the West or of the East, who were to appear in so many of his novels. There,—everywhere,—was the American girl, the sovereign of her world, as all the writers of Howells's epoch thought,[10] in this big brick house or that showing, through the trees, the thrilling light of evening parties. The music of dancing burst through the windows, and on winter evenings one found these beautiful creatures waiting beside the grates of sea-coal fire. Or so it seemed to Howells in this free, simple untrammelled world where in summer the girls sat on the steps at dusk, perhaps with "the devil in them . . . the most lively and amusing," as Howells remembered in a diary that he presently kept. For, as he added, "with us in America this amiable power is not strange to the minds of young ladies." Yet with all this liberty one found the American "innocence" the novelists were to picture and that Mark Twain found in his youth a little further West.[11]

Howells's novels were to abound in young girl characters, sometimes capricious, inconsequent, whimsical, sometimes of a pathetic charm, a gay, ignorant courage and contempt of danger. There were the "hopelessly pretty brides" of *Their*

[10] And as the case really was among many country people. Mrs. Gaylord, in Howells's *A Modern Instance*, "spoke with awe of her daughter and her judgments which is one of the pathetic idiosyncrasies of a certain class of American mothers. They feel themselves to be not so well educated as their daughters, whose fancied knowledge of the world they let outweigh their own experience of life; they are used to deferring to them, and they shrink willingly into household drudges before them, and leave them to order the social affairs of the family."

[11] "There was the utmost liberty among young people,—but no young girl was ever insulted, or seduced, or even scandalously gossiped about. Such things were not even dreamed of in that society, much less spoken of and referred to as possibilities."—Mark Twain, quoted in Bernard De Voto's *Mark Twain at Work.*

Wedding Journey, "with parasols and impertinent little boots
. . . the blushing and trembling joy" one found at Niagara;
and there was many another young woman "sailing through
time, through youthful space, with her electrical lures all out."
Howells, Henry James was to say, was "one of the few writers who hold a key to feminine logic and detect a method in
feminine madness," and he knew the bold bounds over se-
quence and the passion for manœuvring and intrigue of some
of the best women. He was aware of the girlhood that "does
the cheekiest things without knowing what it's about and
fetches down its game whenever it shuts its eyes and fires at
nothing." He knew, moreover, how the helpless male follows
the magic of a voice, heard perhaps in the corridor of a summer hotel, and tracks the invisible girl until he finds her, and
how a girl's name on the case of a piano, seen on a truck on
a Boston street, can obsess the young man who also follows
and finds her. Then he knew the conventional headaches that
keep young ladies from being seen and the devastating effects
of artful dress.[12]

This knowledge was all a development of the experiences
of Howells's youth, long before he came East, in Columbus,
where sometimes the girls sang and played and sometimes
read and talked, perhaps about *Adam Bede,* Thackeray or
Dickens. Or about *The Marble Faun,* the touchstone of the
hour with young people who wished to be thought elect.
"Don't you hate to be *told* to read a book? . . . Don't you
like Thackeray? He's so *cynical* . . . Don't you think Brown-

12 "Who . . . can deny that the cut, the colour, the texture, the stylish
set of dresses, has not had everything to do with the rapture of love's young
dream? Are not certain bits of lace and knots of ribbon as much a part of
it as any smile or sidelong glance of them all? And hath not the long experience of the fair taught them that artful dress is half the virtue of their
spells?"—Howells, *A Chance Acquaintance.*

ing's *The Statue and the Bust* is splendid? . . . Oh, Tennyson, yes! *He's* fascinating . . . Oh, don't you think *Romeo
and Juliet* is divine? . . . Don't you love weird things? . . .
Do you ever have prophetic dreams?" So, in *Indian Summer*,
spoke Imogene Graham; and Theodore Colville, who was
Howells himself, recognized in this the way the girls had
talked in his youth in the West. So also Basil March remembered, in *An Open-Eyed Conspiracy*, that he had "compared
weird experiences" with the girls he knew, asking, "What
was the strangest feeling you ever had?" Howells wrote to a
new friend about one of these girls whose "glowing dark
eyes" were "so different from the glitter and shallow twinkle
of most dark eyes"; they were eyes with "the divine languor in
them." He confessed that he was afraid of her tongue, for his
vanity was thin-skinned and she knew very well "where to
strike." He had known this girl in the "desolate little village"
before he arrived in Columbus, while there, he wrote to the
same friend, he had "fallen in love with a white-faced being
in a blue dress, good heaven! I met her," he continued, "three
times yesterday and died three several divine deaths . . . She
has one of those lily-pale faces . . . night-black eyes, a light
straw hat, mantle indescribable, a blue dress and an angelic
glide. She goes by the office nearly every day and plays the
deuce with the editorials"; and Howells enclosed in his letter
a two-stanza poem about her, written in the "most abominable
German."

The new friend to whom he wrote was the young Oliver
Wendell Holmes, the Mr. Justice Holmes of the far future,
whom he had met in 1860 on a brief visit to Boston, wandering with him on the Common until two in the morning.
Holmes, a Harvard senior at the time, continued to correspond
with him, saying that he liked *The Pilot's Story* when it ap-

peared in *The Atlantic* much better than the Tennysonian piece that followed. "I prefer pure Howells," he said, "to any foreign flavoured productions." Howells, persuading Holmes to read Heine's essay on German philosophy, asked Holmes to send him "your article on Plato"; while, as for himself, he was going in for scepticism, cultivating his incredulity with a course of Voltaire. His father had read to him, some years before, Strauss's *Life of Jesus,* which made Christian belief almost impossible for him, although he had been baptized in the Swedenborgian faith. However, he still felt a religious awe of the seer's lithographic portrait in a full-bottomed wig that hung in the house, and he had bought from an Italian a plaster medallion of the thorn-crowned Christ that stood on his mantel with heads of Shakespeare and Goethe.

Howells had paid his way to Boston with the proceeds of a little book that he had published, with his poems, in 1860, a campaign biography of the presidential candidate, so soon to be elected, Abraham Lincoln. He planned to write letters for the papers at home, fulfilling as well a commission from his Ohio publisher to investigate the factories and mills of the East. He knew whereof he spoke when he wrote in later years of the great paper-mill of Royal Langbrith and the mills of the Mavering family at Ponkwasset Falls. He had found the Lincoln records especially congenial, for, having tasted the pioneer life and known the belated backwoods, he was able to appreciate the wilderness poetry in them.

II

RECONNAISSANCE

YEARS LATER, when Howells was living in Cambridge, he stopped with his father over a night, on one of his visits to Ohio, at the house of Garfield, who had not yet been elected President but who had come home for a summer vacation from Congress. When Howells, who was sitting with the Garfield family on the veranda facing the lawn, began to speak of the poets he had known in New England, Garfield stopped him with a "Just a minute!" and ran down into the grassy space, first to one fence and then to another at the sides. As Howells remembered, Garfield "waved a wild arm of invitation to the neighbours who were also sitting on their back porches. 'Come over here!' he shouted. 'He's telling about Holmes, and Longfellow, and Lowell, and Whittier!' and at his bidding dim forms began to mount the fences and follow him up to the veranda. 'Now go on!' he called to me, when we were all seated, and I went on, while the whippoorwills whirred and whistled round, and the hours drew toward midnight."

Only a few years before, Emily Dickinson, visiting Cambridge, felt it was rather like Westminster Abbey, a poets' corner on a diminished scale; and the writers of whom Howells had spoken were to her "high priests," while *The Atlantic Monthly* was a sort of "temple." Everywhere in the still pas-

toral republic writers felt as she did; most of them were eager
to appear in *The Atlantic*, whether they lived in the East or
the West or the South; and especially in the Western Reserve,
a part of New England transplanted, Boston was the spiritual
capital and Cambridge was revered. Where else could one
catch sight of men like the author of the *Biglow Papers*,
which Howells's father had read to him years before, or the
Autocrat of the Breakfast Table, or the poet of *Hiawatha*, or
William Lloyd Garrison, Sumner, Emerson or Hawthorne?
And where could one find so many spots with stirring associations as the Bunker Hill monument, Faneuil Hall, the South
Church, the Granary Burial Ground, the State House, the
North Church, the old Colonial House and the Old Corner
Bookstore? Two-thirds of the American literature that was
worth speaking of had been written in this corner of New
England; and Howells's Dr. Ellison was typical of the Middle
West in his romantic view of an "ideal" Boston.[1] It was a
political as well as a literary holy land for lovers of free
thought and open speech at a time when the literary life still
had some of the glamour that great wealth had in the time that
was coming.

In short, what Howells called the law of metropolitan attraction led him to Boston naturally at this moment, just as,
when Boston became the play of Hamlet with Hamlet left out,
the same law was to lead him to New York. The region meant
more to him because, "born cultivated," as Lowell was to say,
he was at home with scholars as well as with poets, and be-

[1] "There everything that is noble and grand and liberal and enlightened
in the national life has originated, and I cannot doubt that you will find the
character of its people marked by every attribute of a magnanimous de-
mocracy. . . . A city where man is valued simply and solely for what he is
in himself, and where colour, wealth, family, occupation, and other vulgar
meretricious distinctions are wholly lost sight of in the consideration of individual excellence."—Dr. Ellison, in Howells's *A Chance Acquaintance*.

cause the writers he especially admired never uttered, regarding the West, the slighting things he was to hear in the East so often. Howells, who was always proud of the West, was to find Lowell and Hawthorne, and Emerson also, curious and hopeful about it, feeling almost as much as Whitman that it held the promise of an authentic national literature. Hawthorne said he would like to see "some part of the country on which the damned shadow of Europe had not fallen"; though Howells could not share Lowell's feeling that he ought to go back to Ohio and build up there a career as a Western writer. Unlike so many, he did not believe that the East was in a conspiracy to rob the West of recognition, and he felt, like Mark Twain, that the East was best for his career. Cambridge and Boston were to justify this feeling. Just now he was on a tour of reconnaissance.

Meanwhile, the antiquity he found in New England,—the relative antiquity,—powerfully seized upon Howells's imagination. Like his Kitty Ellison, coming from a world where all was "new and square," he was more than attracted by things that were "old and crooked,"[2] and first of all by Quebec with its narrow irregular streets, its quaint roofs, huddling gables and high-swung calashes. There the picturesque confusion of forms that yet seemed so harmonious, the balconies, the weather-beaten galleries, the balustrades suggested stories to him at once, as if the queer little houses were "the very place

[2] "I go about in a perfect haze of romances, and meet people at every turn who have nothing to do but invite the passing novelist into their houses and have their likenesses done at once for heroes and heroines."— Kitty's letter in Howells's *A Chance Acquaintance*.

Howells wrote later in *Literary Friends and Acquaintance* that, first meeting Lowell, he "began to rave of the beauty and quaintness of French Canada, and to pour out my joy in Quebec." This was obviously the potential novelist's joy that was to lead Howells back to Quebec in two of his early novels.

for things to happen in," as if the people had stepped out of stories and might step back at any moment. So they seemed to Howells as they seemed to Kitty, for whom "the possibilities of fiction" were "overpowering in Quebec." For Howells approached Boston by way of Niagara and the St. Lawrence, the scene of his first novel, *Their Wedding Journey*,—"where the whole landscape looked just like a dream of Evangeline,"— presently reaching Longfellow's Portland, his first old New England town, and the fine square mansions of Salem. He became aware at once of a more complex civilization than he had known in the West, and the big houses, withdrawing themselves in quiet reserve from the tranquil streets, first gave him the idea of family as an actuality and force. Then, driving in the stage from Cambridge to Concord, he found a difference as great between the East and the West as he was soon to find between America and Europe. The stony hillsides, the staggering orchards, the old farmhouses, the grey stone walls, the thick-brackened valleys, the woodland roads, together with the trees, so small after the primeval forests he had known, filled his mind with strange impressions. They gave him, in short, the edge of contrast that was to furnish his novels for twenty years.

Nor were the luminaries disappointing whom he had come to venerate and who were all cordial kindness to the young man from the West, passing him on from one to another as if time did not exist in their calm safe world of thought and leisure. Lowell, whom Howells always saw as a shade larger than life and who especially "ruled my fancy," as he was to write in later years, sent him to Concord with a letter to Hawthorne whose look he found "full of a dark repose." The author of *The Blithedale Romance*, Howells's favourite among his books, seemed to him "always merging into the shadow,"

with a kind of apparitional quality that kept him in a way unknown even to those who thought they knew him best. But,
lighting a cigar, he led the young man up the hill where they
sat together talking on a log in the woods, looking through
the pines over the Concord meadows, while Hawthorne questioned him about the West and spoke with concern of New
England where emotion had been suppressed for generations.
He in turn passed Howells on to Emerson, who lived near by
and who looked at him "with a vague serenity," inviting him,
however, to stay for dinner, after which, walking in the
garden, he spoke of Edgar Allan Poe as "the jingle man."
Howells might have felt that Emerson and Poe were two men
of genius who could not have been themselves if they had
liked each other; and, though Howells was to illustrate Emerson's notion of "embracing the common" and "sitting at the feet
of the familiar,"—for he might have taken for his motto
Emerson's phrase, "I ask not for the great, the remote, the romantic,"—he was ill at ease in the presence of abstract minds.[3]
Thoreau, whom he presently stopped to see, made even John
Brown,—to Howells a pulsating reality,—a kind of essence, a
sublimation of all that John Brown stood for. Thoreau, sitting
against the wall on the opposite side of the room, remained, as
Howells remembered, in a dreamy muse.

Terrestrially minded, Howells himself was less at ease in
Concord than he was in Lowell's Cambridge and Holmes's
Boston, where, invited to dine at the Parker House, he also
met James T. Fields, the editor of *The Atlantic,* Lowell's successor. Knowing his own mind, at twenty-three, and confident
enough, he proposed himself as an assistant under Fields, who

[3] "I was a helplessly concrete young person, and all forms of the abstract,
the air-drawn, afflicted me like physical discomforts."—Howells, *Literary
Friends and Acquaintance.*

may have regretted that he had just filled the post but who was to remember the young man a few years later. Meanwhile, during these four hours,—for they dined at three and broke up at seven,—Holmes said to Lowell, in Howells's presence, "Well, James, this is something like the apostolic succession; this is the laying on of hands," a caressingly ironical phrase that was also prophetic. Howells already looked forward vaguely to living in Boston some day, perhaps as the "linchpin in the hub," as he said in a letter; and before he left the town, by the night-boat to New York, he was also invited to supper by Dr. Holmes. The doctor said that Hawthorne was "like a dim room with a little taper of personality burning on the corner of the mantel," and Howells apparently related to him certain facts of his morbid youth and some of "those messages from the tremulous nerves that we take for prophecies." They talked of presentiments and forebodings, such as Holmes himself was writing about and Howells was to write about in later stories; and then, too excited to think of sleeping, he roamed the streets with the doctor's son, both of whom promised to continue their talk by letter. The two young men explored one another's minds. Holmes's "deeply schooled and definitely regulated life" seemed as anomalous to Howells "as my own desultory and self-found way must have seemed to him."

In New York presently, Howells betook himself at once to the office of *The Saturday Press*, which had published his poems, along with the poems of Thomas Bailey Aldrich and Edmund Clarence Stedman and the writings of John Burroughs and Fitz James O'Brien. The so-called Bohemians gathered there, the Greenwich Villagers of an earlier day who detested what they considered the stuffiness of Boston: "The thought of Boston makes me as ugly as sin," the editor, Henry Clapp, said to Howells. But Howells, who was somewhat in awe of Boston, was right at the moment in thinking that fifty years there were better than a cycle of New York; and, if he did not like the Bohemians, neither did Hawthorne, who had ignored the Bohemian centre in Rome. Or, for that matter, Herman Melville, who had seen them in New York. Although Howells was not to live long enough to know very well the Greenwich Village that blossomed just before the first World War, he remarked of the Bohemians of his time that their generally "unfermented condition" showed that Americans were "too innocent" for Bohemia really. At the moment the only one of the circle who could rank with the New England men was the recently commencing author of *Leaves of Grass,* whom, with an instant liking, Howells met at Pfaff's. The poet leaned back in his chair, reaching out his hand "as if he was giving it to me for good and all," and Howells felt in him a spiritual dignity that was neighbourly, fatherly, brotherly, wholly benign. No one could have been gentler or more winning and endearing. *Leaves of Grass* itself both baffled and impressed him; he thought it "overrated and underrated," and although he had moments of great pleasure in it, he felt it was "the materials of poetry" rather than poetry itself. In this respect, he was scarcely more appreciative than Henry James, who reviewed Whitman's poetry very harshly, while Howells, who saw his own father's ideas in Whitman, was much more sympathetic with his prose. He found this, like Whitman himself, rich, genial and cordial, and he came to see Whitman as a liberating force, an "imperial anarch," and even, years later, as a "Titan."[4]

4 In the *Editor's Study,* in *Harper's,* January 1889, Howells spoke of Whitman's poetry as "eloquent, suggestive, moving, with a lawless, formless beauty of its own."

In his turn, Whitman, referring to Howells, said, "The story writers do not as a rule attract me. Howells is more serious—seems to have something

Returning to Columbus, by way of the night-boat to Albany
—the boat that was to appear in his first novel,—Howells met
Elinor Mead, whom he was to marry the following year, a
girl who had grown up in Vermont, in Brattleboro. She had
come West to visit her cousin, the President Hayes of the future, a cultivated lawyer who lived in Cincinnati, sympathetic
politically with Howells's father and later a sympathetic reader
of Howells himself. One of Elinor Mead's first remarks, when
she appeared in Columbus, was, "Why, have you got *The Atlantic Monthly out here?*" For Ohio was still wild and woolly,
as New Englanders saw it;[5] and Elinor Mead was still more
surprised when Howells told her that in Columbus there were
two or three contributors to the great magazine. As the daughter of a well-known family in Vermont, she knew much more
of the world than he, and, fair and blue-eyed, lively and witty,
she delighted Howells with her gaiety and her intuitive flashes
of wisdom. She was to appear in many of his books as Mrs.
Basil March, whose feminine caprices so amused her husband,
—for one, the perennial enthusiasm for all sorts of love affairs
for which Basil March affectionately teased her. She was, like
all her sex, a bitter aristocrat at heart, or so her husband said
in *Their Wedding Journey,* and, like most New Englanders,
ignorant of the barbarous regions beyond the border of her
native province. But their common pleasure in the droll and
amusing, and especially their willingness to find poetry in
things around them, was to keep their life constantly fresh for
forty-eight years. In short, when the Howellses were married,

---

to say. James is only feathers to me."—*With Walt Whitman in Camden,*
April 28, 1888. Whitman said further, "Howells is genial and ample, rather
inclined to be big, full size."—*ibid,* May 6, 1888.

[5] More than once Howells referred to "those expressions of surprise at
the existence of civilization in a Westerner which Westerners find it so hard
to receive graciously."

they were happily married, something that occasionally occurs even with good writers.

The two evidently became engaged in the course of 1861, before Howells sailed to Europe as consul in Venice, where Elinor Mead followed him in 1862 in the company of her brother, a young sculptor. Those were the easy-going days, before Civil Service reform, when writers and artists were appointed as ambassadors and consuls, a tribute to the imaginative minds whom later governments ignored, though they often had small interest in politics or commerce. Howells had some thought at first of enlisting for the Civil War. "I seriously contemplate a zouave company," he wrote to Dr. Holmes's son, "now forming here of my young men friends . . . But who knows himself nowadays?" he also said; and with him, as with his contemporaries, Mark Twain and Henry James, the question of active service went little further. Meanwhile, after the election of Lincoln, whose life he had written,[6] it seemed to be taken for granted in Columbus that he should have a consul's post, and every important Republican, from the Governor down, signed a petition to the President to give him one. Just so Hawthorne had been rewarded for writing a life of Franklin Pierce. Howells could even feel that a consulate was a public service, if only to keep an eye out for the Confederate privateers that were supposedly at large in the Adriatic. Howells set out for Washington to look into the matter.

There he met Stedman, the poet and critic, a war correspondent at the moment, his good friend in after years, and, in the White House offices, Lincoln's secretary John Hay, who was interested in helping another Western writer. It was Hay who suggested Howells's going to Venice. But among the horde of

[6] It is known that Lincoln drew this book twice out of the Library of Congress and that he annotated a copy of it.

office-seekers, the disappointed who thronged the streets "like uneasy ghosts," as Howells put it, there was one writer whom he did not observe but whom he was to praise in time when this great man had been generally forgotten. In Herman Melville's *Battle-pieces and Aspects of the War,* he was to find "a tender and subtle music," and Howells, the one American writer who was aware of all the others, was still aware of this poet fifty years later. All the romances of that time were "as nothing," he was to write, "in the presence of one such romancer as Herman Melville."

III

IN VENICE

IT WAS A clear blue starlight morning when Howells arrived in Venice, just before dawn at five o'clock, and when the gondola carried him past pale and stately palaces with no sound but the plash of the gondolier's oar. There, surrounded with wondrous grandeur, he was to spend the next four years with virtually nothing to do but write and study, for the city was in a state of commercial decline. The Confederate privateers that he was expected to sweep from the sea never came up the Adriatic, or at least beyond Ancona, where one was sighted; but he could not forget that the British government was fitting them out to prey on the sparse Mediterranean American commerce. Howells was bitter against the English for many years to come. He could not abide the arrogance of these lovers of the "Southrons" who liked to tell the Northerners that they were going to the dogs while they themselves did their best to destroy the republic. Every day at Galignani's he was to read the vitriolic news exulting over Northern disasters in the London papers; and, sailing to Europe by way of England, he had left almost at once, insulted by the brutal comments on Americans he heard there. He had put up in London at the Golden Cross Hotel because David Copperfield had stayed there; then he had travelled overland from Paris to Vienna, approaching Venice by way of the Semmering Pass.

Howells had studied Italian grammar on the voyage from New York, and Venice was to be for him the "Harvard and Yale" that the whale-ship had been for Herman Melville. He was to learn the world there and fit himself, if need were, to teach modern languages at home; and he set to work reading Dante at once with a young priest who sat beside him and entered with tremulous eagerness into his joy in the poet. The young priest kept knotting in his lap the calico handkerchief of the snuff-taker, and sometimes he was so lost in the beatific vision that he left his pupil stumbling in the philological darkness. He was the baffled inventor, the sceptic, whom Howells was to picture in his Don Ippolito and who remarked, "The saints are the gods baptized." Howells himself attempted a long poem in *terza rima*, a tale of the Civil War that was never published, but *The Atlantic* accepted another, *Louis Lebeau's Conversion*, a camp-meeting story that his father had told him. It was written in hexameters and modelled on *Evangeline*, and Louis Lebeau had been a French-Canadian *voyageur*, a boatman and hunter on one of the Western rivers. Howells had been homesick, at first, for Columbus, and, filled with "black fancies," as he wrote in his journal, he dreamed of evening calls there and of a "ravishing little muff," a "jaunty hat with shining plumes" and "feet bounding down the broad stairs."

But, soon absorbed in this new world, he also dreamed of a history of Venice, a subject that he hoped to "set in a new light before himself," like the consul who was also to appear in one of his novels. This project he was never quite to relinquish.[1] Meanwhile, he made friends of several Venetians,

[1] As late as 1900 Howells was still planning a history of Venice, and he drew up in that year a synopsis for the publishers of the book that was never written.

"So many literary Americans have projected such a work that it may now fairly be regarded as a national enterprise."—Professor Elmore, the

among them Biondini, a young man who liked to share his interminable rambles. They went on long evening strolls together from the Campo di Marti to the Public Gardens, through narrow footways between the open spaces, where the ground was often strewn with the shells of pumpkin seeds and the air was rank with the smell of frying cakes. To the sound of the shrieking vendors and the sharp click of women's heels, they talked about the Italian poets and romancers and the accidence and prosody of the French. Howells tried to convert Biondini to his own love of Dickens, about whom he was to have reservations later; but Dickens's humour, which intoxicated Howells, seemed to hurt this Italian's classical sense with something that was like a physical wound. The operatic notion of Italian things bore no relation to the people Howells met, to Tortorini, for instance, who had picked up in England Webster's Unabridged Dictionary, his favourite book. Howells fell in also with an older smooth-shaven man who said he had once swum with Byron from the Port of San Nicolo to his palace door, and he formed a serious friendship with Eugenio Brunetta,[2] a professor at the University of Verona later. It was Brunetta, a lover of Italian poetry and plays, who introduced Howells to the work of the playwright Goldoni, a crucial discovery for the poet from Ohio and one that really changed him into a writer of prose.

For it was Goldoni who brought this young man down to earth, destroying his ideal of romantic glamour, taking him out of his own life and putting him into the lives of others, "whom I felt to be human beings as much as myself." So

consul, in Howells's *A Fearful Responsibility*. Donald G. Mitchell planned to write a history of Venice, and William Roscoe Thayer, F. Marion Crawford and Henry Dwight Sedgwick each wrote one.

2 Towards the end of his life, Howells used the name "Eugenio" as one of his pseudonyms. This was evidently a reminiscence of Eugenio Brunetta.

Howells was to write later in *My Literary Passions*. He had
been riding, as he also said, a "very high aesthetic horse," trying to see things as other poets had seen them, seeing life
through books, in short, and wishing so to see it, instead of as
it was, through his own eyes. He did not abandon poetry; he
was always to pursue it more or less, and with more authenticity
as time went on; and he wrote several poems in Venice, among
them a ballad of mediæval Mantua and *Saint Christopher*,
suggested by a statue on an ivy-covered wall. He even wrote
a short novel in verse, *No Love Lost*, about two American
lovers, engaged before the war, who had fallen in love with
others when they met again in Venice; and *Pordenone*, a
competent poem but imitative still, was also a Venetian compo-
sition. On the wall of an old courtyard through which he
passed every day there remained traces of frescoes by Pordenone, painted at the period of his rivalry with Titian over
Violante, the elder Palma's daughter. The legend was that,
painting there, Pordenone wore a dagger and a sword to repel
an unexpected attack from his furious rival. The story had
given a singular relish to Howells's daily walks. But long before
he left Venice he realized that poetry was not his forte; and
this was very largely the doing of Goldoni.

Fascinated now by Venetian life, Howells saw Goldoni
everywhere, in the lanes and alleys, on bridges, in piazzas and
churches, as if nothing had changed since the eighteenth
century when this Italian Oliver Goldsmith had created the
modern Italian comedy of manners. Replacing the old conventional *commedia dell' arte*, he had brought nature and
reality back to the stage with the types, characters and situations one still observed every day, especially among the middle
and lower classes. He had not been permitted to satirize the

vices of priests or patricians, so his people were often gondoliers, servants, dancers, policemen, publicans and ordinary husbands and wives, or the dark-eyed white-faced Venetian girls
one saw moving about with Southern grace. "If possible, we
avoid a scene," Howells soon wrote, while, "if possible, the
Italians make one"; for they were dramatic by temperament,
usually having the best of times making love, eating and sing-
ing, as Goldoni saw them; and this cunning workman in
human nature was so natural and simple, so cheerful and
sweet, so light, gay, good-hearted, merry and modest that Howells fell in love with him, lastingly, at once. Goldoni might
have written, moreover, *virginibus puerisque*. In a Venice that
was supposed to have been Sodomitic, reputedly filthy and
wicked, this good husband and loyal friend, full of decent
laughter, was as free from the scatological as Trollope or
Dickens. He humanized the romantic city for Howells.

As gradually Howells mastered Italian, he haunted the
theatre more and more, and he never forgot his arrivals in a
gondola, slipping to the water-gate with the sudden waft and
arrest of the gondolier's oar. The red plunge of the lamps
pierced the blackness of the tide, and the water gurgled and
chuckled as the gondola lurched off, while a beggar helped
him up the slippery steps. Then he lost himself in the magic
of Goldoni, whose plays, dramatic soufflés, so slight in texture,
and so graceful and light, were yet so abundant in masterly
and exquisite touches. He read Goldoni's *Memoirs*, which he
was to edit in after years, and visited all the spots in Chioggia
and Venice that were connected with the playwright's life;
and Goldoni's influence was to appear in his own work,
especially in his comedies and farces. In these one was soon
to see practical jokes, absurd situations and cases of mistaken

identity that were borrowed from Goldoni and adapted to American conditions.[3] Meanwhile, this observer of manners and the world, this keen discerner of the springs of action,—who also pleased Howells by deriding the pretensions of rank and always presented merit as the only true distinction,—went far to teach the young American how to look at life, among the Italians as among the Americans later. He showed Howells how to study people in all their variety and how to relate real life to literature; and Howells's earlier novels were also to exhibit the lightness of touch that he had so admired in Goldoni.

Besides this, Howells's marriage, along with the problems of keeping house, brought him into close contact with the life of the people, with the fishermen who stopped at the door with baskets of eels and fish on their heads, the pedlars of firewood, the old woman who brought fresh milk. There were glaziers, too, and the chair-menders with rushes who sat down and plaited forthwith the seats of the chairs, while Elinor Howells filled her sketch-book with scenes from Venetian life, for she was an artist also like her brother, the sculptor. In fact, she drew the illustrations for at least one of his early books. Howells had not been able to go home to be married, so Elinor Mead had come abroad with Larkin Goodhue Mead, and the marriage had presently taken place in Paris. Larkin Mead had surprised his fellow-Vermonters in Brattleboro by modelling in snow a colossal "Recording Angel," and he was on his way to Florence to study the art of sculpture, of which he was to become a professor in the Florentine Academy. He was to spend in Florence the rest of his life, and in the meantime he fell in love with a Venetian girl who lived above the Howellses in the same palazzo. He had seen her walking with

[3] In *Howells and Italy*, James L. Woodress, Jr. enumerates the many striking parallels between the plays of Howells and those of Goldoni.

her parents to and fro, and he had married her when he returned to Venice to act, during Howells's absence, as the vice-consul.

The Howellses had established themselves in an old palace on the Grand Canal where Howells set up the national eagle on a casement of his consulate. It was the Casa Falier, where Marino Faliero was supposed to have been born and where a descendant still lived, Canonico Falier, a mild white-headed priest with crimson stockings. On other floors lived a Dalmatian family, the family of a Modenese marquis, a Frenchwoman and an Englishman, who was the landlord. From the balcony the Howellses could watch the life of the canal, where they came to distinguish at a glance the boats of the various artisans,—carpenters, masons, plasterers and vegetable vendors, —and the gondoliers of the tourists of different nations. The gondolas themselves, both "hearse-like and swan-like," as Fanny said in *No Love Lost*, fascinated Howells who had watched rafts on the Ohio river with a feeling of the joy it must be to navigate one. Imposingly solemn were the funeral processions with the coffin mounted on a catafalque on a boat flanked by two others moving abreast; and there were the regattas that were supposed to have begun at a very early period among the lagoons. From the dining-room the Howellses looked down into a tiny garden that was full of blossoming oleanders; and there was the motley life of the streets with polyglot Russians moving about and gorgeous Levantine figures, Albanian and Turkish. Occasionally a magnificent Greek flashed through the long arcades in dazzling white petticoat and gold-embroidered jacket; and there were the white-coated Austrian officers with whom one could have no relations on pain of losing one's Venetian friends. For conquered Venice was a city in mourning; it had a suppressed look, and the

prouder Venetians never entered the Piazza when the Austrian
military band was playing there. Even the priests were suspected of being spies for the Austrians in these days of the
"Demonstration" of passive resistance when one knew the
opinions of men by the cut of their beards. The Howellses
delighted in the marionettes, with their touches of verisimilitude, and the circuses where many Venetians could see a horse
for the first time; while the little *campi* rang with the music of
the canaries and finches that were hung at the balconies in
cages. On summer evenings, the Piazza of San Marco, with
music and promenades and people drinking coffee and eating
ices, suggested a great soirée in a vast drawing-room. So
Howells felt, as Henry James felt later.

Meanwhile, with her bright active spirit and her cultivated
mind, Howells's young wife set him to reading Ruskin, and
she led him to study Venetian art and the history of painting
and architecture, more or less, naturally enough, through Ruskin's eyes. For virtually all English-speaking people at that
time sat at the feet of this arbiter of the world of art, and they
felt somehow guilty when, defying his adoration of the Gothic,
they dared to find pleasure in the Renaissance. Their talk
became "a jargon, more unintelligible on my part and less on
Elinor's," Howells wrote, "of Titians and Tintorettos, of paint-
ings and sculptures and mosaics, of schools and of manners,
and our reading naturally took that direction, too." Howells
himself was drawn to Sansovino even more than to Titian, the
architect's friend: and in general he was less interested in painting than in architecture. He was even attracted later to Baroque, as one saw in his travel books about Germany and
Spain. It was true that he delighted in Tintoretto's "Paradise,"
which served him as a criterion in the study of painting, but,
characteristically, he enjoyed most Carpaccio and Giovanni

Bellini, who were so full of everyday character and life. He was
rather sceptical regarding art-criticism and the attempt to convey in words the difference between the styles of the various
painters; and, writing about Venice soon, he was happy to
throw no additional darkness on pictures that were obscured
already by the dimness of the churches.[4] Yet he came to know
Venice well from the Lido to the Spanish synagogue, the fish-
market at the Rialto, the house of Othello, Byron's palace and
the prison in the Palace of the Doges; and he translated for a
bookseller there the German guide-book to Venice that he
could perhaps have composed himself.

In point of fact, he was composing, or planning to compose,
a book that omitted most of the facts in the guide-books, along
with all the conventional descriptions and historical sentimen-
talities with which romantic writers had invested the city.
"I've no patience with the follies people think and say about
Venice!" said the consul Ferris in *A Foregone Conclusion*,
expressing Howells's own mind in this matter. Howells was
annoyed by Byron's fol-de-rol about the Bridge of Sighs and
Marino Faliero, as well as by the droll mistakes of Fenimore
Cooper, so unfaithful to Venetian reality in *The Bravo;*[5] and

4 "One does not, if one is as wise as I, attempt to depict pictures."—
Howells, *Familiar Spanish Travels.*

5 Howells shared more or less Mark Twain's feeling about Fenimore
Cooper, failing to see in him the myth-maker and epic poet that appealed
to a later generation. "My knowledge of Cooper was at best vague and of
remote date," he wrote in *Heroines of Fiction;* and he found in Cooper only
"females" of "such an extremely conventional and ladylike deportment in
all circumstances that you wished to kill them."

In his Venetian diary he spoke of Cooper, with his Venice of bravoes and
cutthroats, as "that atrocious old impostor," but he said that Cooper's mistakes did not greatly disturb him. "I never insist on material reality," he
added, and "it would be a matter of indifference to me if Cooper had placed
the Giardini Pubblici on top of the Campanile if he had only dealt more
airily and less tediously with human feeling."

he found that the sights they falsified lost little when the illusions about them were removed. For the rest, he was resolved to tell what the books of travel were slow to present, the everyday life that strangers were most likely to miss and that he was led to observe by the necessities of keeping house and living in the frugal Venetian fashion. Having few social interruptions, Howells and his wife studied the people for amusement, seeing in a day's shopping a sort of campaign from which the shopper returned discomfited and plundered, or laden with the spoils of vanquished shopmen; while it pleased Howells that the artisans worked in old-world, awkward, picturesque ways and not in the handy commonplace modern fashion. Many of their tools were inconvenient and clumsy, yet the handiwork was beautiful in everything they did. Howells, moreover, was always encountering types that pleased his eye, such as the statuesque ancient in the near-by court who was turning a sheet-iron cylinder over a fire with the dignity of a senator and the beard of a saint. The old man might have been turning the wheel of fortune, for, illumined as he was by the red of the flame, he could not have looked more severely grand, although he was only roasting coffee. Then Howells was impressed by the aesthetic perfection of a certain urchin who sold baked cakes of meal near the Piazza and whose cap of red flannel was drawn down over his dark hair and olive skin to the big eyes of lustrous black. Howells learned to row in the gondolier fashion, voyaging with his own boat, like Mr. Erwin, the Englishman, in *The Lady of the Aroostook,* and he found that to keep the gondola's head straight required no small degree of skill.

Elsewhere Howells noted that Cooper was the American author best known to the Italians after Mrs. Stowe. He found that Longfellow was the next best known, and, after him, Washington Irving.

Howells observed, too, with a devouring eye, the Americans who appeared there, mostly travelling women in these war years, occasionally appealing to the consul in their unprotected state, assuming that consuls existed to look after their interests. The daughters, often charming, whom they brought with them involved both their mothers and the consul in complications, and Howells was struck by what he called the mystery of women's nerves, for they seemed always to be having some "old attack." Or something perhaps in the nature of strategic headaches. He noted in his diary their sometimes flabby egoism, or their insipid vanity and watery pride, though often with good nature at the bottom of their folly; and he was also badgered by Austrians who were seeking for brigadier-generalships which they thought they could easily obtain in the Federal armies (if the consul would pay their expenses across the Atlantic). There were other visitors who pleased the consul more. Samuel P. Langley appeared in Venice, later the famous inventor of the heavier-than-air flying-machine, who told Howells the story of *The Lady of the Aroostook,* for he had actually come over from America on a ship with only one woman on board. Henry Ward Beecher appeared on his way to England for a speaking tour on behalf of the Northern cause, followed by Howells's old friend in Ohio, Moncure D. Conway, who was soon to establish himself in a chapel in London. It was thanks to him that Browning read Howells's poems, saying that he found "power and beauty" in them. For John Lothrop Motley, Howells's chief, the Minister to Austria, who drifted about Venice in a gondola with him, he arranged to have documents copied in the Venetian archives to be used in *The United Netherlands;* and Charles Hale arrived, the brother of Edward Everett Hale and at present the American consul-general for Egypt.

For Howells this was a great event because Charles Hale was
the editor of the widely read *Boston Advertiser*, and he accepted for serial publication there the book that Howells had
been writing about Venice. *Venetian Life*, Howells's first real
book, was to remain for many years, as a popular and critical
success, virtually a classic. A generation later, a young man,
Rudyard Kipling, found, in a rest-house on the edge of the Indian desert, a broken copy of these Venetian studies that some
wandering traveller had left behind. Later he wrote, "I spent
most of a hot night reading it by the light of an unsteady oil
lamp . . . It awakened in me—as in who knows how many
young men since?—a deep desire to know this city of mixed
nationalities and fantastic lives described by this consul of the
United States. When at last fate allowed me my desire, and I
came to Venice, phrases and sentences from the pages read so
long ago returned automatically to my memory . . . [The
studies were] the most careful and picturesque I have ever seen
on any part of Italy. They were the thing itself, and that, once
read, they held good and revived themselves in the mind of
a reader after more than a generation is proof, were any
needed, of the justice of the Master's verdict."[6]

Before he left Venice, in 1865, Howells had assembled the
materials for another book, *Italian Journeys*, drawn from notes
about various tours that he and his wife had made, mostly by
diligence, to certain cities. Near by they had followed the
Brenta, with its picturesque villas, recalling Goldoni's day and
Casanova's, where dilapidated rococo statues stood in tangled
gardens and the eighteenth century came once more to life.
They had visited Vicenza, the birthplace of Palladio, and Pe-

[6] *Proceedings of the American Academy of Arts and Letters, 1921.*

Venetian Life, published as a book in 1866, passed through seventeen
editions in twenty-five years. As late as 1907–1908, three new editions were
brought out.

trarch's Arquà in the Euganean hills, and Howells felt that the old ducal cities of Mantua, Modena, Parma, Ferrara should be locked up within their walls to crumble away. He had a sense of outrage at finding them inhabited and their rest broken by sounds of toil and traffic, and he thought it was a shame to tempt these sad old cities into an activity that was unnatural for them. The Howellses stopped at Passagno, Canova's birthplace, on the brink of a declivity all planted with vines, figs and peaches to the watercourse below, where the great man had built a copy of the Pantheon containing casts of all his works in sculpture. Among these was the statue of Washington dressed as a Roman general the original of which had been burned in North Carolina. The venerable custodian had been Canova's body-servant, and he loved to talk of his old master, while he pointed out to Howells the niece of Canova, still living there and evidently used to being looked at. Howells admired this artist because he "rescued the world from swaggering in sculpture," turning it away from Bernini to whom Howells was temperamentally opposed as he was to the romantic extravagance of writers like Byron.

The Howellses visited the Sette Commune, the seven villages where the Cimbri lived, the descendants of the ancient Cimbrian invaders of Rome, now settled in the hills near Bassano, still speaking their own dialect as wood-cutters, hunters and charcoal-burners. Then, sailing from Genoa to Naples, Howells and his wife went on to Rome where they stayed in a modest little street very near the Pantheon. Their apartment, "though small, was apt for me, as Ariosto said of his house," Howells wrote many years later, and there the Armenian archbishop came in his red coach one day to carry the consul off to the Sistine chapel. Pope Pius IX was to say Mass there. Howells, who said he had "no grudge against priests of any rank," unlike many of his countrymen in Rome, was struck by the fierce faces of the French officers in the streets and the red legs of the French soldiers. They were the troops of Napoleon III who had put down Mazzini's republic and were still to guard the Pope for several years. William J. Stillman was established as consul, the painter and founder of the first American art-journal, *The Crayon,* with whom Howells took long walks on the Campagna. Stillman, a follower of Ruskin, had wished for the post that Howells obtained, for he had hoped to carry on Ruskin's work in Venice with a book of his own on Venetian painting. In Rome, Howells also encountered Joseph Severn, the British consul, always eager to talk of his friendship with Keats, and the old Welsh sculptor John Gibson, who had been there when Keats and Severn arrived. Howells touched the right spring when he spoke of his own pleasure in John Gibson's coloured marbles, and the old man went on to talk of his favourite theory with visible delight.

Meanwhile, Howells already had more or less in mind what he described in his diary as an American romance, the scene of which was to be laid in Venice, and he wrote for the *North American Review,* of which Lowell was the editor, an essay that he called "the turning-point of my life." For he felt it had finally turned him from poetry to prose. This was a long and masterly paper, *Recent Italian Comedy,* about the new plays that covered modern life in a country where the novel was all but unknown except in the form of the historical romance in the vein of Manzoni, Scott and Fenimore Cooper. Howells himself had begun to feel that he was almost expatriated, and he had "seen enough of uncountryed Americans in Europe to disgust me with voluntary exile," as he wrote to Lowell. While, as he said in his diary, he looked forward despondently to "the hard and earnest struggle of my native land," he was also convinced that "there is no life in the whole world so cheerful, so social, so beautiful as the American." He was to go home with impressions of Italy that appeared in many of his books, novels and essays of travel, to the end of his days, and he was to return there later for long visits.

ROUNDABOUT TO CAMBRIDGE

O NCE MORE in America, in 1865, Howells cast about for
what his Bartley Hubbard described as a "basis," calling first on Lowell to whom he brought an inkstand in the
shape of a bronze Italian lobster. Lowell, now at the height of
his power as a poet and a critic, no doubt at the moment the
best of American critics, had praised Howells's *Venetian Life*
as "the most careful and picturesque study of any part of
Italy" he had ever seen. It was "the thing itself," he said, adding, to Howells, "You have enough in you to do honour to
our literature." Moreover, he had written to James T. Fields,
his successor on *The Atlantic,* "Howells is sure to be somebody
if he lives." But Fields had nothing at the moment to offer
Howells, and Lowell urged him again to return to the West.
Howells, in fact, went back to Ohio, although he did not in-
tend to remain where, as he had written to his father, he had
been "so wretched"; he had not shaken off, he said, his "old
morbid horror of going back to live" there. He was bent on
making his way in the great literary centres.[1]

[1] "I must profit by this éclat at once. A three months' residence in Ohio
would dissipate it all. . . . I should be dispirited and discouraged. Many
subjects that I could write up at once in New York or Boston, and thus
open place for me, would pass from my mind, and the struggle for position
would be twice as hard."—Howells, Letter to his father from Venice, 1864.

Howells felt about Ohio as Lydia, in *The Lady of the Aroostook,* felt
about South Bradfield, "I could have stayed there, but I couldn't go back."

So at first Howells settled in New York as a free-lance journalist who was soon asked to join *The Nation,* the new intellectual weekly, just established in 1865 by the North of Ireland Protestant, E. L. Godkin. *The Nation* had been printing letters about his Italian journeys that were left over from the Boston *Advertiser,* and Godkin, so often cold and harsh, was drawn at once to Howells, whom he found not only able but "gentle and winning." Howells, on his side, felt "the warmth, the human glow" of Godkin and "the honest greatness" of his mind, as he was to write many years later, recalling "the prevailing brightness" of the office of *The Nation,* to so many others the symbol of censorious gloom. Godkin's weekly had set out to check the shoddy tendencies of this opening age of Reconstruction, the political corruption, the greed and the graft as well as the low standards of the literary world, at least throughout the country beyond New England. It became at once an organ of the universities, focussing the mind of the new generation, expressing the views of older men like Francis Parkman and Charles Eliot Norton, whom Howells first met in New York. It was also building up a staff of first-rate reviewers, among them Henry James and Henry Adams, both of whom lived in Cambridge or were soon to live there. Howells worked at a desk in Godkin's own room, writing a weekly column called "Minor Topics,"—literary gossip, for the most part,—and together, at the end of the afternoon, they walked up Broadway until they reached the corner where Howells turned off. With his wife and little daughter he was living on Ninth Avenue, in "Berickity-Barackity," as they called their boarding-house.

The Nation, Howells wrote in a retrospective article, was "an English liberal journal on American terms, with a strong infusion of Irish wit and fight," and it was his own wit and humour that Godkin chiefly prized him for, the satirical touch that he shared with his young wife. For no one was readier than she to laugh at affectation or, above everything else, at the sentimental, and she could not have failed to enjoy her husband's attack in *The Nation* on "Timothy Titcomb," Josiah Gilbert Holland. The first editor, as he was to be, of the future *Scribner's Monthly* might have been called sanctimonious and was certainly mawkish, and Howells pursued him with ridicule as a writer who poisoned the wells of life by falsifying and distorting all straight feeling. His pages were "flowery," his fancy was "feeble," Howells was presently to say, his work was "puerile" in conception and "crude" in treatment; and this reviewer added that we have a right to expect "some fidelity to our contemporaries and neighbours." Already beginning to formulate his own realistic point of view, Howells made a life-long enemy of this influential personage who did his best in turn to checkmate him. Besides humour, Howells and Godkin had in common "Celtic juices," Howells's phrase for the Irishness of Godkin's mind that matched the Welshness of his own.[2] For the rest, Howells cared little at the moment, much as he cared later, for the great cause of *The Nation*, social reform. He presently voted for General Grant whose administration was to stand for everything that Godkin most detested, and he was by no means sympathetic with Godkin's Cassandra-like prophecies of doom. In fact, he fully shared the "innocent confidence" of the post-war mood of which Henry James was to write in his recollections. Americans felt "publicly purged," said James, "of the dreadful disease which had come within an

[2] Elizabeth Stoddard, the novelist, held a somewhat different view of the relations of these two men. "By the way," she wrote to Howells in 1866, when she was at work on *Temple House*, "I met Mr. Godkin after you left town. I found him a contracted prig in an irreproachable coat. He spoke well of you, but to my amusement and surprise he patronized your mind."

inch of being fatal to us, and . . . by that token warranted sound forever, superlatively safe."

So Howells was to feel for many years until he became convinced that all was going *wrong* with the American republic, and he was to write to Lowell in 1874, "I hated to have you say, 'Land of Broken Promise.' I don't believe you believe it." He shared the general feeling that somehow the Civil War had settled all the troubles of the world, that any more battles were inconceivable[3] and that the "true American Gospel" was "It will all come right in time" (the phrase of the old minister Mr. Waters, in his later novel, *Indian Summer*). Meanwhile, during the three or four months of his connection with Godkin, he wrote a weekly "Letter from New York" to Cincinnati, and he asked Norton if he knew of "some genial little college where a man's ignorance would not be counted against him." He felt competent to teach modern languages there. Then he resumed his old friendship with Edmund Clarence Stedman, who introduced him to others of the New York literati. Whitman had gone to Washington, and the Bohemians he had once encountered had largely lost their former focus, but he always enjoyed the "brave, clear, bright presence" of Stedman himself and the wit of Thomas Bailey Aldrich. Then there was Bayard Taylor, whom he had met in Columbus and at whose New Year's party he fell in again with James T. Fields, who at last offered him the prize for which he had hoped. In short, Fields invited Howells to come to Boston and become the assistant editor of *The Atlantic*.

Now it happened that Aldrich, who had been asked a few weeks before him to edit *Every Saturday*, also in Boston,—an-

---

[3] "Of all things of the past a battle is the least conceivable. I have heard men who fought in many battles say that the recollection was like a dream to them."—Howells, *Their Wedding Journey*.

other magazine published by Ticknor and Fields,—had expressed in one of his letters Howells's own feeling about the relative merits of Boston and New York. The people of Boston were "full-blooded readers," appreciative and trained, he said, and the humblest man of letters had a position there that he did not have in New York. "A knight of the quill" was "supposed necessarily to be a gentleman" there, whereas in New York, said Aldrich, he had "no standing"; and Howells felt all the force of this and much else besides, when, on his twenty-ninth birthday, he went up to Boston. This was in March, 1866. Howells was by no means without reservations regarding not only Boston, which he was always to view with critical detachment, but also regarding New England literature and its "colourless rigidities," the result of generations of puritanism. He was aware that the New England poets felt their vocation as prophets too much for their own good in poetry and that New England had no novels because of an instinct to be true rather to an ideal of life than to life itself. But he was also aware that, whatever its limitations were, this literature was the best the country had produced,—incomparably the best, with two or three exceptions,—and he knew that Boston was the most intellectually civilized city, at the moment, in the Western hemisphere.

As a matter of fact, the Howellses stayed in Boston only two months before they were enabled to buy a house in Cambridge, a "carpenter's box" on the obscurest of streets where they were to live for three or four years. There were pine-trees on either side of the gate, with sweetbriar over the door, there were grapes, currants and blackberries in the garden, and in "cottage quiet" there the Howellses began a life they were to look back upon as intense and simple. It was true that Howells's little study had no sunlight and no heat, but he could have written in an ice-box, one of his friends said; and nothing could have been remoter from the tumult of cities. Events, he wrote, were rarer than genius in Cambridge. Everything was so tranquil that Howells found stimulating the agitation of a cow in a near-by pasture, and he felt even excited when two men walked up the street and a large dog appeared at the corner of the fence. It seemed actually incredible when, a few minutes later, a man drove by in a trotting-buggy, or so he wrote to Charles Eliot Norton, who had found the house for him and who lived at Shady Hill, not far away. There, in the golden-brown study, lighted by candles and student-lamps, with the great Tintoretto and the long windows, Howells's friend Henry James was to have within a year what he called his first initiation into letters. There was no room in Cambridge where Howells was to feel more at home, with the exception of Lowell's study at Elmwood, for Norton who shared Lowell's admiration for *Venetian Life* in the *Advertiser,* was also to remain a faithful and intimate friend. Both were involved in "that afterglow of Italy" which Howells seemed to find everywhere in Cambridge.[4]

While Howells did most of his work at home, he went constantly to Boston on the horse-car that ran to Bowdoin Square and that was often so full of people whom he knew that it had all the elements of an afternoon tea. One often saw some literary celebrity swaying from a strap, Richard Henry Dana, perhaps, who rode to town every day, with his green lawyer's bag, from Harvard Square. In his own office on Tremont Street, where the firm of Ticknor and Fields housed the *North American Review* along with *The Atlantic,* and Aldrich's *Every Saturday* on the floor above, Howells

[4] Norton urged Howells to write a series of portraits of Italian women of the Renaissance. He began a sketch of Lucretia Borgia but gave it up because he could not find enough material in the Boston libraries.

sifted manuscripts, wrote book notices;[5] corrected proofs and corresponded with the contributors he discovered or those whom he found there. His long experience as a practical printer had been largely counted on, and he was expected to take charge of all the new talent of which he knew much more than anyone else. For, whether in Columbus, New York, Washington or Venice, he had met many, at least, of the emerging writers, and he was to know all the talents of the coming generation. Already, before he became editor-in-chief, he developed the eagerness for "the strange voice, the novel scene, the odour of fresh woods and pastures new, the breath of morning, the dawn of tomorrow," as he was to write years later in *Literature and Life.* He was obliged to negotiate with the Olympians, as they seemed to him, the veterans who had founded *The Atlantic* and who were sometimes inaccurate and had to be corrected by this neophyte from the all but unknown West. He waited once, with heart in mouth, in Charles Sumner's study, to submit his doubts regarding a classical quotation of this most scholarly senator who was also touchy, and he called down upon himself even the wrath of Emerson who had kept too long one of his proofs.[6] He concluded that it was not for him to play the censor in a magazine that, after all, these great men had created. They had set it in authority over American literature and he could not assume authority over them.

As time went on, the editor, Fields, placed Howells more

[5] "Outside of Cambridge and Godkin, it appears to me that our literary review-writing world is only one vast Tuckerman . . . Horrible, isn't it, to have only one critic [*The Nation*] for 40,000,000 of people?"—Howells, Letter to Henry James, 1869.

[6] In Emerson's verse, Howells found "a certain beautiful lawlessness," as he wrote later, that "expresses now and then his impatience of smoothness and regularity, his joy in a fractured surface, a broken edge, his exaltation in a pace or two outside the traces."

and more in charge until he took over the editorship in 1871,
—the genial, burly, hirsute Fields, whom Henry James was to
remember as resembling the wire-haired fox terrier who lived
with him in England.[7] James was to enjoy as much as Howells the salon of Mr. and Mrs. Fields,—Fields, with the "singularly graceful young wife," who, he wrote, in those earlier
days, seemed to be "invested with a stately past." Under their
fostering roof, James added, "*The Atlantic Monthly* had virtually come into being." But James, too, like Howells, lived
mostly in Cambridge, and he too saw much of Lowell, to
whom Howells was devoted and who returned the devotion
of this younger friend. Howells remembered later how he
used to falter at Lowell's gate and walk up to his door with
the same palpitations he had felt when he called upon the
girl he was first in love with. But before long he was dining at
Lowell's every week,[8] and often Lowell appeared at his own
little house, suggesting an afternoon's walk, perhaps to Dub-
lin. This was an Irish district built around a graveyard, one
that led Howells to express a grudge against the Irish that
Lowell persuaded him to feel was mean and cruel. It was
Howells's only prejudice except his dislike of the English, and
he was to outgrow both within a few years.

Lowell's Elmwood was two miles from Sacramento Street,
but this did not interfere with these all but weekly pedestrian

[7] "My lamp burns still, my servants are long since at roost, and my faithful hound (a wire-haired fox terrier of celestial breed) looks up from his
dozing in an armchair hard by to present to me his extraordinary facial resemblance to the late James T. Fields. It's one of the funniest likenesses I
ever saw (and most startling), and yet I can't write to Mrs. Fields of my
daily joy in it."—Letter of Henry James to Howells, 1902.

[8] Once when the Christian Socialist, Thomas Hughes, was there, the
warm-hearted author of *Tom Brown's School-Days*. Later Hughes founded
a Utopian colony, "Rugby," in Tennessee; and no doubt Howells had him
in mind in creating the character of David Hughes, the grand old radical
dreamer in *The World of Chance*.

tours, often through the half-frozen Cambridge mud. The two trudged through snow and rain, sometimes along horse-car tracks, perhaps discussing Howells's studies of the Yankee character and country speech that Lowell had made his own in the *Biglow Papers*. At other times, Howells, dropping in, found Lowell sitting among his books, reading some old French poet, or Calderón, or Dante, and turning round "rounder," Howells remembered, than anybody else when he turned to put a log on the fire. Lowell's personal influence in the small world of American letters was at this time all-pervasive, and Howells delighted especially in the care and distinction with which he avoided the slovenliness of American speech. He in turn spoke of Howells as worthy in this respect or that,—sensitiveness of observation, perfection of style,—to be ranked with Longfellow and Hawthorne.

It was a pleasure to Howells in Cambridge that everyone he met in the street seemed to be all liberality and appreciation, that he virtually never heard anything common or mean in this ripe Harvard world of poets and scholars. One day on Brattle Street he was introduced to Longfellow, with his white hair and beard and autumnal bloom, on whose *Evangeline* he had modelled his own long narrative poems and who was at the moment translating Dante. Longfellow's more important poems had been written years before, but he was now writing some of his best sonnets, and he asked Howells, who admired his courage in treating the personal as the universal, to come to his house for meetings of the Dante Club. With the main object of discussing his translation, this brought together the lovers of Italy in Cambridge, all of whom read *Venetian Life,* "the book that made friends with fortune for me," as Howells wrote when it was published in 1866. (*Italian Journeys* followed in 1867.) Ten or twelve scholarly men appeared at these meetings in the Craigie house, among them Holmes, Agassiz, Dana, Lowell and Longfellow's friend, George W. Greene, who had been for many years the consul in Rome. Greene reminded Howells of an old Italian house-priest, cultivated in all the elegances of literary taste, quoting with an exquisite Roman accent the modern Italian poets about whom he was himself soon lecturing at Harvard. Before the supper at nine o'clock, Longfellow read a canto and the others considered it in detail. One evening Lowell read aloud another Biglow paper which he had just written for a second series.

At Longfellow's, Howells was invited to meet and sit beside Dickens at dinner, and both there and at Fields's presently he had good talks with this extraordinary genius and sovereign romancer. Dickens, who was genial and easy in talk, had "everything in manner that his books could make you wish him to be." So Howells wrote, still under the spell of Dickens's mighty imagination. Later, although he never gainsaid the power of the great master, or the wholesome allegiance to life of this wonderful artist, he was to have reservations about the many times when he was not an artist and not a master. But this was after he had developed the method and theory of realism that were naturally antipathetic to much in Dickens, his "air of the theatre" and that "love of stage effect" to which he seemed always willing to sacrifice truth. As for Longfellow, he was always to remain a favourite of Howells, who, though no believer in heroes or hero-worship, exalted into heroes two or three Cambridge authors. It would have pleased him, when Longfellow's name was seldom mentioned except in dispraise, that he remained a world-poet among other peoples, that in his sesquicentennial year his poems were to appear in Communist China and

Russia was to issue a postage-stamp with his portrait on it.

That Cambridge and Boston had reservations about Whittier and Harriet Beecher Stowe, Howells soon learned in *The Atlantic* circle, perhaps before he met the old abolitionist poet and the author of *Uncle Tom's Cabin*. Both seemed no doubt a little too rough and ready. But no one questioned the right of Mrs. Stowe to use the magazine whenever she wished, and she overrode certain objections when she insisted on publishing there the story that Lady Byron had told her. It was the apparently true story of Byron's incestuous relation with his half-sister Augusta Leigh, and Howells, who detested Byron, felt it was worth all it cost, though fifteen thousand subscribers withdrew from *The Atlantic*. With Francis J. Child, the great ballad collector who read him with peculiar zest, Howells had the warmest of friendships, and one day Child drove all the Howellses to the circus in East Cambridge to see a "pancratist, an equilibrist and a splendid strange equestrienne" (as he had promised in his invitation). In Boston, there was Dr. Holmes, who had welcomed the Howellses at once and from whose windows over the bay one saw clouds of gulls and wild ducks in the spring when the ice broke up; and there was Francis Parkman, whom Howells reviewed again and again and who was to write to Howells constantly in praise. That Parkman was the greatest of American historians Howells never doubted, and he said this great writer had made French Canada, the scene of two of his own early books, "the beautiful inheritance of all dreamers." Once at the house of George Ticknor, the historian of Spanish literature and the frosty old man of letters of an earlier epoch, Howells met two English noblemen who had been travelling through the South and who shared his own feeling about the Civil War. Ticknor shook his head in the presence of these liberals, for he was himself a sad reactionary, but it is more than probable that Howells's feeling about the English was modified by his meeting with these men. That, as Sir Walter Besant said, Howells "hated" the English seemed to be true in his first novels,—in the character of Mr. Rose-Black, for one example, the impudent and pushing young dilettante in *A Fearful Responsibility,*—but this was plainly a result of the embittered war-time when Americans had good reasons for resenting the English. How different were the Englishmen who appeared in Howells's later books, Lord Rainford, for instance, in *A Woman's Reason,* with his Utopian ideas, so like those that were latent in Howells's own mind. Then there was the good-natured Westgate of *A Letter of Introduction* and the natural and simple Lord Lioncourt of *Ragged Lady,* who so preferred hunting to being hunted. These characters undoubtedly had some of the traits that Howells had observed in George Ticknor's house years before.

It was usually by horse-car that Howells went to Boston, whether on his way to the office or to see his friends, and also to visit the theatre, a passion already developed in the West, that was by no means shared by the élite of Boston. For the Boston that made itself known to the world in letters, politics and reform cared as little for the stage as fashionable Boston,—or so, at least, it seemed to Howells,—while he who had delighted in Italian comedies and farces still relished burlesque and opera-bouffe. He was soon to experiment with his own comedies and farces. Meanwhile, he studied the horse-car types and even began to weave stories about them. More than once he encountered a young woman in black, for instance, with eyes of a liquid splendour, with heavy bracelets, with arms of an exquisite roundness, great hoops of earrings and a *morbidezza* that made her a startling apparition. She was so precious to wonderment that he felt it would be a kind of loss to learn anything actual about her.

For the rest, unlike most husbands and fathers inhabiting this suburb, this Cambridge frontier between city and country, Howells, working at home by day, while others had gone to Boston, saw the strange characters who came to the door. There was an Irish pedlar of starch, a one-armed soldier who sat down on the steps one afternoon and told him all about the fight at Vicksburg, and there was a sailor, just back from the sea, whose wife was dead and his family lost and who had come to Cambridge to find his daughter. This was a piece of literature made to one's hand, for the sailor was actually just out of prison where he had been sent for bigamy, and the episode that had appeared so perfect as a tragedy did not seem less finished as a farce. Italian harpers came to the door, vendors of plaster statuettes, Canovan deities and dancers, figures of Apollo, a Lombard scissors-grinder, a little old woman from Genoa with packets of needles and pins, thread and tape. Among Howells's doorstep acquaintances were an ex-journalist from Trieste, a green-grocer from Milan who had lived in Athens, a Venetian who carolled a barcarole and a Neapolitan chestnut-roaster all of whom were glad to tell their stories. Howells, who loved gaiety of colour and who knew so well the Italian scene, saw Cambridge as half Italianized, and it seemed to his receptive spirit that all the people of romance, Greeks, fairies and genii, were at his door. They had only to be hospitably treated, he was convinced, to surpass, for the purposes of fiction, the cunningest inventions. To his Emersonian imagination, it was indifferent that Harvard Square was adorned only with a pump and horse-trough instead of the fountain one saw in the piazza at Lucca.

Then his walks about Cambridge, sometimes with Lowell, past outlying cornfields and vacant lots, also yielded scenes that were comic or tragic, like the grocer's cart containing the body of a young girl who had drowned herself, a foretaste of his admired Stephen Crane's *Maggie*. There were, moreover, the simple joys of a trip down the harbour, on the "Rose Standish," to Nantasket Beach, where Silas Lapham was to have his summer cottage, passing green-shuttered passenger boats, steamships of coastwise lines and sailing craft skimming round about them. Howells had noticed that the shabby wharves, with their barrels and bales, hacks and trucks, turned beautiful when you saw them from a little distance; and his light-hearted *A Day's Pleasure* was all the more amusing when the family, arriving, did not go on shore. They decided to stay on the boat and "respect their illusions," and it was then that Cousin Frank defined for Aunt Lucy "our Boston look."[9] Such were the *Suburban Sketches* that appeared in *The Atlantic* and that Howells soon collected in a book, the book that Henry James described as "one of the least known of his productions, but one of the most perfect." James went on to speak of Howells's "unerring sentiment of the American character . . . Other Americans have considered and discoursed upon American life, but no one, surely, has *felt* it so completely as he."

[9] "Why, that's what we call our Boston look . . . You needn't have written anything to have it,—it's as general as tubercular consumption, and is the effect of our universal culture and habit of reading. I heard a New Yorker say once, that if you went into a corner grocery in Boston to buy a codfish, the man would ask you how you liked 'Lucile' whilst he was tying it up."

V

YOUNG CAMBRIDGE

THE JAMES FAMILY had settled in Cambridge in the summer of 1866, only a few months after Howells, who could not remember later where he had first seen Henry James, though the two became almost at once intimate friends. Every other day they met at the James house in Quincy Street or in Howells's carpenter's box, especially on Sundays, when James stayed to supper, eating very little, for he suffered at the time from indigestion. Sitting in winter near the stove, under the kerosene lamp, they read to one another what each was writing. James read to Howells his *Gabrielle de Bergerac*. As much as Howells loved Italy, he loved France.

On other evenings, or afternoons, the two friends roamed the streets or strolled perhaps to the Botanical Garden, where they sat in the sun on the edge of a hotbed of violets, punching their walking-sticks into the sandy path. Or they rambled round Fresh Pond where, one day later, while Howells rowed, James told him the plot of *Roderick Hudson*. Howells was seven years older than James but, as he said in after days, "I did not yet feel my fiction definitely in me." He thought of himself as a poet and a writer of travels, although he was at work on *Suburban Sketches*, while James had already published stories and was dedicated heart and soul to the writing of novels. In the interest of art, as he put it, he re-

54

lated to Howells the tale of his mostly ill-fated uncles and cousins, while he talked about methods of fiction and certain French novelists to whom he was especially devoted. He had spent much of his childhood abroad and his literary tastes were altogether French.

During their largely nocturnal rambles, they settled the true principles of literary art, as Howells wrote to Stedman in New York, adding that James was "a very earnest fellow and I think extremely gifted,—gifted enough to do better than anyone has yet done toward making us a real American novel." He thought James had "every element of success in fiction." One of the questions they talked about was how to eliminate the everlasting young man and young woman, and they imagined a great many intrigues in which these two should not be the principal personages. They dreamed of a kind of novel that would not be obsessed with the monotonous theme of young people in love, and James developed a notable scheme for a story whose interest was to centre in a mother and son. Howells, however, had to admit, when he looked back in later days, that the young man and young woman were everlasting, and that he and James had continued to write about them, though they had somehow moderated the importance of these characters and ascertained more clearly their place in fiction. James had been at once successful with all the American magazines, and he had published two stories in *The Atlantic*,—one before Howells had been connected with it,—and Howells, who said, "I would willingly give you half the magazine," was bent on keeping James for *The Atlantic* alone.[1] Of *The Passionate Pilgrim*,

[1] "There seems at last to be a general waking-up to your merits; and when you've a fame as great as Hawthorne's, you won't forget who was the first, warmest and truest of your admirers, will you?"—Howells, Letter to James, 1869.

which he procured, he was to say in time that it was "an intense piece of American fiction . . . with a life, a feeling, a colour, and above all a prompt distinctness" that were absent from his perhaps more masterly fiction. James, from the first, for him, was an "unrivalled artist . . . a metaphysical genius working to aesthetic results," while, to James, Howells was an "artist born" whose two early travel books belonged "to literature and to the centre and core of it." A year or two later, James wrote to Norton, "Howells edits, and observes and produces—the latter in his own particular line with more and more perfection. His recent *Suburban Sketches* belong, I think, by the wondrous cunning of their manner, to very good literature."

Before long, as editor-in-chief, Howells agreed in advance to serialize James's first novel, *Roderick Hudson,* and James himself was to say, "The new American novel had . . . its first seeds . . . sown very exactly in *Atlantic* soil." Meanwhile, Howells had induced James to write a monthly report on the fine arts in Boston, for he had quite as passionate an enjoyment of pictures as his own fictional character, Rowland Mallet. Howells, confident as a critic of plays, was diffident as an art critic, while James had few doubts in judging art; and John La Farge had said of him, when James studied drawing with William Morris Hunt, that he had "the painter's eye." So he gladly set about writing on pictures not only in Boston but in New York, though he felt obliged to say, "When today we look for 'American art,' we find it mainly in Paris." First or last, he reported on exhibitions of Chase, Eastman Johnson and Winslow Homer, together with William Morris Hunt and certain Barbizon pictures that were shown privately in Boston, and he reviewed a collection of "authentic old masters" at the Athenæum, still an unfamiliar sight for the American public. He spoke of John La Farge's "complex and suggestive work," but he detested Winslow Homer's subjects, his barren plank fences, bald blue skies, big dreary vacant lots, calico sunbonnets and flat-breasted maidens. There was too much in all this that brought before his mind the image of a dish of pie and rural doughnuts.

In short, James found distasteful much in the local scene that Howells was to find amusing and picturesque, beginning with Cambridge,—Howells's delight,—which to James was "dry, flat, hot, sterile and odious," as he wrote in a notebook. To him the town was "about as lively as the inner sepulchre," and the New England that fascinated Howells was generally unpleasant to the author of *A New England Tale* and other stories. A New Yorker born, he was an alien quite as much as Howells there, and one who thoroughly disliked the temper of the region, from which his Southern hero was to rescue violently the heroine of *The Bostonians*, his later novel.[2] He was to betake himself more and more to Europe until in the end he settled there for good, looking back thence on the Cambridge winter, "with the earth like a stone and the sky like a feather." In England, he wrote, the earth was "like a Persian rug—a hearth rug well sprinkled with soot."[3]

But nothing was ever to interrupt the friendship of Henry James and Howells or of Howells and James's brothers, Robertson and William, both of whom often wrote to him, praising his books, in after years, while he saw much of both at the moment in Cambridge. Moreover, the genial wit and sage,

[2] "There is something in all the regular New England scenes and subjects, in fiction, which strikes a chill upon my soul."—James, Letter to Howells, 1873.

[3] In 1875 James wrote to Howells, "I am glad you are dining out and liking Boston. I'm afraid the tender grace of a day that is dead will not revisit *this* stagnant heart. But I come back to New York with a real relish. I feel vastly at home here and really like it."

Henry James the elder, a benevolent Swedenborgian, like his own father, took Howells also under the paternal wing that sheltered all the brothers and Alice, their sister. The most celestial angels, the irrepressible old man said, quoting Swedenborg, his master, were quite unconscious of their own perfection, and for this reason James disliked the consciously ethical "moral men," the Unitarians who supremely worshipped conduct. He had just parted, he said to Howells, with a group of Bostonians who were "simmering in their own fat and putting a nice brown on one another," for to him the complacent were more hopelessly lost than sinners; and one day he went with Howells to call on an old Shaker elder who said his people believed they were living the angelic life. The sage replied that if the Shakers felt that way they were in all probability the sport of hell. Because of the American sentiment of human brotherhood, he preferred the "thin wilderness" he found at home to the "thick wilderness" of England. Howells was amused by the visible constraint put upon the kind old man when he uttered "Father's Ideas" at the dinner-table. Now and then he would break out with some outrageous paradox which the others felt obliged to modify or explain away, and then, Howells wrote in one of his letters, he would be "clapped back into durance again."

One day, from a summer hotel in Maine, he wrote to Howells in Cambridge, sending him a round-robin signed by himself and William, Henry and Alice and a number of their friends[4] who were all gathered there at the end of August. One of them had been reading aloud, as they sat on the piazza, Howells's last effusion in *The Atlantic,* and, fanned by the sea breeze, they were so delighted with it that they

[4] Francis Boott and his daughter Elizabeth, Miss Grace Ashburner and Arthur G. Sedgwick, all well-known in the story of Henry James and Howells.

wished to pay homage to the author. They were eager to tell him, the generous old philosopher said, "how dear you are to the heart of the people here assembled," and, while one of them painted the robin, and another wrote the verses, he did the chirography and all together the signatures. "We shall be extremely glad to impart to you," he said, "a little bit of the great pleasure you have given us"; and this was an illustration of the kind of response that Howells encountered from the first in Cambridge and Boston. He had been there only a year when, in 1867, his old friend from Columbus days, J. Q. A. Ward, wrote to him of a dinner at which, in Boston, he had listened to the youthful writer's praises. The young sculptor had heard Howells "very highly spoken of . . . amongst Cambridge and Harvard men, 'keen' fellows, who are jealous of outsiders and love their New England." It was a party of "literary and artistic" men, and he had listened to "a thorough overhauling" of Howells and his work. "There was not a word said but you would have been pleased to hear," he wrote. "I wanted to hear an impartial opinion of a man who was not supposed to have a personal friend in the room. It was not mean, was it?—for my fist was hard clenched to knock down the first man that abused you . . . I felt proud of my early knowledge of you."

Who were these "literary and artistic" men with whom J. Q. A. Ward had dined when Howells was still virtually a stranger in the region of Boston? No doubt most or many of them were members of The Club that was founded in 1870 in Cambridge, a group of young men of about Howells's age who dined together once a month in winter. Among them, besides Howells, were Charles S. Peirce, William and Henry James, Oliver Wendell Holmes the younger, John Fiske, Henry Adams, Brooks Adams and Thomas Sergeant

Perry. It was an understatement when Perry remarked that they had "the best talk in town" there, for, taken together, the members stood for a good half of the American literature of the coming generation. Howells was to see most of them constantly for several years at least, and in many cases even to the end of his life.

Henry Adams, whom Howells called "always preëminently civilized," had had a bitter taste of Washington, but, now a professor of history at Harvard, he was editing in Cambridge the *North American Review*. The regular editors, Norton and Lowell, had both gone abroad, and Norton wrote to Howells from England, "I once more begin to *feel* European. I am gradually getting rid of some American angularities and drynesses. My roots feel the refreshment of unfamiliar waters flowing from the deep old world springs of culture and imagination." But, while his eyes were delighted, his American heart afflicted him where the horses were "stabled like princes" and men and women were "ill-fed, ill-clothed and disregarded." In short, he added, "to live here would be intolerable, and I shall come back to the barrenness of America more American in heart than ever." Henry Adams, too, was to share this divided state of mind, exemplified above all by Henry James, but now, taking over the great review, he was "making the old tea-kettle" realize, said Lowell, that it was a steam engine, or belonged to the same race. Howells himself had edited one number of the magazine, and once he dined at Adams's house with Lord Houghton, Richard Monckton Milnes, the patron of letters who had known Heinrich Heine and who talked about this favourite poet of Howells.

In two respects Henry Adams was a type of the new generation. He was an agnostic, like most of the cultivated world of the time,—even Lowell, Longfellow and Norton among the older men,—and he was a Darwinian, prepared for some years at least to accept the new gospel of Evolution. This was the special theme of Howells's neighbour, John Fiske, the prodigiously learned young man with the round bespectacled eyes who had published his first book in *The Atlantic*. Howells had suggested the title, *Myths and Myth-Makers*, and Fiske had dedicated the book to him "in remembrance of pleasant autumn evenings spent among were-wolves and trolls and nixies." His object was to show the essential unity of all myths as the first efforts of the human imagination, instinctively endowing inanimate nature with the dimly understood attributes of primeval man. Fiske's greatest concern at the moment was Herbert Spencer's interpretation of Darwin's ideas of Evolution, while with his astonishing memory, he could repeat whole pages of his friend Howells's writing. Often, as Howells remembered, the two neighbours walked back and forth, till dinner-time, the chicory-bordered paths of their dusty suburb. To Howells the new doctrine of Evolution was self-evidently true, and he was to refer to "our finer morality" and "our finer art" as naturally superior to those of more primitive epochs. He was also convinced that humankind had evolved beyond pornography, as the art of the novel had also evolved since the ruder days of Richardson and Fielding. He too, moreover, was an agnostic who had believed in immortality until he became a member of the Cambridge circle; and, though deeply religious in temperament, he could only say henceforth that his faith was "hope-in-doubt."

Howells had met Thomas Sergeant Perry, Henry James's early friend, at Quebec, in 1869, when he and his wife were taking the summer vacation that was more or less described in *Their Wedding Journey*. Perry, who had just returned from Europe, whither he had gone with William James, to study in Berlin, was bored with the St. Lawrence, with the vulgarity of the passengers and the wonders of the Saguenay, and he said later,—though Howells denied it,—that his unseemly conduct had given rise to the portrait of Mr. Arbuton in *A Chance Acquaintance*. This was the very superior young man who was so Europeanized that he did not think much of America, "though I can't find," said Kitty Ellison, the young girl in the novel, "that he quite approves of Europe either." He even made one doubtful whether there wasn't something a little common in breathing and the circulation of the blood and whether it wouldn't be true refinement to stop them, and he was not sure it was the Saguenay's place to have a legend of its own and snubbed the legend because the Saguenay had it. He was so used to the rich effects of the old world that he patronized the landscape and even the cows, and almost expected the cows to go down on their knees out of gratitude when he finally said it was just like Normandy. Mr. Arbuton, no doubt, had been suggested by Perry, and this character was unquestionably a Boston type,—Francis Parkman said he had known three Mr. Arbutons,—but "I bear no malice," Perry said; and Howells inscribed to him a copy of the novel as "the book's first friend."

Perry had tried to find Howells in Venice two or three years before when the author of *Venetian Life* had already left, but he and Howells and Henry James soon formed a triumvirate for the study of foreign literatures and realistic fiction. Perry was a Harvard tutor at the moment who edited the *North American Review* when Henry Adams went abroad, and Howells persuaded him to start a department called "Recent Literature" in *The Atlantic* to follow the new departures, especially in France.[5] Henry James said that Perry had revealed Balzac to him, and he introduced both James and Howells to Turgenev, whom he translated, beginning with the novel *Virgin Soil*. He reviewed for *The Atlantic* many new European books, and it was he who first led Howells to read Gogol and Dostoievsky and, above all, Tolstoy a few years later. As an older man, enthralled with Chekhov, Perry visited Russia; and meanwhile he and Howells met almost every other day, "and we talk literature perpetually," said Howells.

Among others of the younger generation who appeared in Sacramento Street were John Hay, who had written *Pike County Ballads* and who had recently returned from Spain where he held a diplomatic post, and contributed *Castilian Days* to *The Atlantic*. Howells delighted in his turning from a half-European refinement to the crude potentialities of the frontier West in his *Jim Bludso* and *Little Breeches* at this moment when American literature on the continental terms was ceasing to be New England literature. He was full of Spain and the Prado museum, which had the best Titians in the world, he said, and he had written well of Velasquez, who was only beginning to be properly known when the king had sent his pictures to the Prado. Then Bret Harte came on from California, sending in advance to Mrs. Howells a rustic flower-stand "for your drawing-room window" in the new house the Howellses had built in Berkeley Street, where they were to live for half a dozen years. He promised to telegraph from Chicago when they could meet him at the

[5] During the years of Howells's editorship, *The Atlantic* published essays on Baudelaire, Flaubert, Zola (three articles), Stendhal, Dostoievsky, Musset, the Goncourts, Mérimée, Gautier, Mistral, Bourget, Björnson, Scribe, Dumas the elder, Sainte-Beuve, Renan, etc., many of them written by Howells, Henry James or Perry.

station, saying, "Then will step from the cars a tired man, in the habit of an American pilgrim . . . with an expression like Malvoglio's of being 'sad and civil' "; and thereupon began the furore with which he was received by a Cambridge and a Boston that were eager to recognize talent. He was entertained every night by Longfellow, Lowell, Agassiz and Fields, and Howells found him quite unspoiled by his great popularity as "one of the most refined and delicate of artists." Struck by Harte's powers of characterization, he had urged him to come East, and Harte had been happy to do so at a time when Boston criticism was accepted and supremely valued all over the country. News of his progress across the Middle West was reported almost from hour to hour in the papers. "You have such a rare faculty," Harte had written, "of not liking things in a likable manner. Anyone can be charmingly enthusiastic, but so few can be even tolerably sceptical"; and he added, to Howells, referring to the exuberance of the writers for the *Overland Monthly,* "How superior is your cultivated repose."

These were the days when Bret Harte was creating for Germany, Russia, England and France the idea of the Far West in literature. *The Atlantic* contracted to pay him ten thousand a year for his stories; but he was soon up to the ears in debt, and Howells was present when he was arrested in Boston. Meanwhile, Thomas Bailey Aldrich had published in 1870 his influential *The Story of a Bad Boy,* a book that Howells instantly praised for telling "what life is," instead of "what it ought to be. No one else seems to have thought of telling the story of a boy's life, with so great desire to show what a boy's life is, and so little purpose of teaching what it should be," Howells wrote about this tale of Aldrich's own boyhood that suggested other books by friends of his. For it seems to have given rise not only to Howells's *A Boy's Town* and Charles Dudley Warner's *Being a Boy* but to Mark Twain's *Tom Sawyer* and *Huckleberry Finn*.

It was at about this time that Godkin wrote to Norton in Europe, "Howells *grows* steadily, I think, and in all ways, for he has become very stout," and others, falling in with Howells, were struck by his quiet air, his dense dark eyes and square strong face. The lively Aldrich excited one more, but Howells left the deeper impression, perhaps because he did not seem to care about making one, and, silently observant, talking little, he had the composure of one who had already a record and a future. With his belief that fiction should help humanity to know itself better, he had no doubt learned something directly from *The Story of a Bad Boy*. He had learned, at any rate, that one might well fictionalize one's own life, and he did so in *Their Wedding Journey* a year or two later.

VI

FIRST NOVELS

"I WAS A traveller before I was a noveler," Howells wrote years later in *The House of Harper*, "and I had mounted somewhat timidly to the threshold of fiction from the high-roads and by-roads where I had studied manners and men." It was not until 1872 that he published *Their Wedding Journey,* his first attempt to mingle travel and fiction, using for this novelized account of a summer vacation with his wife some of his old newspaper letters of ten years before. The Howellses had gone from Boston to New York, to Albany by the night-boat, to Niagara and then to Quebec by the Saint Lawrence. In the three other short novels he published in the seventies, the story unfolded itself with a background of travel, either on "the sad great river of the awful North" or in Venice or on a ship thither. All these novels were cases in point of what Howells called in a review "the ante-natal phantom, pleading to be born into the world, the American novel."

For Howells was attempting something new, in the spirit of a moment when Taine's ideas of the time and the place were finding illustrations in the realistic fiction of several countries. One of the Russian critics had said, "We are Russians; for heaven's sake then give us Russian characters. Let us behold our own follies, our own foibles, our own perversities"; and the great Russian novelists had arisen to do so. As for Howells, who had read and seen Goldoni, he had also read Björnstjerne Björnson, who was creating with one or two others a literature for Norway. Howells had not read Turgenev yet, but he was more drawn to Björnson's "realism of the spiritual type" than to that of "the sensual type," such as the French; and he shared Henry James's preference for Edmond de Goncourt's description of the realism which the Goncourts did not always practise. This realism existed not to picture "what is low, revolting and unsavory, but to define in artistic writing the lofty, attractive, agreeable"; and Björnson's *Anne, The Happy Boy* and *The Fisher Maiden* seemed to Howells free, bold and full of colour. He thought that in these sagas, which had given the author an all-European reputation, Björnson had invented almost a new pleasure. Fairy tales in real life, they had the simplest characters, with little that was surprising in incident or circumstance, for Björnson believed in giving only a few distinct touches in representing a character or a situation. This was the opposite, Howells said, "of all that is Trollopian," for, although he thought better of Trollope later, he was in reaction at the time against "the bad school we were all brought up in." He meant the English novelists and "the heavy and awkward traditions of the craft" that Dickens and George Eliot perpetuated. Björnson, beside them, was natural and graceful, and he had, moreover, a poetic atmosphere. Fullness in brevity might have been his motto. Howells was to turn away more and more from English traditions in the novel in favour of Russian, French, Spanish, Norwegian and Italian. Their fiction, he was to say, was "the only living movement in imaginative literature."

Now Howells, who had written *Suburban Sketches* before

he read Björnson, had developed already a form and a style, and he might have said that Björnson rather confirmed than influenced the trend of his own work in fiction. He instinctively liked the subtly simple, the brief, the natural, the real, and in all this Björnson corroborated his own tendencies, just as Turgenev did a little later. He liked what Michelangelo called "the light of the piazza" as the best light for a statue or a novel, and, feeling that obscurity was a crime, he was enamoured of clearness: anything left in the vague was intolerable to him. Wishing to be flexible, he was indifferent to intrigue and plots: he might almost have agreed with Sartre about "the foolish business of mere story-telling,"—in fact, Howells used a phrase that was much like Sartre's, "The foolish joys of mere fable." For he felt that the power to dazzle with impossible characters and strange events was something that hundreds could do,—therefore why do it? To interest with the ordinary events of life and truly human characters was something that only a handful were able to do;[1] and he was severe with his former self, as he was with other authors, for looking through somebody else's literary telescope. As one to whom all things of everyday life, he said, presented themselves in periods more or less rounded, and capable of use as facts or illustrations, he was bent on seeing

[1] "It was in all respects an ordinary carful of human beings, and it was perhaps the more worthy to be studied on that account. As in literature the true artist will shun the use even of real events if they are of an improbable character, so the sincere observer of man will not desire to look upon his heroic or occasional phases, but will seek him in his habitual moods of vacancy or tiresomeness. To me, at any rate, he is at such times very precious, and I never perceive him to be so much a man and a brother as when I feel the pressure of his vast, natural, unaffected dullness."—Howells, *Their Wedding Journey*.
"Oh, why didn't something happen?"
"Ah, my dear! What could have been half so good as the nothing that did happen?"—*ibid.*

character, not as it was in other novels, but as it abounded outside all fiction.

In short, Howells set out to look straight at American life without any of the literary glosses that had been thought desirable, just as, in history, Francis Parkman had looked straight at our meagre past and thrown a bright light on its savage solitudes.[2] He was to escape soon enough from what a painter later called "the persistent glamour of the European scene,"—to which Henry James yielded, with unique results, —but he was still too far under the spell of the "elderly enchantress" to give himself wholly at first to the native scene. In *Their Wedding Journey* he argued with himself, "Why should we wish to find America like Europe? Are the ruins . . . and miseries . . . which beset the traveller abroad so precious that he should desire to imagine them . . . in his own hemisphere?" Yet he had seen Italy in Cambridge, and, while Venice long lingered in his mind, he was almost obsessed with the half-European Quebec where Parkman, to whom he owed so much, had given him the stories of the Ursulines, Madame de Peltrie and Château-Bigot. Rochester, enchanted in the moonlight, suggested Verona to the bride and groom, and the dingy railroad restaurant recalled a small station in the south of France where they had once stopped for breakfast. How different from what they saw now were the fresh bright little tables, the plates, the napkins, the half bottles of wine. In fact, the tourists of *Their Wedding Journey* strove for "the feelings of foreign travel," and they placed villas and castles and palaces upon all the eligible building

2 Howells was convinced, moreover, that "the constitution of our society is more picturesque, more dramatic, more poetical than any in the world," as he was to say in *Imaginary Interviews*, and that "the American who chooses to enjoy his birthright to the full . . . breathes a rarefied and nimble air full of shining possibilities and radiant promises."

sites on the train to Niagara, casting an absurd poetry over the landscape. It was, moreover, the non-American character of the old streets of Quebec that commended it to the Marches and to Kitty. It was so full of the charm of old-world travel in "the enviably deplorable countries we all love."

It was not until 1878 that Howells could write to his friend Mark Twain, "I find that I have outlived all longing for Europe"; and he might have added that travel itself played a small part in his mind when he had become absorbed in the American scene. Yet, for certain reasons,—and, not the least, his own pleasure in it,—his novels continued to abound in scenes of travel on night-boats, on river-boats, in sleeping cars and parlour cars, in railway waiting-rooms and especially hotels. It "amused" Howells himself "to check his baggage and depart from stations, to arrive at hotels and settle himself in new rooms; the very domiciliation in sleeping-cars or the domestication in diners had a charm which was apparently perennial; a trip in a river-boat was rapture; an ocean voyage was ecstasy. The succession of strange faces, new minds, was an unfailing interest, and there was no occurrence, in or out of the ordinary, which did not give him release from self and form a true recreation." So Howells wrote later, referring to his own case, but this was not the only reason that his novels were so full of the bustle of travel, the chaos of wharves and docks and jolting stages. One found oneself there in sleeping-cars lunging through the darkness and hearing only the rhythmical clangour of the wheels, the burly roar of the locomotives and the clatter of the rails, when the door was opened, that struck through the car like a demoniac yell. One felt the long irregular jolt when the progress of the train was reduced to an incessant shudder and a quick lateral motion, and one knew that the engineer was "making time," or when the train creaked, stopping and starting, and one knew it was crunching along on a bed of snow. Then there were the flaring gas-jets of the stations and the hissing and coughing of the locomotives, backing and advancing in the railroad yards at night.

In Howells's novels, early and late, one happened on these moments, and there were the ships and the Fall River boats with so much upholstery and so much music, so many white cabins and plush sofas and prismatic chandeliers, and the great city hotels, all marble mantel and tessellated floor, glossy paint, Brussels carpets and fluted pillars. There were hotels by the dozen, all kinds of hotels, in Howells's books, from the St. Alban of *The Minister's Charge* to the Dutch hotel in *The Kentons,* and others in *Their Silver Wedding Journey.* Especially there were summer hotels in New Hampshire, at "Lion's Head," or at Magnolia in *The Story of a Play,* where pony-carriages passed on the beach, followed by horsemen on crop-tailed roans, and there were sail-boats and dories swinging off-shore. Howells pictured many a summer hotel that stretched like the shore of a continent beside the ocean, so that walking on the veranda one might have been going from Mount Desert to St. Augustine, or at least Savannah. A summer hotel was the *mise en scène* of *A Traveler from Altruria,* where the doctor, the manufacturer, the minister, the lawyer and the romantic novelist fell in with Mrs. Makely and Mr. Homos. In a later essay, *The Closing of the Hotel,* Howells followed the phases of the last weeks of a summer hotel when the band "vanished as it were in a sudden crash of silence" and then the elevator ceased to run. The hotel was invaded by a multitude of crickets, shrilling in the gloomy reaches, and a slowly creeping desolation and gradual paresis seized upon the late full and happy life there.

Then there were the delays in waiting-rooms where one made up stories about the people who were flitting to and fro, and the chorus of consuls and cabin-boys, hotel clerks and stewards who ministered to the needs and desires of the people of Howells. It is true that at this time Americans were generally on the move, going and coming, in Europe, in the East and the West; but also, in our thin, scattered society, there were few occasions on which people of the different regions met one another; and there were still fewer spots where they could meet. East, West, Middle West and South were then far apart, while Howells's own outlook was always continental. It was his wish and aim to bring together characters of all the sections and of all types and classes; and where could Kitty, from western New York, have met Mr. Arbuton of Boston except on a river-boat on the Saint Lawrence? Where, except on the "Aroostook" could Lydia from South Bradfield have fallen in with Staniford, whom she was to marry? Stations, hotels, boats and trains were inevitable settings for an all-American novelist at that moment.

It was a moment, for the rest, which gave birth naturally to a notion that Howells held for a good many years, that "the more smiling aspects of life" were "the more American . . . the large cheerful average of health and success and happy life." He used these phrases twenty years later when he had begun to see how much evil there was in American life, the evil that already appeared in some of his novels; but how could he not have been impressed by the smiling aspects of American life in the post-war epoch of confidence, security and hope? (That is to say, except in the unhappy South.) Mark Twain was similarly struck even in *The Gilded Age*, and Howells was aware in *Their Wedding Journey* of "the swindling railroad kings" whom Henry Adams was exposing in *Chapters of Erie*. Henry James took it for granted that, as he said, America was "more innocent" than other countries, adding that this innocence was "nowhere more patent" than in Howells's novels and that no one else knew so much about the American character. His sentiment of this character was "unerring," James remarked, and Howells himself saw nothing more typical of the time than "the innocently adventurous, mettlesome American maiden." He was referring to Daisy Miller in whom many a girl saw herself,—in that "still flattering if a little mocking mirror,"—and hastened to efface herself almost as soon as she saw herself there between 1870 and 1880. But he might have been referring to his own Lily Mayhew, to Kitty, to the Florida Vervain of *A Foregone Conclusion,* or to Lydia, on the Aroostook, "voyaging under the chaperonage of her own innocence."[3] In their frank, trustful ingenuousness and their childlike gaiety of heart, natural, fearless, ready to be taken command of, none of these girls was aware of the havoc she was causing. They were all bold or helpless, generous and proud, capricious, self-reliant and with an instinctive confidence in others. This "American girl who swarmed abroad to play such a prominent part in international fiction," as Howells put it,—even if "abroad" meant only Quebec,—was the principal character of his own earliest novels; and it might have been said that in these novels, along with those of Henry James, Americans first saw themselves in print.

For the "females" of Fenimore Cooper, the types of Mrs. Stowe or even the somewhat peripheral characters of Hawthorne scarcely had the clear actuality that Henry Adams

[3] But not from the point of view of the French lady to whom Henry James lent a copy of *The Lady of the Aroostook.* This mother of daughters said that the situation imagined in the novel was immoral and quite unfit to be presented to a young girl's mind.

signalized in his review of Howells's *Their Wedding Journey*.
"Our descendants will find nowhere so faithful and pleasing
a picture," Adams said, "of our American existence"; and
"Why should it not live?" he added. "If extreme and almost
photographic truth to nature, and remarkable delicacy and
lightness of touch, can give permanent life to a story, why
should this one not be read with curiosity and enjoyment
a hundred or two hundred years hence?" Howells had seen
that, if he was going to do anything worth while, he would
have to get into fiction from life the things that had not been
got into fiction before; and at a time when we were still "literary colonists," as he said, "beginning to observe the aspects of
our own life," he realized for the first time many of these aspects, scenes, types of character, contrasts of section and setting.
There was, first of all, the contrast between city mouse and
country mouse, between the cultivated Yankees and the raw
material, between the unconscious and the conscious that he
was to sustain throughout his work,—in the Coreys and the
Laphams, for instance, in the minister Sewell and the farm
boy Lemuel, in many other novels.

There was the contrast between East and West, in small
symbolic matters[4] as well as in matters of character in *A
Chance Acquaintance*, there was the contrast of Boston and
New York,[5] and there were the characters who were also

[4] "It seems true that on a westering line the blacking fades gradually
from the boots, the hat softens and sinks, the coat loses its rigour of cut,
and the whole person lounges with increasing informality of costume. I
speak of the undressful sex alone; woman, wherever she is, appears in the
last attainable effects of fashion, which are now all but telegraphic and
universal."—*Their Wedding Journey*.

[5] The Boston ladies in *A Chance Acquaintance* were no doubt happy not
to have possessed "the vivid New York stylishness." On the contrary, "a
peculiar restraint of line, an effect of lady-like concession to the ruling
mode, a temperance of ornament marked the whole array, and stamped it
with the unmistakable character of Boston."

typical of the place and the moment. Mr. Arbuton was the kind of Boston prig who took Henry Adams "morally out of Beacon Street"; and Staniford and Dunham were new Boston types,—Staniford, the post-Civil War Bostonian who was planning to ranch in Colorado and Dunham who had forsaken the pale Unitarian worship of the past. Dunham had even expected to unite with a celibate order, and he read the London weekly papers that gave him the foreign standpoint from which he liked to view his native world. There was Lily "who laughed at everything not because she was amused but because she was happy," and the competent military travelling widow "who knew herself too well ever to unpack anything that would not spoil by remaining unpacked." Perhaps above all there was Kitty from Eriecreek, New York, with her unsnubbed fearlessness of heart, to whom the world was all fresh and whose light and eager laugh was as quick and sympathetic as her imagination. Every face she saw in Quebec told its pathetic story to her, and she entered in thought every cottage and dreamed out there its humble dream. "It's the chief business," Staniford said, "of the youth of one sex to think of the youth of the other sex"; and Howells created a roseate atmosphere of youth and hope in which young people were felt to be really in love.[6] In this respect he was more successful than the more brilliant Henry James, whose men and women generally approached one another as precious articles of *virtu* rather than as lovers. One saw them in love but did not feel them so.

[6] "Some such pair is in the foreground of every famous American landscape; and when I think of the amount of public love-making in the season of pleasure travel from Mount Desert to the Yosemite, and from the parks of Colorado to the Keys of Florida, I feel that our continent is but a larger Arcady, that the middle of the nineteenth century is the golden age, and that we want very little of being a nation of shepherds and shepherdesses."—Howells, *Their Wedding Journey.*

It was of Kitty that Henry James wrote in his review, "So! In the House of Fable she stands firm on her little pedestal"; adding in a letter to Howells, "I wish I could talk over her successes with you, sitting on the pine needles by Fresh Pond." Again, reviewing *A Foregone Conclusion*, James said that "this genuine artist . . . has ranked himself with the few writers on whom one counts with luxurious certainty." Howells had been from the first both a critical and popular success with the older New Englanders,[7] the not so old[8] and with readers everywhere, such as John Hay[9] and Bayard Taylor,[10] all of whom relished the constant felicity and the unobtrusive humour and wit that marked Howells's earliest light-hearted novels. There was no cunning design in the

[7] "We are perfectly charmed with your 'lady' [of the Aroostook]! I am almost envious that you should have kicked up out of the soil of Maine such a nugget which all of us have walked over never dreaming how to coin it. . . . When in Genoa I saw a ship from Bath and the captain standing in his glossy black backed vest and white shirt sleeves—the very image of Yankeedom, and you can't think how my heart yearned to him."—Harriet Beecher Stowe to Howells, 1878.

[8] "My sister read to me *The Lady of the Aroostook,* and we were both delighted. It seems to me as near to perfection in its kind as anything terrestrial can be. I hear but one opinion of it—without drawback, even in the most critical corners of this critical town—that it is charming."—Francis Parkman, Letter to Howells, 1879.

Writing to Howells of *A Chance Acquaintance,* Parkman also praised "the truth, freshness, subtle penetration of character, kindly satire and wholesome genuine feeling that fills it throughout."

[9] "Where did you find that impossibly happy way of saying everything?" John Hay wrote to Howells about *Their Wedding Journey.* "It is a thing that the rest of us blunder on, once in a while, but you never miss. You see the critics all notice this, and, not knowing what else to say, they say Hawthorne and Irving, etc."

[10] Bayard Taylor had written to Howells about his *Venetian Life.* "The style is exquisite. . . . It is remarkably plastic. . . . It becomes grave without the slightest heaviness or dullness and runs, as if spontaneously, into light and sparkle. . . . Then over the whole book there is the bloom, the subtle something (always suggesting perfume to my mind) which the poetic faculty gives to the prose of a poet."

loosely knit stories that seemed as inconsequential to the reader as life was, ending well or not well, happily or otherwise but with no effects that were false or overdramatic. These novels were graceful and compact, subtle in flavour, with an elastic style and feathery touches that said much while seeming to say little, with a fullness in brevity recalling Björnson and a charm of perfect naturalness that gave one the effect of reality Howells cared most for.

Howells had long doubted his fitness for a sustained narration, but no wonder he was soon able to say, in a letter to his father, "I see clear before me a path in literature which no one else has tried, and which I believe I can make most distinctly my own."

VII

MARK TWAIN

MORE THAN half consciously, meanwhile, Howells had been studying the New England scene, the background of many of his future novels, spending summers, or weeks, or months, by the seashore, in the mountains, in Maine, at Nahant, Jaffrey, Lake Winnepesaukee. It was a rule with him never to spend two summers in the same place.

Howells was enchanted at Newport by the sea-washed quaint old place and dreamed of living in the winter there, and he spent a few days with his wife at Plymouth in a hotel that was kept by the widow of a spiritualist sea-captain. Here the late timothy lay in the vegetable garden under a marble obelisk, the widow's pride. At Kennebunkport there were loverless maidens, twenty girls to every man, in the rowboats on the river, in the summer hotels, enough to provide a novelist with heroines forever. There was an old garden in Little Nahant with greenhouses tumbling in and a belvedere trembling on posts over the rocks, with neglected rose-bushes and terraced beds full of weeds and witch-grass that served as a setting for a later novel. It had a disordered loveliness that was full of sad poetry as it overlooked the illimitable welter of the sea. At Annisquam he spent one summer in the former home of a quarry magnate, walled and terraced, overlooking

Ipswich Bay, with an avenue of roses, syringas and smoke-trees, and with burning heaps of flowers in the neighbouring dooryards. Then there were the farm boarding-houses among the New Hampshire hills where the silent Yankees gave up to the visitors their habitable rooms and moved for the summer into nooks and crannies, and there were the Equitys and the South Bradfields where the "lady of the Aroostook" had taught school and where Marcia, in *A Modern Instance,* met Bartley Hubbard. There was often a disused academy on the village green with a neo-classic pediment and fluted pillars, and the boarders took walks and drives through white birch groves.

First or last, in short, Howells saw New England from end to end,—from Ponkwasset Falls in New Hampshire, where the Maverings lived, to Lumberville whose name had been changed to Lapham,—at a time when the old puritan culture was visibly decaying, when life in Willoughby Pastures or Lower Merritt or West Pekin had shrunken till it rattled in its shell. There were often three times as many gravestones as there were living persons in the village, and crazy heresies had taken the place of the ancient orthodoxy, as the railroads had killed the country taverns. Often in the remains of these one found big dusty ball-rooms where for half a century no one had danced, and common schools had replaced most of the old academies that had once yielded a rude but solid learning. The old scriptural nomenclature had also given place to made-up story-book names like Lurella and Zerrilla.[1] Howells, who was to draw inimitable pictures of all this life,—the vil-

[1] Or Idella, "a particularly repulsive invention, a combination of Ella, the mother's name and the grandmother's name, Ida. Annie abhorred those made-up names in which the New England country-people sometimes indulge their fancy."—Howells, *Annie Kilburn.*

lage parties, for instance, at which Bartley Hubbard was the first to break the ice "and set the angular fragments grating and grinding upon one another,"—observed it as in itself it really was, leaving Matthew Arnold to draw the moral.[2] He knew well the lonely women in the lonely villages "lingering upon the neutral ground between the faded hopes of marriage and the yet unrisen prospects of consumption."

Howells had discussed with Lowell the Yankee speech of *The Biglow Papers* and, seldom using dialect, he was eager to get, as he told John Hay, "the conscientiously-cunningly-reluctant arbitrarily emphatic Yankee *manner*." At the same time he shared Lowell's pleasure in the landscape and the flowers, in the breath of the pines, the smell of the oaks, pungent where the balsam failed, in the spaces where red field-lilies tilted in the wind. He knew the woods where the tall brakes grew, with delicate ferns waving and swaying, the starry profusion of the laurel coming into bloom, and the wild raspberries, dog-roses and bay when "the fog came in . . . like a visible reverie" and blurred with its whiteness some valley by the sea. His novels were to follow the seasons, June with its odour of clover-heads and blackberry blossoms beside the road, with the bobolinks and orioles in the fields and dooryards, and the end of summer when the fire crept

[2] "Think of the turn of the good people of our race for producing a life of hideousness and immense ennui; think of that specimen of your own New England life which Mr. Howells gives us in one of his charming stories which I was reading lately; think of the life of that ragged New England farm in *The Lady of the Aroostook*; think of Deacon Blood and Aunt Maria and the straight-backed chairs with black horse-hair seats, and Ezra Perkins with perfect self-reliance depositing his travellers in the snow! In the New England, as in the old, our people have to learn, I suppose, not that their modes of life are beautiful and excellent already, they have rather to learn that they must transform them."—Matthew Arnold, *Discourses in America*.

from sumac to sumac and lighted the vines in the grass and over the walls.

*

*   *

Howells had first met Mark Twain in the autumn of 1869 in his *Atlantic* office at Ticknor and Fields's, where he had recently written a review of *The Innocents Abroad* and the author had dropped in to thank him for it. Mark Twain, who was lecturing in Boston, said he felt "like the woman who was so glad her baby had come white," for he regarded Howells as "the literary court of last resort" and Boston opinion as far more important than others. He was wearing a sealskin coat with the fur outside, and, with his crest of red hair and wild moustache, he was a startling sight in the streets of Boston. But he liked nothing better than to attract attention. Short, five feet four inches tall, about the height of Howells, he was erect and slender and seemed to be taller, for Howells was stout, short-necked and rather chunky. The two at once became friends, as close as Howells and Henry James. Mark Twain called James "Henrietta Maria," while James, in his turn, said that Mark was a writer who was fit only for primitive minds.

At this time Mark Twain was already "de-Southernized," as Howells said, for, having been a Confederate soldier of slave-holding stock, he had become a rampant pro-Negro Republican; and Howells, who felt that *The Atlantic* must change from a New England magazine and accept an American literary situation, hospitable to the talents of the whole country, was eager for Mark Twain's compositions. The new friends had much in common. Both were natives of the Mississippi valley, familiar with its woods and fields; both had known piloting on the Western rivers; and they had both been country printers and shared an interest in printing-presses, in the hand-press and the steam-power press and in all manner of printing shops. As Westerners, moreover, they had both chosen to live in the East, and Mark Twain had settled in Hartford in a sort of suburban grove near Harriet Beecher Stowe and Charles Dudley Warner. He said that New England was the freest corner of the country and he preferred Boston to New York. Mark Twain was indifferent to what Howells called "the incredulous sniff of the polite," and, though Lowell and Longfellow did not make much of him, the fastidious Norton and Child delighted in the stranger. Mark Twain liked the *Atlantic* audience before which he could sit down serene because it did not require a "humorist" to stand on his head; for he was usually considered a mere buffoon. Howells suggested and urged him to write *Life on the Mississippi,* which he published serially in *The Atlantic,* saying, as he read the manuscript, that it almost made the water in his ice pitcher turn muddy.

Mark Twain constantly wrote to Howells. First or last he wrote to Howells more letters than to any other living man, and sometimes they were twenty or even forty pages long, longer than Henry James's voluminous letters, which ran now and then to twenty-five pages. Meanwhile, he came to Boston often, to *Atlantic* lunches, where he talked away whole afternoons with Howells and Aldrich, or for evenings in Cambridge with those scalloped oysters without which no party was really a party. Once, with a friend from Hartford, he set out to walk there; and, although he stayed ostensibly at the Parker House in Boston, he would sometimes come out to Cambridge for two or three days, lounging through the rooms in his long nightgown, telling the story of his life. Howells could never have tired of this, but he felt hollow at the end, "like one of those locust shells one finds sticking to the bark of trees at the end of summer." After lecturing in town, Mark Twain appeared once in evening clothes and covered them with an overcoat the following morning when he and Howells went out for a walk; or he came out in slippers and put on rubbers. He often went to sleep with a lighted cigar in his mouth. Every human impulse was selfish, he insisted, the sacrifice of a mother for a child, of a martyr at the stake, of a lover saving his mistress from drowning or burning; self-love was at the bottom of it all, the dread of greater pain in relinquishing the sacrifice, said Mark. Once he came on for a luncheon that Ralph Keeler gave,—the author of *Vagabond Adventures,* which appeared in *The Atlantic,*—for Howells and himself, Bret Harte, Fields and Aldrich. Ralph Keeler, who was living in Cambridge where the Brahmins ignored him, was a true American picaro, Howells thought. He had run away from home as a boy in Ohio and travelled as a black-faced minstrel on Southern rivers. He had been a clog-dancer and tambourinist on Mississippi showboats among the people whom Mark Twain wrote about, Arkansans with bowie-knives, prize-fighters and balloonists, and his story was a veritable American picaresque romance. Later he was to appear as Fulkerson in *A Hazard of New Fortunes.*

This was the sort of man and book that Mark Twain liked to meet and read, and all the more interesting because Keeler disappeared on a ship that was sailing to Havana. He had gone down as a reporter and was probably murdered. Howells shared Mark Twain's delight in autobiography and the picaresque,—which he had first loved in *Don Quixote,*—because these books depicted character for him and widened his own knowledge of human nature.[3] Nothing, Howells felt, contributed more than autobiography to men's understanding of one another, and he edited during the seventies a series of autobiographies, the romantic courtier Lord Herbert's, Marmontel's and others. One was Goldoni's autobiography, associated with his first summer in Venice, another was Alfieri's, about which he lectured, and there were the Memoirs of Wilhelmina, Margravine of Bayreuth, Frederick the Great's extraordinary sister. He included Gibbon's autobiography, incomparable for its noble manner and for the martial vigor of its style, a book suggesting to Howells that the Swiss society of Gibbon's day had the innocence and blameless freedom of an American town (in the circles that he himself had known there). For the young ladies of Lausanne met at one another's houses without any sort of chaperonage, laughing, dancing, playing cards with young men of all nations, yet, as a chronicler of the time observed, "respecting themselves and respected by the men." Howells, the devotee of marriage, did not let Gibbon off easily for "sighing as a lover" but "obeying as a son," giving up the Swiss pastor's daughter who was to become the mother of Madame de Staël. He could scarcely forgive Gibbon because he had permitted himself to lose this girl who presently suffered so many hardships; but his critical introductions to all these books showed a remarkable sympathy for many different types. It was evident that Howells understood all sorts and conditions of men. Only one so organized could have been equally intimate with both Mark Twain and Henry James.

[3] "Did you ever read Defoe's *Roxana*? If not, then read it, not merely for some of the deepest insights into the lying, suffering, sinning, well-meaning human soul, but the best and most natural English that a book was ever written in."—Howells, Letter to Mark Twain, 1886.

Sometimes Howells visited Hartford, where his own contagious laugh set the whole Clemens household laughing, and Mark Twain himself would come into a room in white cowskin slippers and perform a Crippled Coloured Uncle. Mark Twain was the best reader aloud whom Howells ever heard, and he sang with great feeling the Negro spirituals when the Jubilee singers first came north.[4] He told stories of Uncle Remus, the Tar Baby and others, as he had heard them told in his Missouri boyhood, and Howells could never forget Mark Twain's voice as he read George W. Cable's *Jean-ah-Poquelin*. This was the story of the old New Orleans trader who concealed from the authorities his leper brother, and Mark Twain took a tragic pleasure in it. He was soon to go on a lecturing tour with Cable, who at about this time visited Howells, a great admirer of *The Grandissimes,* "charming, powerful, exquisite" and "full of atmosphere," as he said in a review. Howells and Mark Twain together walked and talked in the billiard-room with high windows overlooking the pretty Hartford landscape, and Mark Twain tried to interest Howells in the "Blindfold Novelettes" that would make "a stunning book," he said, "to sell on railway trains." Together they planned a river trip down to New Orleans, which they were obliged to abandon, and Mark Twain teased Howells about his "dear favourite" Jane Austen, who was Mark's abhorrence. He wrote on shipboard once that Jane Austen's books were not to be found in the ship's library, and "just this one omission," he said, "would make a fairly good library out of a library that hadn't a book in it." He would send Howells,

---

[4] "I believe that if the Negroes ever have their turn, and if the meek shall inherit the earth they must come to it, we shall have a civilization of such sweetness and good will as the world has never known yet. Perhaps we shall have to wait their turn for any real Christian civilization."—Dr. Olney in Howells's *An Imperative Duty.*

with a contribution, some such note as, "Say, boss, do you want this to lighten up your old freight-train with?" or he would send a telegram, "All right come down with me Friday the superior value of birds in the hand over those that still sport in joyous freedom amid the leafy depths of their native woodland is so universally recognized that I cannot feel necessitated to enlarge upon it to one of the first minds of the age at three cents a word by telegraph."

When Howells read *Tom Sawyer* in proof, he wrote to Mark Twain, "Give me a hint when it's to be out, and I'll start the sheep jumping in the right places," for he reviewed almost all of Mark Twain's books, and he knew that *Atlantic* reviews called the dance. Visiting Mark, he wrote to John Hay, "We confessed to each other that the years had tamed us, and we no longer had any literary ambition. Before we went to bed, we had planned a play, a lecturing tour, a book of travel and a library of humour. He has life enough in him for ten generations, but his moods are now all colossal." In the end Howells edited the *Library of Humour* that was called Mark Twain's, with funny, or perhaps more often facetious, pen-drawings by E. W. Kemble,—a great collection of passages from every American period and section from the days of Washington Irving down. Then Mark Twain wrote to him about a domestic tragedy, "Yesterday a thunder stroke fell upon me out of the most unsuspected of skies . . . I found that all their lives my children have been afraid of me! have stood all their days in uneasy dread of my sharp tongue and uncertain temper. The accusing instances stretch back to their babyhood, and are burnt into their memories, and I never suspected and the fact was never guessed by anybody until yesterday. Well, all the concentrated griefs of fifty years seemed colourless by the side of that pathetic revelation." But oftener Mark Twain's note was ironical or witty. On Election Day he wrote once, "I love to steal a while away from every cumbering care and when returns come in today lift up my voice and swear." He added, "I have noticed that a little judicious profanity helps out an otherwise ineffectual sketch or poem remarkably. I attribute the feebleness of many of Tupper's noblest efforts to the lack of this element."

At this point of profanity, and similar manifestations, Mark Twain's wife entered the picture, and what Howells called her "ladyhood limitations" sometimes interfered with Mark's literary freedom. The fact was that Mark himself was very uncertain in matters of taste, and rather at sea as well in social matters, and, visiting the Howellses, he committed blunders for which his wife presently took him to task. "O dear!" he wrote once, "I came home jubilant, thinking that for once I had gone through a two days' trip and come out without a crime on my soul: but it was all a delusion,—as I soon found out as I glided along in my narrative . . . I have suffered enough through Mrs. Clemens's measureless scorn and almost measureless vituperation [Mark Twain's phrase for soft reproaches] . . . The sudden damnation drops on a body like the released pile-driver, and he finds himself in the earth down to his chin, when he supposed he was merely being entertaining." He condemned himself after the Whittier birthday speech when, knowing it was all a blunder, he was "fatally helpless to stop," said Howells, and stood "solitary amid his appalled and appalling listeners, with his joke dead on his hands." Mark was crushed, as Howells remembered. He thought he had injured himself all over the country and felt he should not publish at all for a while.

Mark Twain needed guidance. Therefore he always asked for it, and the trouble with what Howells called Mrs. Clemens's "female fears" was that she could not draw the line. As for Howells, face to face with Mark Twain's "breadth of parlance,"—whether Elizabethan or Southwestern,—he was first of all concerned as editor of a magazine that had to work within the taboos of the moment.[5] Just so Thackeray had been concerned when he edited the *Cornhill* and Dickens as editor of *Household Words* and *All the Year Round;* and Howells himself recalled how Thackeray editorially admonished Trollope to remember the modesty of their young girl readers. Thinking himself of the serial form in which novels of the time appeared, he considered "the young married pair beside the evening lamp, or the well-grown family around it," and he was obliged to play the censor now and then with Mark Twain when he tried "a little stronger language than *The Atlantic* had stomach for." But Howells's objections were actually few. How serious was the pressure that was brought then on all magazines one saw in the case of a story of Howells later when the editor of *The Century* asked him to omit a word that he had innocently used. The word "dynamite" had acquired sinister associations with the rise of anarchism, and Richard Watson Gilder asked him to wire a new line to take the place of the phrase including this word. "I hope you will not think us supersensitive," Gilder wrote. Howells

[5] It was mainly on practical grounds that he advised young writers,—Owen Wister, for instance,—not to attempt to publish books that offended these taboos; for, at a time when magazine serialization brought all the rewards of publishing, no magazine editor would consent to publish the work. In *Criticism and Fiction* he said, "Everyone recognizes *Anna Karenina* and *Madame Bovary* as supreme. . . . If, by any chance, by some prodigious miracle, any American should now arise to treat illicit love on the level of those books, he would be absolutely sure of success and of a fame and gratitude as great as those books have won for their authors. But no editor would print the work, and here again our novelist must submit to conditions."

himself had also learned the conditions that were necessary to conduct a great magazine.

But Mark Twain was usually his own censor, and, for the rest, he appealed to Howells to handle all his manuscripts "with entire freedom. . . . Please correct mercilessly the *Conscience* article," he wrote, and, regarding *Life on the Mississippi*, "cut it, scarify it, reject it." Mark Twain's "squeamishness was greater than Howells's," Bernard De Voto was to say. "I am sure that his conception of what was proper to written literature was more prudish than that of his mentors—it was demonstrably more prudish than Howells's"; and Bernard De Voto, who read Mark Twain's manuscripts, spoke of his "timorous circumlocutions, published and unpublished" as "astonishing."[6] As for Howells's own prudery, it was that of the later Victorian time, scarcely more marked than Anthony Trollope's; and when he said, "I am still very Victorian in my preference of decency," one might have added, How could he not have felt so? For who can be far removed from the feeling of his own time? He shared Anthony Trollope's belief that the novelist was the chosen guide, the tutor whom young people chose for themselves, that they received from novels their moral teaching, and that he ought to be careful what words he used, what thought he expressed when he sat in counsel with his friends and readers.[7] For this reason

[6] In *Mark Twain at Work*. Mr. E. H. Cady (in *The Road to Realism*) seems to be right in saying, "Certainly Howells was not responsible for the war which raged deep in Twain's psyche between a prudish country boy and an expert smoking-car pornographer."

[7] "I should be said to insist absurdly on the power of my own confraternity if I were to declare that the bulk of the young people in the upper and middle classes receive their moral teaching from the novels they read. . . . But the novelist creeps in closer than the schoolmaster, closer than the father, closer almost than the mother. He is the chosen guide, the tutor,

Howells wrote to John Hay, "My children are my censors
. . . I could not have palpitating divans in my stories"; while
his fine essay on Zola was to show how far apart in his mind
were the "indecent" and the "immoral." He was to write, "The
truth may be indecent but it cannot be vicious, it can never
corrupt or deprave; and I should say this in defence of the
grossest material honestly treated in modern novels as against
the painted and perfumed meretriciousness of the novels that
went before them."

Later Howells was to be attacked for defending Tolstoy,
the "obscene," as he was attacked for defending the "immoralities" of Zola, "that most virtuous and veracious spirit,"
as he called him; and this was at a time when the cautious
Gilder was to say that a greater freedom in fiction was approaching. But no one raised these questions when Howells
was still young.

---

whom the young pupil chooses for himself. Shall he, then, to whom this
close fellowship is allowed—this inner confidence—shall he not be careful
what words he uses, and what thought he expresses, when he sits in counsel
with his young friend?"—Trollope, *Thackeray*.

Howells himself said, reviewing John Hay's *The Breadwinners*, "Among
us at least the novelist is hereafter to be held to account as a public teacher."
Later he added, in *Novel-Writing and Novel-Reading*, "The novel can
teach . . . but only by painting life truly"; and he spoke in *Heroines of
Fiction* of "the supreme ethics which consist in portraying life truly and
letting the lesson take care of itself."

VIII

EDITOR AND PLAYWRIGHT

DURING THESE YEARS, from 1871 to 1881, Howells was the chief editor of *The Atlantic,* and, doing most of his work at home, he went in to Boston in the afternoon, sometimes only once a week. For editing took up a small part of his time. As a young man, he had written at night, but, finding his mornings free in Venice, he had begun to work then and had continued to do so ever since. He was a methodical writer, working from nine till twelve or one, and turning out a thousand words or fifteen hundred words a day; and, wherever he happened to be, in his own study, in hotels, on trains, he worked as regularly as Anthony Trollope. "An author," he said, "is merely one who has had the fortune to remember more than other men . . . Writing is only remembering the history of your life."

Where Howells's writing ended, his editing began, and in this he did more than anyone else to transform a New England literature into a literature that was broadly continental. These were the years when, as he said, Americans were "striving to evolve, to become a distinctive condition of the English race in literature," when American life was "not only getting looked at but getting fairly well represented . . . in details of motive and character slowly and honestly assembled by many hands from its vast spaces and varieties."

Through his encouragement most of these hands wrote for Howells's magazine, beginning with Mark Twain and Bret Harte speaking for the Far West, with Henry James for the American in Europe and with writers from every other section. There was "a tendency to seize with joy upon the expanding national life," Howells also wrote, in these post-Civil War years, and by 1879 he was able to say, "It seems to me that we are in a fair way to have a pretty school of really native American fiction." In the South, there had been scarcely anything but what the Spaniards called "Walter-Scottismo," with "the moral principles all standing on their heads in defence of slavery," and Howells brought in "Charles Egbert Craddock," George W. Cable, Joel Chandler Harris and many others. He serialized George Eggleston's *A Rebel's Recollections*, a bombshell from the point of view of Boston. Howells did not think writers should "try to write Americanly," but that, being born Americans, they should use their countrypeople whenever American characters served their turn: and it delighted him that writers were trying to make each part of the country and each phase of its civilization known to all the others. He encouraged even the use of local dialects, hoping that "our inherited English may be constantly freshened and revived" from these diverse native sources.[1]

Howells drew into the magazine various Western and Southern writers with Edward Eggleston, as well as George, H. H. Boyesen, John Hay, Charles Warren Stoddard and Sarah Orne Jewett. He had surely suggested to Miss Jewett her first book, *Deephaven,* published in 1877, which was simply a working out of Kitty Ellison's idea of a book in his

[1] Howells once quoted Alphonse Daudet who, apropos of Turgenev, said, "What a luxury it must be to have a great big untrodden barbaric language to wade into!"

own second novel, *A Chance Acquaintance*.² This had appeared as a serial in *The Atlantic* four years earlier. Then he was the first to feel Charles Warren Stoddard's rare quality when this other San Franciscan who had been Mark Twain's secretary³ sent him *A Prodigal in Tahiti*. "Respectability bores me horribly," Stoddard wrote to Howells. "I know that I shall hate heaven without a change of angels . . . between the acts of the endless oratorio," and he had gone off to become the author of the *South Sea Idylls*, "of the best prose then anywhere written," in Howells's opinion, "light, easy, whimsical, pictorial, touching." There were two other contributors to whom he was closely drawn as writers of realistic novels, H. H. Boyesen, a Norwegian immigrant whom he met in 1872, and the New Haven ex-officer, John W. De Forest. Howells had reviewed in *The Atlantic* in 1867

---

² Said Kitty in Quebec, in *A Chance Acquaintance*, "These queer little houses: they're the very places for things to happen in! I suppose there's a pleasure in finding out the small graces and beauties of the poverty-stricken subjects that they wouldn't have in better ones, isn't there? At any rate, if I were to write a story, I should want to take the slightest sort of plot, and lay the scene in the dullest kind of place, and then bring out all the possibilities. I'll tell you a book after my own heart, *Details*—just the history of a week in the life of some young people who happen together in an old New England country-house; nothing extraordinary, little every-day things told so exquisitely, and all fading naturally away without any particular result, only the full meaning of everything brought out."

This was a perfect description in advance of Sarah Orne Jewett's first novel.

³ "Poor, sweet, pure-hearted, good-intentioned, impotent Stoddard," Mark Twain wrote to Howells in 1880, "I have known him twelve years now and in all that time he has never been fit for anything but a consul. When I was at the Langham Hotel in London, I hired him for three months at $15 a week and board and lodging, to sit up nights with me and dissipate. At the end of the time he wouldn't take a cent. I had to finally smuggle it to him through Dolby after leaving England. . . . He is just the stuff for a consul. . . . Now you pitch in and leg for him. Get a quiet consulship *created* at Tierra del Fuego, if there shouldn't be a vacancy."

De Forest's *Miss Ravenel's Conversion*, "the only great novel," he called it, "which the Civil War produced . . . the first to treat the war really and artistically," with characters that were just like people in life. "His soldiers are the soldiers we actually know," Howells continued, "the green wood of the volunteers, the warped stuff of men torn from civilization and cast suddenly into the barbarism of camps, the hard, dry, tough, true fibre of the veterans that came out of the struggle." Their talk, moreover, was as natural and free as the soldiers' talk he was to admire in Stephen Crane and Tolstoy.

With this experienced novelist, Howells had a long correspondence, and he published as serials two or three of De Forest's books, describing him as "a realist before realism was named" and as "an admirably equipped artist." De Forest's work, he added, "has in some respects not only not been surpassed, but not approached among us," and he wrote about him again and again, reviewing this novel and that, and also in his later *Heroines of Fiction*. As a young man living in France, in that respect like Henry James, De Forest had read the French realistic writers, and Howells said he was "the pioneer in the path which the American novelists were to take," although Henry James came hard upon him. But he had offended what Tennyson called "the finer female sense," in whose favour the prosperity of American fiction resided, and, dealing with the disguises in which women's natures revealed themselves, he had a certain scornful bluntness. He was a man's novelist where men seldom read novels, for he could not flatter women's faults or foibles; and therefore, as women disliked him, he was never widely read in what Howells saw as a nation of women readers. As Howells said, referring to himself and Henry James, "Finer, not stronger, workmen succeeded him, and a delicate realism, more responsive to the claims and appeals of the feminine over-soul, replaced his inexorable veracity."

"Your appreciation," De Forest wrote in 1879 to Howells, who had fought valiantly for him, "thaws out a heart frozen by neglect," and later he wrote again in 1886, when Howells himself had grown more astringent, "I admire your honesty and courage. How dare you speak out your beliefs as you do? You spare neither manhood nor womanhood, and especially not the latter, though it furnishes four-fifths of the novel-reading public. It is a wonder that the females of America, at least the common born and bred of them, do not stone you in the streets." Long before this, H. H. Boyesen had recognized with Howells "the duty of unswerving fealty to the real thing in whatever you did," Howells's phrase that was realized later in *The Mammon of Unrighteousness*, Boyesen's somewhat bitter realistic novel. In that story of the family affairs of a self-made millionaire who founds a university in the state of New York, Boyesen showed how quickly an immigrant can become an American and one who has been sharply disillusioned. But Boyesen was at first a poet in romantic prose, a disciple of Björnstjerne Björnson in *Gunnar*, the story of a Norwegian cattle-boy which Howells also serialized in *The Atlantic*. With its goats and milkmaids, hulders and trolls, pine forests, fjords and snow-fields, the story might almost have been one of Björnson's, and yet in less than twenty years Boyesen was completely naturalized and wrote like an Anglo-Saxon born in the West. His diction was "apt and elect," said Howells, and he had learned the difference between good American English and newspaper English,—whenever he touched a phrase of the latter, he felt in his nerves its difference from true American and true English. Boyesen was teaching in the West, wretchedly lonely one day, then happy and full of great aspirations and dreams, and Professor Child had found him in the stacks of the Harvard Library and introduced him to Howells, to whom he read *Gunnar*. Howells was delighted with this Norwegian-American writer, and he took with Boyesen the long walks he had taken with Lowell and Henry James, talking about novels and the literary movement in Norway.

*

*   *

Meanwhile, in 1878, Howells wrote to Mark Twain, "To tell you the truth, I would ten times rather write plays than anything else." At that time he had already produced *Out of the Question, A Counterfeit Presentment* and his first so-called farce, *The Parlour Car*. Longfellow had come with him to a rehearsal of one of these plays,—which Lawrence Barrett brought to the Boston Museum,—and sat with him on the stage during the four acts with the keenest zest for all the details of the performance. Longfellow even thought that if he had been younger he would himself have composed altogether for the stage. Howells, who had written plays before he was thirteen, and who had been enraptured in Venice by Goldoni, often went to the theatre in Boston to see Salvini, Bernhardt, Ristori, the younger Kean and others who lured the upper classes. There, even the meteoric Offenbach "misled them," he wrote, "from the truth illustrated by the Symphony Concerts." Longfellow, who often asked Howells to dine, and always when George W. Greene was there, invited him once with Salvini for an Italian dinner.

Mark Twain, who disliked the theatre, was constantly tempted to write plays, just as Henry James was later in England, and he had begun to talk plays with Howells in 1875, suggesting this or that collaboration.[4] Howells urged him to dramatize Colonel Sellers, crazed by his own inventions and his belief that he was the rightful heir of an English earldom, and Howells himself wrote certain scenes of a play that was never produced, while Mark Twain wrote his own play, which was produced with success. Then Mark asked Howells to work with him on a second *Colonel Sellers,* establishing him permanently as *the* American character to be used by future generations of authors and actors. ("*Nobody* created Sellers," he added. "I simply put him on paper as I found him in life.") Mark would rise from the table, flinging his napkin into the chair, walking up and down, exulting in the thousands of dollars he was going to make; and he urged Howells to write another Sellers play to be called *Colonel Mulberry Sellers in Age.* "Your refined people and purity of speech would make the best possible background for this coarse old ass," he wrote; "and when you were done, I could take your manuscript and rewrite the Colonel's speeches and make him properly vulgar and extravagant . . . Shall we think this over? or drop it, as being nonsense?" For he never knew whether a plan was feasible or not.

Then Mark Twain proposed that he and Howells should write a comedy founded on the character of his brother Orion: "Do not fail to note the hopeful, glad-hearted, schoolboy cheeriness which bubbles out of every pore of this man who has been *always* a failure." Soon he said, *"Now* let's write a tragedy!" and he sent Howells a possible closing scene. He had noted an incident in Carlyle's *Cromwell,* and "Come," he said, "let's do this tragedy and do it well." He had another idea for a play, adding a new character to *Hamlet,* and in 1877

[4] But "we won't simultane,"—a made-up word of Mark Twain's, meaning, "produce simultaneously,"—with Canada.

he wrote that he had finished *Simon Wheeler, Detective*. "It had been conceived, plotted out, written and completed in 6½ working days of 6½ hours each: just a fraction under 250 manuscript pages . . . If the play's a success, it is worth $50,000 or more—if it fails it is worth nothing, and yet even the worst of failures can't rob me of the 6½ days of booming pleasure I have had in writing it."

Mark Twain tried to interest Howells in all manner of subjects,—"Have you blocked out the Sandwich Island play yet?"—while Howells's work was all of a piece and seldom strayed far from the realistic treatment of Americans he had seen and remembered. *Out of the Question*, a poorish play in fact, might have been suggested by Mark Twain's own story; for the hero is a self-made man, a Mississippi steamboat engineer, and he marries an Eastern girl who is socially above him. Stephen Blake is a "natural gentleman," but it is "out of the question" for Leslie Bellingham to marry him until it becomes "out of the question" for her not to do so: he has saved her brother from drowning and saved her from the tramps who have stolen her watch and broken Blake's own wrist. It was another vindication of Howells's repeated theme that merit has the right of way over breeding and station. *A Counterfeit Presentment* was a better play, and moreover it was produced with great success. The life of Constance Wyatt, a general's daughter, has been ruined by her engagement to a scoundrel,—a bigamist, a forger, a liar and a coward,—and she is shocked at first sight by his "counterfeit presentment," his physical double, in a summer hotel in New Hampshire. Bartlett is a landscape painter with a prodigious resemblance to the villain she has left behind in Paris, but, giving her lessons in sketching scenes of goldenrod and granite, he finally succeeds in winning her over. Howells was never so charming as in his courting episodes, through grape-trellises, in row-boats, in the parlours of summer hotels.

With all his passion for realism, Howells liked almost equally well the "absolutely unreal," as he called it, the purely fanciful in all the arts which he felt was on a lower plane,[5] but which always delighted him none the less. He liked comic operas and pantomimes that had their being wholly outside the realm of the probabilities, aware that they belonged to the decorative arts and were not to be ranked with imaginative works that represented and bodied forth human experience. He had vastly enjoyed Tasso's *Aminta* and Guarini's *Pastor Fido* with their "divinely excellent artificialities," with their "enamelled meadows," as he had once liked Pope. Indeed, he revelled in their "pretty impossibilities": what he objected to was the romantic or fantastic thing that asked to be accepted on the ground of reality. He loved Italian opera, that "divinely impossible thing which defies nature and triumphs over prostrate probability." He loved the Gilbert and Sullivan operas, "the most charming things in the world," he called them, and, seeing on the stage their impossible people, he breathed an atmosphere that was like the ether beyond the pull of our planet. It was far from all earthly laws and limitations. So he was happy to write a comic opera of his own, a libretto called *A Sea Change* for George Henschel's music. Unhappily, the manager of the theatre that was to produce it tried to climb into his yacht in a fog, fractured his skull and presently died. So Howells's comic opera was not produced.

The scene of *A Sea Change*, a "lyricated farce," was the promenade deck of a steamer, just out of Boston, with Muriel,

[5] But he also said, in *Imaginary Interviews*, "There is no inequality in the region of art."

the daughter of Mr. and Mrs. Vane, flying from Theron Gay, her lover. But Theron, to be near her, has stowed away on the ship, and Muriel's father and mother, discovering him, censure the young man, though Mr. Vane cannot see that he is so much to blame. He is, after all, a young man of respectable standing, a point the Vanes make in song and dance. Muriel, however, insists that Theron shall be put on shore—"Right away, right away, right away!" as Björnson said,—Björnstjerne Björnson who remarked that American women wanted things "right away," if they wanted things at all. But as the ship is two days out, this is quite impossible, so Muriel says that Theron must be put off on an iceberg; then, realizing that the ice-princess will get him, Muriel changes her mind, and they all make up and are happy. This libretto was a clear expression of the comic spirit, "like a gentle bubbling spring, always close beneath the surface," that one of Howells's friends noted in him, and that appeared and continued to appear in the farces he wrote until he was seventy-one years old. In that year, so far away, he wrote, for *Harper's Weekly, Saved: an Emotional Drama*, a "New Year's Story," a burlesque in which everyone is "saved," the burglar in the library, the little girl who finds him, and her father and mother. The little girl saves the burglar, the father is saved from forging a cheque and the mother is saved from running away with Arthur Fortesque. "Yes," says the child, "and we've *all* been saved, this happy New Year's morn; saved from robbing, from crime, from shame, from heedless fibbing, from good resolutions, from faintness for want of coffee"; and the burglar adds, "You never said a truer word, deary. Take the word of an honest man for that."

Howells's farces, dramatic scenes that were privately presented all over the United States and sometimes in England,

and even by professionals now and then, were often based on Goldoni's plays and occasionally resembled the witty little *proverbes* of Alfred de Musset. Some grew out of his own adventures, hiring a cook for his wife, for one, the theme of a later piece, *The Albany Depot;* some, like the *Parlour Car, The Register, The Elevator,* used situations suggested by recent inventions. What happens when elevators refuse to budge between the fourth and fifth floors and half a dinner-party is caught inside them? Then what may not be heard through a register between two rooms in which two separated lovers happen to be sitting? And what may occur when a wife goes out forgetting to tell her husband where she has hidden his dress coat? Many of the scenes take place in one of the new apartment hotels where the Robertses, the Willis Campbells and their friends rejoice in this "ideal way of living . . . all on one floor," and many shrewd remarks pass in these little compositions that are miracles now and then of taste and brightness.

Later Sir Henry Arthur Jones said that the delightful little plays were properly one-act comedies rather than farces. "In their stage quality," he wrote to Howells, "and assuredly in their literary quality, they are much higher than the average comedy of the English and American theatre . . . I found true comedy in the dialogue and characters of all of them. Surely it is in dialogue, and in individual scenes, and in character, that the true comedy touch can be recognized, rather than in the general scheme which may be quite farcical,—witness Molière." To this Howells replied, "Let us compromise in a foreign tongue"; and he agreed to call the plays *comediettas.*

IX

THE REALIST

DURING THEIR walks in Cambridge, H. H. Boyesen had talked with Howells about Turgenev, to whom he had dedicated *Gunnar*. The Russian novelist was corresponding with him, writing at first from Baden-Baden and presently from Paris and speaking of both Henry James and Howells. Turgenev was amused by James's reference to his aristocratic features, for his nose seemed to him rather plebeian, and then he continued about Howells, "I have read *Venetian Life* and *A Chance Acquaintance* and like both books very much indeed. I think I even prefer the former. There is in both a delightful freshness and *naturel,* and a gay, subtle, artless, elegant humour which I enjoyed thoroughly. Please to present my best compliments to Mr. Howells and tell him that I would be very glad to receive a copy of *Their Wedding Journey* from his hands."

This was in 1874, and Howells evidently sent the book, for Turgenev replied on October 28th, saying he had read it "with the same pleasure I experienced before in reading the *Chance Acquaintance* and *Venetian Life* . . . Your literary physiognomy," he continued, "is a most sympathetic one; it is natural, simple and clear—and in the same time it is full of unobtrusive poetry and fine humour. Then I feel the peculiar American stamp on it—and that is not one of the least causes of my relishing so much your work." For Turgenev had long been drawn to Americans and their literature and had read Bret Harte, Hawthorne and Whitman also. Turgenev himself was more widely read in America than in England and had been translated earlier in New York and Boston. There had been sixteen translations in America by 1874 and even a collected edition of them, when there were only five or six in England.

Thomas Sergeant Perry, who had met Turgenev in Paris, had told both Howells and Henry James about him. He was a great relief, said Perry, after "the London ball-room novel" in which no one was really moved by passion. "The biggest thing I have seen abroad is Mont Blanc, but the greatest is Turgenev," said one of the writers in the "Contributors' Club" in *The Atlantic,* a department that Howells established for light essays and letters. Indeed, the "Contributors' Club" buzzed for several months with notes about Turgenev's radiant young women, the Natalies, Elenas, Tatianas, Lizas who seemed to many readers like American girls. There was a long debate about Marianne in *Virgin Soil,* her insolence, her short hair and her opinions, and one writer noted that every character in this book could be matched by an anti-slavery, woman's suffrage or Fourierite American. Another compared Russians and Americans, in reviewing *Smoke,* which Boyesen had read with Howells in 1872: "One sadly recognizes in the Russians' grotesqueness, their tall talk, their fondness for all sorts of psychological, social and political quackery, their likeness to Americans, whom they resemble in the recentness and the geographical vastness of their country." By 1877, in fact, the interest in Turgenev had grown to the proportions of a veritable cult.

For Howells, Turgenev was, quite simply, "the man who

has set the standard for the novel of the future"; and he wrote later, "Life showed itself to me in different colours after I had once read Turgenev; it became more serious, more awful; and with mystical responsibilities I had not known before my gay American horizons were bathed in the vast melancholy of the Slav, patient, agnostic, truthful." Turgenev affected him both technically and spiritually, partly because he was free from the French preoccupation with the squalid, the base and the diseased, because of his elevation, the tenderness of many of his heroines and the simplicity and poetry of all that he wrote. His heroes, however weak, were never mean or unprincipled, and he was "profoundly serious," said Howells, "in behalf of what is just and good, even when he appears most impassive in respect to his characters . . . The Russians," Howells added, were "the great race which has more than any other fully and freely uttered human nature, without either false pride or false shame in its nakedness," and this first Russian author whom he read moved him almost as deeply for a while as the idol of his later years, Tolstoy. Turgenev too had a keen delight in reality for its own sake, and, following Björnson's influence, he contributed to rescue Howells from "the gross darkness of English fiction" (a phrase from Howells's later *My Literary Passions*). Abounding in poetry, colour and warmth, he was entirely free from the moralizing of Thackeray, the exegesis of George Eliot, the "stage-carpentry and limelighting" of Dickens, even the fine and important analysis of Hawthorne, and he stood aside and let the characters work the story out, with no assistance from the invisible author. "He seems the most self-forgetful of the story-telling tribe," Howells wrote in 1873, "and he is no more enamoured of his creations than of himself. He pets none of them; he upbraids none; you like them or hate them for what they are; it does not seem to be his affair."

For Howells, like Henry James,—and George Moore presently,—was more concerned than English critics with craftsmanship in the novel, with the art of fiction, just as he was more interested in Continental fiction than in the English novelists whom his countrymen admired. "All Continental Europe," he said, "has the light of aesthetic truth," and he shared what he called "the universal impulse which has given us the work, not only of Zola, but of Turgenev and Tolstoy in Russia, of Björnson and Ibsen in Norway, of Valdès and Galdós in Spain, of Verga in Italy." He was, in his tastes, cosmopolitan, and he was to go on to Zola's "epic greatness" and the realistic novelists of Italy and Spain.[1] He was responsive to the international tendencies in fiction as Americans later were to these tendencies in poetry. Meanwhile, in Turgenev, the "novelist's novelist," as Henry James called him, he found analogues with American novel-writing, in the withdrawal of the author from the scene, in singleness of theme, in restrictions of time and space and other matters; and again, as in Björnson's case, these ratified his own principles more than they actually influenced his work. Turgenev dealt "nearly always with small groups," he wrote, "isolated and analyzed in the most American fashion," adding that "in most American novels . . . the people are segregated if not sequestered, and the scene is sparsely populated."[2] "This effect

[1] Howells wrote introductions to the English translations of Galdós's *Doña Perfecta* and Verga's *The House by the Medlar Tree*. The latter was a translation of *I Malevoglia*, the first novel of a series of which the second, *Mastro-Don Gesualdo*, was translated by D. H. Lawrence. This story of a Sicilian fishing village was full of the "poetry," Howells said, "that resides in facts and resides nowhere else."

[2] "I suppose my tendency would always be to get my characters away from their belongings, and let four or five people act upon each other. . . .

may be," he added, "in instinctive response to the vacancy of our social life. There are few places and few occasions among us, in which a novelist can get a large number of polite people together, or at least keep them together," and that is why "we excel in small pieces with three or four figures, or in studies of rustic communities, where there is propinquity, if not society."

Howells might have been speaking here of his own earlier novels, which had, in this respect, so much in common with Turgenev; and among the characters in two of his later novels Turgenev was a subject of conversation. "The samovar sends up its agreeable odour all through his books," says Colville, in *Indian Summer*, to Imogene Grahame. "Read *Liza* if you want your heart really broken . . . If there are so many sad things in life that is a very good reason for putting them in books too." Then, in *April Hopes*, at Campobello, a group of ladies in the summer hotel talk about *Smoke* and *Liza*, the *Nichée des Gentilshommes*, as Mrs. Pasmer calls it ("with the involuntary superiority of a woman who reads her Turgenev in French"). "I must get *Liza*," this lady says. "I like a good heart-break, don't you? If that's what gave you the bad moment." But "there couldn't be an American *Liza*," another interposes, "and that's the charm of these Russian tragedies. You feel that they're so perfectly true there and so impossible here. Lavretsky would simply have got himself divorced from Varvara Pavlovna, and no clergyman could have objected to

---

I suppose I shall always have my people so few that their fates can be interwoven and kept constantly in common before the reader."—Howells, Letter of 1877.

"To put it paradoxically, our life is too large for our art to be broad. In despair at the immense scope and variety of the material offered it by American civilization, American fiction must specialize."—Howells, *Heroines of Fiction*.

marrying him to Liza." To this replies Miss Cotton, the sentimental old maid, "That's what I mean by his pessimism. He
leaves you no hope, and I think that despair should never be
used in a novel except for some good purpose, don't you, Mrs.
Brinkley?"—and the ladies continue for several pages this very
New England, or very American, discussion.

Turgenev was a great ally who strengthened Howells's own
beliefs,—his work was soon to show in *A Modern Instance*
some of the "sad things" that Turgenev wrote of,—while
Turgenev shared not only certain of his methods but also
his transparency of style. He shared especially the "truthfulness" that to Howells was all-important and that led Howells
to attack, for the harm they do, the "romanticistic" novelists
who falsified life. For while in general he disliked the "monstrous rag baby of Romanticism," he said the romanticistic
was as different from the romantic as the romantic was from
the realistic; and, preferring the realistic, he accepted the
romantic if it did not go in for too many "effects,"—"dire
catastrophes, sentimentality, prodigies, the flare of theatrical
facts," the "excess of Dickensosity" and so on. For these led
to sad results in those who read them. Howells was to be
impressed by the remark of another writer that modern minds
were largely fashioned by the novelists who wrote about them,
a perfect expression of his belief that the novelist must see
life straightforwardly and render a straight and truthful picture of it. "We believe fiction in the past to have been largely
injurious," he said, with this question always in mind.

One of Howells's readers wrote to him, "whatever in my
mental makeup is wild and visionary, whatever is untrue,
whatever is injurious, I can trace to the perusal of some work
of fiction"; and Howells himself liked to show this process of
cause and effect in many novels of his own. In fact, he never

ceased to do so, and in one of his last books, *The Vacation of the Kelwyns,* he showed how Parthenope Brook was misled by novels. She had drawn all her views from Grace Greenwood, Fanny Fern, Matilda Muffin and various other authors who had written sentimental nonsense, some of it in *The Atlantic* before his time there; and he pilloried this in book after book in the spirit of *Don Quixote,* which had lampooned false chivalry in a similar fashion. These novelists had inculcated "a varying doctrine of eager conscience, romanticized actuality, painful devotion and bullied adoration, with auroral gleams of religious sentimentality," he wrote. "Womanhood stood high in the temple of the cult where the votaries of these authors worshipped. Parthenope herself had never observed among her acquaintance that girls were really nicer than young men, but she believed that they ought to be won by heroes who sacrificed or ventured a great deal for them, rescued them from some sort of peril, or risked their lives for them even when they were not in danger." Howells, referring to his own work, continued (in *Novel-Writing and Novel-Reading*), "When I began to write fiction, we were under the romantic superstition that the hero must do something to *win* the heroine; perform some valorous or generous act; save her from danger, as a burning building or a breaking bridge, or the like . . . In compliance with this burdensome tradition, I had my hero rescue my heroine from a ferocious bulldog . . . This was in my first novel; but, after I began to look about me and consider, I observed that none of the loved husbands of the happy wives I knew had done anything to 'win' them except pay a certain number of visits, send them flowers, dance or sit out dances with them at parties, then muster courage to ask if they would have them. Amongst the young people of my acquaintance, I noticed that this simple and convenient sort of conquest was still going on; and I asked myself why it should be different in books. It was certainly very delightful as I saw it in nature, and why try to paint the lily or tint the rose?"

So, regarding untruth to nature as the eighth of the deadly sins, he continued to attack this "false school in literature," with its absurd heroics and counterfeit ideals and its "all-compelling lady's-novel hero." If the women in these books did not "burst into tears" or "choke with sobs" or, like many earlier heroines, "fall lifeless," they were too often filled with notions of self-sacrifice that were only weakening and blinding. What was "sublime" or "ennobling" in a young girl's marrying a man to punish herself for liking someone else, in the novel admired by Sibyl Vane whose "romantic benefi-cence" and "unselfish interest" made so much trouble for Lemuel in *The Minister's Charge?* The pretty little self-righteous prig, Alice Pasmer, in *April Hopes,* who has so many scruples and preposterous ideals, has been "taught to believe" in them by "the novels," as Howells says, "to which we all trust our instruction in such matters."[3] To Dan, who is simple and single-minded, Alice exclaims, in the words that Romola addresses to Tito in George Eliot's romance, "You are a faithless man!" and she throws him over, not at all perceiving, in her "high-minded piety," how very different Dan is from Tito. It was Imogene's false romanticism that caused such havoc in *Indian Summer,* and this could be said of Penelope Lapham also; and Howells never tired of ex-

[3] "Isn't there a theory that women forgive injuries, but never ignominies?"
"That's what the novelists teach, and we bachelors get most of our doc-trine about women from them. . . . We don't go to nature for our impres-sions, but neither do the novelists, for that matter. Now and then, however, in the way of business,"—Atherton is a Boston lawyer,—"I get a glimpse of realities that makes me doubt my prophets."—Atherton in Howells's *A Modern Instance.*

posing this moralistic folly and the silly romantic notions acquired from novels. At the great dinner-party in *The Rise of Silas Lapham* the company discusses "Tears, Idle Tears," in which the hero and heroine keep dying for each other and sacrificing for each other in the most satisfactory and unnecessary way. It is nothing but "psychical suicide," says the minister Sewell, who adds that there never was a time when novels did more to shape people's minds and that "they do more mischief than ever."

No doubt there was more to be said than Howells admitted for the romantic novels that "befool and debauch us." But he was convinced that Thackeray, Dickens, Bulwer, Charles Reade and all their living followers were "untruthful," Dickens, with his "Gothic tendency to grotesque and monstrous decoration" and Thackeray with his preference of caricature to character. In Dickens, he said, "there is never the open air, never the light of day, always the air of the theatre, always the light of the lamps," and he disliked Thackeray's "willingness to dawdle," not to say "twaddle over his scene, when it was his affair to represent it: he stood about, with his hands in his pockets, interrupting the action and spoiling the illusion in which alone the truth of art resides." It was true that, reading *Great Expectations* many years later, he was ashamed of having slighted Dickens and "the wholesome allegiance to life of his game of make-believe." Amazed by the variety and fullness of the book, he recovered his original love of Dickens, and he said we ought to have several lives in order to correct in one the mistakes of another. As for Sir Walter Scott, he said, "You love the man more and more, while you respect the artist less and less," for he was one of the fountainheads of the "rage for effectism" that set Howells against the "bad manners of English fiction." For Scott, with his "great poetic soul," was always "loose, straggling, imperfect and deficient in surplus"; and Charles Reade was "forever at your elbow, winking at you, sticking his tongue in his cheek." Howells felt that George Eliot, with her faithful representing of commonplace things, was the greatest English talent after Jane Austen, or beside Anthony Trollope, "with his immense, quiet, ruminant reality, ox-like cropping the field of English life and converting its succulent juices into the nourishing beef of his fiction." He who had once thought Trollope dull now regarded him as wise, just and sane, with his "simple honesty and instinctive truth, as unphilosophized as the light of common day." But, above all, he admired Jane Austen in whom he saw "the norm and prophecy of most that is excellent in Anglo-Saxon fiction since her time." She was the criterion for "the serene veracity which is the sole law of beauty and lord of all moods and times."

These views of Howells appeared in *Criticism and Fiction,* or in the later *Heroines of Fiction,* or, in 1882, in the essay on Henry James that presently brought a storm of abuse about him. It was not yet known, he said, to the ignorant masses of educated people, that James was one of the greatest masters of fiction, an unrivalled artist in a thick-witted time that was vulgarized by the prevalence of puerile romance. One liked James's characters through their own qualities, not by the author's petting or insinuation, and Howells went on to say that fiction had become a finer art than it had been with Thackeray and Dickens. One could not tolerate any more Dickens's mannerisms or Thackeray's confidential attitude, for the novelist had no more business in the novel than the painter in the picture. Those great men were of the past, along with their methods and interests, while the new school studied human nature in its wonted aspects and "the moving accident" was "certainly not its trade." Literature and art, said Howells, were to be judged only by the test of their fidelity to life, and he continued, "In one manner or another, the stories were all told long ago, and now we want merely to know what the novelist thinks about persons and situations." For, as art advances, character becomes more important than plot and the action must be the action that springs from this. Therefore the American novelists were going to the Continent where art was much more serious than it was in England, except in "the simple verity and refined perfection" of Jane Austen, the most artistic English writer of novels.

X

IN THE SEVENTIES

Two other messages came to Howells from Turgenev. Henry James wrote from Paris that the author of *Liza* and *Smoke* had the "most agreeable memory" of Howells's writings, and he wished James to pass this on to his friend in Boston. Then, a little later, President Hayes, of all men, in Washington,—Rutherford B. Hayes, Mrs. Howells's cousin, —also wrote that he had met a German member of the Reichstag who had known Turgenev, perhaps in Baden-Baden. To this man, who had lived in the United States, Turgenev had said, "I have spent the night reading *A Chance Acquaintance*. Do they have in America such girls as the one from Erie-creek?" and the German said, "Of course. Go and see one."

Howells, in the meantime, had written another campaign biography, *The Life and Character of Rutherford B. Hayes*, to celebrate this cousin by marriage who had vetoed the Chinese Exclusion Act, a "firm-willed, humorous, unpretentiously self-reliant man." Howells had examined old letters and records of his wife's family and produced in three weeks a shapely little book, which he had obviously composed with a certain enjoyment. The book was published in 1876, during which he visited the Centennial in Philadelphia. This he reported for *The Atlantic*, saying that the sculpture was mostly Italian, with two or three American "disgraces." The English sent only story pictures, no doubt their best, but still too literary, in Howells's opinion, while the French sent their second-best; and Howells was struck by the distracting variety of influences in the sometimes excellent American landscapes and portraits. But it was obvious that the national genius spoke most freely in things of iron and steel, and Howells was impressed by the elegance, ingenuity and aptness of the mechanical triumphs of invention and skill. There was, for instance, the Dynamo that was to figure so largely in the mind of Henry Adams, who was also there.

Hayes, whom the Howellses visited later, a Civil War general and Governor of Ohio, had appointed Bayard Taylor as minister to Germany, and, at Howells's suggestion, he appointed Lowell to England, and, earlier, to Spain. ("I *should* like to see a play of Calderón," said Lowell, who had refused an appointment to Vienna.) Then, to Mark Twain's disgust but with Howells's scrupulous recommendation, he had sent Bret Harte to Germany as a consul. (Howells had written an honest letter, speaking as well as he could of Harte, adding, "I should have great hopes of him,—and fears. It would be easy to recall him.") Hayes asked the Howellses to join him, in two private cars, with General Sherman and others, on a trip to California. They could not go, and the plan was abandoned because of a necessary extra session of Congress; but they spent a week in the White House in 1880. With the President, every morning, Howells went for a long walk, and he carefully studied Washington where he soon thought of going to live and which appeared in his novel, *April Hopes*. Hayes talked to him freely, especially about the South, but also, as a discriminating reader, about novelists and novels. As a result of another talk with Howells, he read *Anna Karenina* a few years later. He recorded in his diary

then, "A fine time with W. D. Howells—as charming and
bright as ever, and more and more a man of wisdom and
heart."

During these years, and somewhat later, Howells was
offered professorships at Union College, in St. Louis, at Johns
Hopkins, Yale and eventually Harvard, refusing them all as
a novelist who was devoted to his trade and who knew that
he "could not *teach* by any sort of text-book." He had, however, a literary use of Spanish, Italian, German and French,
and he knew that he could make others feel "the beauty and
importance of literature," so he had accepted for a year or
two President Eliot's invitation to talk at Harvard about new
Italian writers. Then, in Boston, he gave the Lowell Institute
lectures on "Italian Poets of Our Century," and Lowell himself went into town to hear them. Of these lectures there were
twelve, and they formed the substance of his book *Modern
Italian Poets,* the only account in English at the time of these
patriots in verse, some of whom Howells no doubt overrated.
With them in several cases literature was merely an instru-
ment for the redemption of their divided country, but among
them were Parini, who had satirized the Lombard nobles,
Alfieri, Ugo Foscolo, Manzoni of the tragedies and poems,
Leopardi, Niccolini and Giusti. Great and small alike, these
poets had educated Italian readers for their own national freedom, and the series, with Howells's faithful translations,
sketched the history of Italian poetry for the hundred years
ending in 1870. Referring to De Sanctis often, Howells had
shown much independence of judgment, and he revealed by
implication his own constant sympathy for the Risorgimento.[1]

---

[1] "I lived in Italy in the Garibaldi days,"—about which Trevelyan's son
was writing,—"when he was still a god, and the gondoliers expected him as
in a second coming. Once, at the Porto Lago Scuro, in order to pay a boatman thrice his fare, I had to change a five-franc piece, which I did by

Meanwhile, as early as 1868, Howells had written to Charles Eliot Norton that Mrs. Howells's ill-health was his one great drawback,—"for it is hard for her to bear and for me to see." She had never entirely recovered from the birth of her second child and for the rest of her life remained a semi-invalid, "a mere shadow of a little fair woman," as one observer remembered, "but bright and very feminine in her style of talking." She described as a "hideosity" an ugly old table of her husband's, and it was evident that Howells studied her conversation for the talk of certain women in his novels. He listened to her appreciatively, and he discussed with her all his ideas and read to her everything he wrote. Another observer, Hamlin Garland, described her somewhat later as "a tiny figure, a wraith physically, but with a gay, humorous outlook on literature and life . . . almost always with a shawl or scarf over her shoulders, very pale, with a piquant, wrinkled face." With her wit and her disconnected flashes of wisdom, she was eager for news of the world from which she had withdrawn, and Howells was always called upon to report what he had seen and to describe the people he had met. This no doubt helped him to realize the world he was living in, but in time it kept him, Garland thought, from mingling with men, and it caused him to share a little too much what he called Mrs. Basil March's "female instinct for domiciliation." In certain of his novels,—for one, *A Hazard for New Fortunes*,—he went to extraordinary lengths in describing the problems of housekeeping and apartment-hunting, and in general all those questions that were of special

---

grace of a kind fellow who went to get it done. When he came back I offered him half a franc for his trouble but he drew back, hurt. . . . A bystander whispered, awestrickenly, 'E Garibaldini!' So the hero consecrated and ennobled his followers."—Howells, Letter to Sir George Otto Trevelyan, 1907.

concern to what he called a nation of women readers. His editorship undoubtedly accentuated these tendencies, but so did his great devotion to an invalid wife, and he had humorously complained in a letter to Norton, "I began by representing myself as an intellectual ruin . . . I think my state is partially attributable to too much female society; and what becomes of literary men in Paynim lands, where wives, nurses and grandmothers are indefinitely multiplied in households, I couldn't in my enfeebled condition guess." But he also said, "There is no society but that of women for an idler,"—or an author—"in our country; the other men are busy and tired, with little patience and little sympathy for men who are not busy and tired."

*

*   *

In August, 1875, Charles Dudley Warner, Mark Twain's Hartford collaborator, wrote to Howells from Venice, telling him how much he liked *Italian Journeys* and then continuing as follows, "But it is time you quit paddling alongshore and struck out into the ocean. Ask Mrs. Howells (with my love) if it is not so. The time has come for you to make an *opus*—not only a study on a large canvas but a picture. Write a long novel, one that we can dive into with confidence, and not feel that we are to strike bottom in the first plunge. We want to swim with you, not merely to lave our faces." Warner added, "If you won't write the great novel, I hope Mr. James will."

At this moment Henry James was writing *Roderick Hudson,* but Howells, who had developed more slowly, or with greater hesitation, was not ready yet for a long novel, and it was not until he retired from *The Atlantic* that he entered upon his most important phase. As early as Warner's letter, however, he had no doubt been brooding on the theme of *The Undiscovered Country,* for during that summer he had spent six weeks at Shirley near the Shakers, who formed the background of the novel. He had seen the Shakers constantly and watched them at work, making brooms, baskets and hooked rugs, braiding palm-leaf hats and cultivating their corn, raspberries and grapes. The novel itself, if not the "picture" that Warner asked for, was the "study on a large canvas" that appeared in 1880,—"the strongest thing Mr. Howells has done," as Brooks Adams said in a review, "of stronger fibre than his other books . . . Mr. Howells hitherto seems to us to have spent his strength on rather small game . . . But now he has . . . entered upon a broader field."

Why was Howells drawn to the Shakers, with whom he found himself presently "on intimate terms of friendship," as he wrote to Warner, those Yankee monks and nuns who were known to the world for their garden seeds, their brooms, their quaintness in dress and their religious dances? They were objects at the time of as much curiosity as the Indians of New Mexico were to be; and Howells first wrote about them in a little book called *Three Villages,* a "profile" like those in *The New Yorker* decades later. Howells certainly found unsympathetic what they called the "gospel relation," as distinguished from the "marriage relation," in the "Adamic order of life," and as one of the American "worshippers of marriage,"[2] and especially of young love, he was all for the earthly

---

[2] "We Americans are worshippers of marriage."—Howells, *Hither and Thither in Germany.*

It was notable that, in 1877, Howells, writing to Henry James, urged him to let Newman (in *The American*) marry Madame de Cintré. James explained in a letter of sixteen pages why this marriage would have been impossible.

order of the "world outside." He must have detested their phrase for falling in love as "feeling foolish," and he might, on the whole, have agreed with Ford, in *The Undiscovered Country,* that their life was simply "the dream of a sick woman." Yet there was something in Shakerism that still appealed to him, aesthetically and spiritually and as a novelist, for, as Henry James wrote to him, the field of *The Undiscovered Country* was "something really new and unworked . . . a real *trouvaille.*" The Shakers, moreover, represented the ideals of equality and fraternity that Howells had inherited from his father, and their kind of communism was closely akin to the socialism that he was to celebrate later. With their suggestion of the early Christians,—childish as they were, sheltered from most of the experiences that make for growth,—they had at times an innocence that appealed to Howells, although other shrewd observers questioned this.[3] Howells's aesthetic sense, moreover, delighted as much as Charles Sheeler's in their clean-lined furniture and functional buildings, and even their costumes pleased him as they danced their "mystic round." Their low-crowned, broad-brimmed beaver hats and straight-skirted coats of drab, their broad flat shoes and hair that hung low in the back, together with the stiff gauze caps and white kerchiefs of the women, were the rustic American dress of two centuries ago. All this charmed Howells's taste for the picturesque.

[3] "I know the Shakers, having lived many summers near Lebanon, and I am aware that you know all about them. It is quite new material, and capital for a novel. How much they are in earnest is the great question. Old General Porter of Niagara told me that in his business relations he never could get the Shaker chief to own up to anything, not even that any of the Shakers kissed the girls. I was with Fanny Kemble when a girl of a Shaker store at Lebanon sold us baskets. 'I see,' said Fanny to her, 'that you are English; so am I, and we are both alike, only you act at Lebanon, while I act at New York.' "—Thomas G. Appleton, Letter to Howells, 1880.

Howells's feeling for the Shakers stood for one of the twenty characters that, as he said, we all possess, and in a sense it was scarcely more marked than his delight in pretty women or his distaste for slovenliness in dress. But Henry James perceived that the feeling ran very deep and that, for this reason, he had not presented Shakerism as grotesque or pictorial or "whatever-it-may-be" enough. He had described it, James continued, "too un-ironically and as if you were a Shaker yourself. (Perhaps you are—unbeknown to your correspondents and contributors—and this is the secret of your book!)" Howells was, after all, the child of Quakers and Swedenborgians, with a very unworldly element at the bottom of his heart, and he felt in this "angelic life" something that resembled the Swedenborgian notion of the life hereafter. He was struck by the charity and truthfulness of the Shaker elders whom he knew and by "that scarcely less lovable quaintness to which no realism could do perfect justice," and he was taken with their idea of a house for wayfarers,—"Our rule," as they said, "forbids us to turn anyone away." So he came back to the Shakers later in *The Vacation of the Kelwyns* and in two weak brief novels, "idylls in drab," *The Day of Their Wedding* and *A Parting and a Meeting*. In one of these a Shaker couple who have run off to be married find that they cannot live in the world outside. Their training has been too much for them. They cannot enter the earthly order, and they return to Lebanon unmarried.

But the Shakers formed only the background of *The Undiscovered Country,* perhaps the most poetic of Howells's novels, which opens in a shabby Boston street inhabited by "ghost-seers" and fortune-tellers with "Madam" on their doorplates. There Dr. Boynton, the spiritualist, a gullible enthusiast, lives with his daughter Egeria in a queer melancholy

house where he gives public seances during which light taps
are heard on the table and the valves of the sliding doors.
Egeria, a beautiful tall young girl in a robe of white serge
with a pale green scarf acts as the "test-medium" at these
seances, asking, "Is it you, Giorgione?"—to which the reply
comes, "Yes, it is,"—for "He never can keep away when colour
is mentioned." So says Dr. Boynton, who has come from
Maine, like Mrs. Eddy's Dr. Quimby, and who has looked
deeply into mesmerism and expounds his ideas with "a pleased
air of scientific enquiry." Egeria has been his mesmeric
subject almost from birth, and he is sure that "we stand upon
the verge of a new era. The key to the mystery is found!" But
then comes the journalist Ford who is bent on exposing him
and putting an end to his researches. Dr. Boynton flees, taking the lovely pythoness, with whom the determined Ford
has fallen in love, but in his confusion he gets on the wrong
train, while all his possessions and money are carried off to
Portland. He sets out with Egeria to visit the Shakers who are
familiar with "spiritualistic science," and eventually Dr. Boynton dies among them. Egeria, desperately ill, recovers in the
spring and marries Ford, who has found her there.

Up to a point the story might almost have been a sketch
for James's *The Bostonians*, published six years later, with
Egeria for Verena Tarrant and Ford for the rescuer Ransom
in a Boston of innumerable isms. Some of it savoured of
Hawthorne, an influence that William James had noted in
his brother's and Howells's early work,[4] and it savoured espe-

---

[4] "It also tickled my national feeling not a little to note the resemblance
of Hawthorne's style . . . to yours and Howells's. . . . That you and
Howells, with all the models in English literature to follow, should needs
involuntarily have imitated (as it were) this American, seems to point to
the existence of some real American mental quality."—Letter of William
James to Henry James, 1870.

cially of *The Blithedale Romance,* Hawthorne's story of Brook Farm, in the picture of the communal life of the Shakers. Howells suggested an era in Boston, a day of psychic experiments, along with campaigns for women's rights, when trance-speakers invited the crowd in their carryalls and buggies at Walden Pond to "Come, come to spirit-land." Then he had touched off in a few lines Boston characters of the time, Phillips, Ford's friend, the collector, for instance, on the lookout for fiddle-back chairs, old pewter, tin lanterns, spinning-wheels and claw-footed tables. There was Dr. Boynton's landlady, Mrs. Le Roy, who confessed, "I give the spirits a fair chance," and the large watery-eyed Mr. Eccles with the mottled face and the reddish hair and the "dental smile" who towered at the seances ("as a lofty mould of jelly may be said to tower"). The taciturn Ford, avoiding society even more than Phillips,—who consorted mainly with "men of a feminine temperament,"—was the type of new intellectual who had come in after the Civil War and whom one connected rather with *The Nation* in New York.

As for the bland Dr. Boynton, he was a character of the time indeed,—he might almost have been Bronson Alcott,[5]— but an even more memorable figure was Egeria, the victim of the mesmerist who awakens to life and love among the sympathetic Shakers. Nothing could have been more charming than the Hawthornesque tale of her convalescence as the spring comes on in the New England country, with the

----

[5] Many years later, in 1904, H. G. Wells wrote to Howells, "*The Undiscovered Country* is a delightful addition to my knowledge of you—and the Shakers. It's the nearest thing I know of yours to a form I dream of, a novel in which the leading character so to speak is a *topic.* I like the figures of the wandering Boyntons best, the preoccupation of the doctor, and the perplexed young girl, the fading vanishing quest, the snow and the strange people."

velvety new leaves and the unfolding buds,[6] or the picture of Egeria and Ford in the vineyard, she on one side of the trellis, he on the other. They find it easier to be frank with a screen of vines between them, catching glimpses of each other through the tendrils.

It was Howells's belief that a novelist's power was to be tested largely by his success in dealing with women,[7] and he was himself in general perhaps more successful with women than with men, or, one might rather say, than young men. For his older men, Silas Lapham, Dryfoos, Godolphin, Bromfield Corey, were fine, well-drawn characters indeed. But how superior, as both characters and portraits, were the women in *Dr. Breen's Practice,* for one example, and *A Modern Instance,*—novels that followed *The Undiscovered Country,*—the first novel decidedly unimportant and the second one of the best he wrote. Grace Breen was an attractive girl who had become a physician because for a moment she had failed

6 "It might well have seemed to the girl's impatience as she watched the orchard trees, sometimes from her closed window and sometimes from her open door, as the day was chill or soft, that the blossoms would never come; and even when every tip of the mossed and twisted boughs was lit with the pink glimmer of a bud, and the tree's whole round was suffused with a tender glint of colour, that the delicate petals of rose and snow would never unfold. The orioles and bobolinks sang from the airy tops, and from the clover in the grassy alleys among the trees; in a neighbouring field the oats were already high enough to brighten and darken in the wind. . . . The grape-vines on Elder Joseph's trellis were set thick with short, velvety leaves of pinkish olive, when suddenly, in a warm night, the delaying buds unfolded and in the morning the apple blossoms had come. . . . 'It seems right,' said Elder Joseph, 'to be getting well in the spring, when everything is taking a fresh start. I like to see the young woman looking so happy.' . . . 'My getting well,' said Egeria, 'is part of the spring.' . . . With her blue eyes dreamily untroubled, she looked like some sylvan creature, a part of the young terrestrial life that shone and sang and bloomed around her."— *The Undiscovered Country.*

7 "I must still believe that novelists are great in proportion to the accuracy and fullness with which they portray women."—Howells, *Heroines of Fiction.*

where other women's hopes are and who broke down as a doctor because she could not keep men away and because women patients would not trust her. They felt they were safer in the hands of the stupidest boy. It was a topical novel at a time when women physicians were just coming to the front, and the young and pretty Dr. Breen fails in her profession because, as a woman precisely, she succeeds so well.[8] Walter Libbey, whom she marries, is a vague young man, floating round the world, with no object in living until he goes back to direct his family's mills; and he is like many of Howells's other young men, who are often more than a little wishy-washy. There is Dan Mavering, in *April Hopes,* between the pull of two strong women, inconclusive, always asking for help and advice; there is the unstable Emerance, in *The Vacation of the Kelwyns,* with his "groping past and hesitating present"; and there is Easton, in *Mrs. Farrell,* with his "little pursuits," aimless, apologetic and masochistic. Then there is Breckon, in *The Kentons,* asking one and all whether he ought to be a minister or not. Generally speaking, in Howells's work, it is the women who make the decisions, in accordance with Bromfield Corey's remark that "the women in America represent the aristocracy which exists elsewhere in both sexes." For the rest, in *Dr. Breen's Practice,* the scene is one of those seaside hotels with a croquet-ground over the ocean, as in one of Winslow Homer's water-colours. The ladies in the morning gather on the beach, knitting and sewing in the shelter of the cliff while one of them reads aloud, *Middlemarch,* perhaps.

Marcia, too, in *A Modern Instance,* is admirably drawn. She is, in fact, one of the first-rate Howells characters, only

---

[8] "But when did a woman ever mean business, except in the one great business?"—Howells, *Fennel and Rue.*

matched in his work so far by the flashy Bartley Hubbard, the journalist who rises in Boston and then rapidly falls. He is a "poor, cheap sort of a creature, deplorably smart and regrettably handsome," as Ben Halleck remembers from their country college days, but he has the air of a man of the world in the village of Equity where he edits the "Free Press" for a while. There Squire Gaylord, who seems always to be working his rusty jaws, the village deist, takes the young man's measure, but he cannot cure his daughter's infatuation, and Marcia, handsome, jealous, passionate and proud, follows Bartley when he has to leave the village. She obliges him to marry her and take her to Boston where, after many ups and downs and many of Bartley's contemptible tricks, her husband deserts her and vanishes into the West. Finally, on a trumped-up charge, he sues her for divorce, and the terrible old squire, determined to see justice done, induces her to go with him and contest the suit. In the end, Ben Halleck, in love with Marcia, fails, even after Bartley's death, to urge the marriage with him that would probably have been happy. He is a desperate victim of New England scruples.

To the question of "happy endings" Howells was indifferent. "The novel ends well that ends faithfully," he said; and in its equivocal conclusion *A Modern Instance* was not unique among his books. But it was a major novel, beyond any question, in its depth and range of feeling, in its visibility, in its variety of characters and sombreness of theme; and the story of Bartley's deterioration and Marcia's fanatical belief in him was one of the most moving that Howells wrote. The grim village of Equity was singularly real; so was the newspaper world of the "moral vineyard," Bartley Hubbard's phrase for Boston where he himself played for a while a brilliant part. There was nothing that Howells did not know about the journalistic life, and he must have delighted in picturing Bartley's way in journalism, which was so different from his own.[9] For Bartley, with his "reporter's rhetoric," wrote for the effect he was going to make, not from any pleasure in the treatment,—his motive was as different as possible from the literary motive; and, writing about "Boston's Boarding-houses," he gathered all the facts but made no attempt to give them form. He did not try to imagine a young country couple like Marcia and himself finding or hoping to find their place in the city; he set about to produce a "spicy" sketch that had also largely the character of an exposé. For he knew there was nothing the public enjoyed more than an exposé that seemed to be made in the reader's own interest.[10] It was Bartley who got up "Our 'Solid Men' Series," in which he later included Silas Lapham, interviews with "merchant princes and leading manufacturers," one of whom at present was the elder Halleck. This good old man appeared as "A Nestor of the Leather Interest," and he and his family, village people who had risen in business but remained unspoiled, were drawn as carefully and vividly as Marcia and Bartley. Of the other characters, one was to appear in several of Howells's later books, Clara Kingsbury, who made all unhappy people's affairs her own, while she had "a very large streak of silliness in her." A love of luxury and a sense of duty were equally mingled in Miss Kingsbury's mind, and she lived between the extremes of squalor and fashion.

[9] In another novel, *The Quality of Mercy*, Howells contrasted Pinney,— another pushing journalist like Bartley Hubbard,—with the "old-fashioned, quiet ideal of newspaper work," which he liked and remembered.

[10] "Oh, if you knew what I have suffered from the unchallenged predominance of America's Bartley Hubbards you would understand the grateful delight with which I behold them with a ring in their nose at last!"— George W. Cable, Letter to Howells, 1883.

Howells wrote *A Modern Instance* after he left *The At-lantic,* but long before this Charles Dudley Warner praised the authenticity of "this Ohio poacher in our New England." It was true that Thomas Wentworth Higginson, a sort of pro-fessional New Englander, wrote to him asking, "Are you sure you have heard the catbird sing at night? I never did. The robin sings later than the catbird, and the green-finch or vesper-bird in very rural villages is later than the robin; but neither as late as that." Few readers doubted, however, that Howells knew New England, as well as a larger world and a larger life, and before the end of his first phase Oliver Wendell Holmes wrote to him,—his friend of the midnight walk on Boston Common, "I must congratulate you on the brilliant and commanding position you have fairly won for yourself. You have brought us an outside element which Boston needed and have assimilated all that Boston could do for you . . . so completely that it seems as if you had cheated some native Esau out of his birthright."

XI

A VISIT TO ENGLAND

Howells was a wanderer, he was a nomad all his life, and, dwelling in Boston, or the region of Boston, more or less, for fifteen years, he moved constantly even there. From his original carpenter's box, he moved first to Berkeley Street, then to Concord Avenue, in 1872, where he built a new Cambridge house in an old garden, a house with a mansard roof and a library with Eastlake tiles, picturing the seasons in brown and yellow. Then, five years later, he built another at Belmont, a few miles away, designed by McKim, Mead and White, the firm of his wife's brother. "Redtop," this ample cottage with its sloping red roof, looked out over Cambridge and Boston, and the old philosopher Henry James wrote to him in praise of this "fairy abode of light and beauty" on its "cheerful, breezy hill . . . I never saw a house," said James, "that took my fancy more captive at once by its tone of colour—as soon as I had entered the door; and every subsequent impression deepened the effect. All the details struck me as purely lovely, and when I looked from within outwards and over that incomparable landscape . . . I said to myself, 'Well, good fortune can no further go. Let silence muse the amount of it!' "

There Longfellow came to supper to meet Garfield, soon to be President, the old Ohio friend who said to Howells, "I

was thinking how much like your father you carried yourself." Howells was to spend only three years in this remoter
suburb before he resigned from *The Atlantic* where, as he
wrote, "the proofs, the books, the letters have become insupportable," so that he broke down with a serious illness. Besides, he wished to live wholly as a writer, and it seemed
financially safe to resign when such a weak little novel as
Dr. Breen's Practice could go through sixteen editions in ten
years. In fact, all his books, weak and strong, were popular
now, even though they had no element of cheap popular
interest.[1] After the years of editorship, Howells was succeeded
by Thomas Bailey Aldrich. Meanwhile, one of his Belmont
neighbours was the painter George Fuller, who had shown
his pictures in Boston a few years before. Howells was greatly
taken with *The Romany Girl* and *She Was a Witch*, and,
struck by his authentic charm and the delicate glow of his
canvases, he became attached at once to the tall, burly artist.
Later he was to write a sketch of George Fuller's life and
work in the memorial volume that was published about this
luminous painter of the New England landscape,[2] who had
been an itinerant portrait painter and a practical farmer in
Deerfield where he reclaimed great patches of swamp
meadow. George Fuller had painted portraits of Mrs. Howells's father and brother. No doubt, he was one of the painters
who led Howells to remark that Bostonians never bought
American pictures.

Howells set out for a visit to England and a year in Europe in July, 1882, sailing from Quebec, where his father
was now the American consul and one of his sisters had

---

[1] *Suburban Sketches* went through eleven editions in fifteen years; *A
Fearful Responsibility*, ten editions in nine years; *A Foregone Conclusion*,
seventeen editions in seventeen years, etc.
[2] *George Fuller: His Life and Works.*

married a French-Canadian journalist. Mark Twain had recently come to visit him before his own journey down the Mississippi to collect new material for his book on the river; and he and Howells went out to Concord to pay their respects to Emerson who was to die, like Longfellow, a few weeks later. Not long before this, Henry James had written from London, "I have lately seen several times our friend Clemens on his way back to Hartford. He seemed to me a most excellent pleasant fellow and what they call here very 'quaint.' Quaint he is." James had also written, "What has struck me here is the almost absurd facility of success," for it had taken him fifteen years at home to make the reputation he seemed to have acquired in a few months in England. "Continue to Americanize and to realize: that is your mission," he wrote to Howells, "and if you stick to it you will become the Zola of the U.S.A." He added, before Howells arrived, "From here I am greatly struck with the extreme *freshness* of your work. I mean that newness and directness of personal impression, of feeling as to what you write about, which is the most precious thing in literature,—and which is in such vivid contrast with the staleness of tone and flatness of note of most of the writing here."

Now James "housed and started this orphan family in London . . . as an adoptive father," Howells wrote, taking for them in South Kensington a set of very good rooms and introducing Howells here and there. James had given him, years before, a letter to Anthony Trollope, in whose house he had spent a night in 1866; but Howells was still little known in England, in spite of the great popularity of his first book, *Venetian Life*. However, he had gone there largely to see through the press a charming edition of his work in twenty-one volumes. A Scottish publisher, David Douglas,

was bringing them all out in Edinburgh in a sort of minia-
ture form, delightfully attractive, with a paperback shilling
series of other American authors, including Holmes, Burroughs, Cable and Frank R. Stockton.[3] At this time also,
Oscar Wilde, who was travelling in America, attacking American outdoor advertising and finding how prosaic in Utah
polygamy was, said in a lecture in Cincinnati that there was
"no living English novelist" who could be named with Henry
James and Howells. He had read every one of the books of
that "most charming writer, Howells," who found himself
lionized now, mildly, in England. He had acquired a certain
popularity there. He had himself largely outgrown what he
described once as "our historical grudge" against the English,
in his case dating from the day when, during the Civil War,
they had covered Americans with "mockery and contumely."
He had paid them back in his own way for their sneers at
America by many ironical remarks about the English; but the
trouble with this sort of thing is that it always hits the people
who have not been the original offenders.

Howells seemed to Edmund Gosse, who saw much of him,
"tremblingly alive, like an excited child." He had an "airy
playfulness," Gosse wrote later, "a sort of roguishness which
faded from him in years of anxiety and grief." Edmund
Gosse's wife had given him for his birthday the whole
Douglas series of Howells's writings, and *A Modern Instance,*
published that year, seemed to him "the greatest work of fiction that America has given us since the death of Hawthorne.
I am quite sure of that," Gosse continued, and "the end of
A Modern Instance is superb. The old judge [Squire Gay-
lord] remains the most striking character all through, but all

[3] Howells had begun to appear regularly in the Tauchnitz edition in
1879.

is strong and consistent. The railway journey is admirable.
Your journeys are always good," he added, referring to what
might be called a specialty of Howells. Again he wrote, "We
are all talking about you. I see ladies giggling over little books
in the train, and then I know they must be reading *The
Parlour Car*. A quantity of cads have sworn to behave like
gentlemen in consequence of meeting *The Lady of the
Aroostook*, and the question, Have you read *A Wedding Journey* is one of those tiresome things that make one loathe one's
fellow-creatures. I really cannot but think that Douglas's edition must be very successful."

In fact, Howells, who disliked "Society with a capital S
as I heartily do," said Edmund Gosse,—much as they both
liked people, one by one,—fled before long to Switzerland
where he could be undisturbed and finish his new novel,
A Woman's Reason. But he had seen much of Lowell, now
minister to England and "sweetly and beneficently un-
changed," as he wrote to Norton, and almost every afternoon
Lowell had come for a walk with the same brisk light step as
in the old days in Cambridge. Romantic still through and
through, Lowell disliked the realism that he could tolerate
only in his friends, and he abhorred the French naturalists
and had no use for the Russians whose novels meant so much
to Howells. Nor could he endure Ibsen whose "cold fascination" was soon to seize upon Howells, the lover of Björnson.
Lowell had lost interest in his own reforming phase at the
moment when Howells's interest was about to begin, when
it virtually had begun, in fact, in a visit to the London slums
that was to haunt his memory many years later. He had a
vision of certain hapless creatures who fled blinking from one
hole in the wall to another and of other creatures in liquor
quarrelling and scolding, while they had little or nothing on.

There were squalid bits of childhood scattered about underfoot and vague shapes of sickness and mutilation, and all the time a buying and selling of loathsome second-hand rags. He had begun to see sights like this at home. At the same time, the peculiar odour of smoke had made him feel at once at home in London, perhaps because it had saturated his first consciousness in the little black, smoky town where he had been born.

Meanwhile, Howells had also seen, a number of times, Burne-Jones in whose work he delighted at the Grosvenor Gallery and whom, as he wrote to Norton, he had found "full of affectionate questions about you." He had had enough talk with Burne-Jones to feel his "gentle and exquisite spirit"; and then he met at dinner Thomas Hardy, "the one writer in England," he had said, "whom I shall look up." Hardy, who thought of Mark Twain as much more than a humorist, congratulated Howells later on his "powers of work—and none of it ever bears the mark of haste," adding, "I trust that you may long maintain such vigour, with such finish and truth of observation." Later still, in 1892, Howells's "beloved" Thomas Hardy wrote, "How obviously excellent it is that an American novelist should exhibit America, where he cannot be gainsaid, rather than alien countries, as so many able American writers insist on doing." Now, in London, in 1882, Howells dined with a whole circle of Americans who happened to be there at the same time. Among them were Henry James, John Hay, Edwin Booth, Aldrich, Charles Dudley Warner and Bret Harte, who had run down from Glasgow, where he was now consul and who no longer seemed a broken man. He had been transformed by English recognition and renewed success, and, as someone said, he looked like a French marquis of the old regime, or,—another added,—"an actor made up for the part." Mark Twain was one old friend who could never forgive him.

One American with whom Howells fell in at this London dinner was Henry Adams's "young hero of the American type," Clarence King, whom Howells had first seen in Cambridge when King was correcting proofs of his first book. Fields had taken for *The Atlantic* his *Mountaineering in the Sierra Nevada,* and Howells had been struck at once by the "sunny gaiety" of this "brilliant beaming creature." Then King had written to Howells in 1871 from Arizona, in connection with *Their Wedding Journey,* "As to describing people you and Harte hold letters patent; there should be written over against *The Atlantic,* 'None genuine unless stamped H. and H.' " He invited Howells to join him in a spring visit to the Yosemite, saying it might suggest a journey of Basil and Isabel in the Sierras, "with plenty of points made out of the herd of travellers"; and now he wrote to praise *A Modern Instance* and "all the mellow mannered strings of your genial irony." He had been much worked up by this novel: "It has seemed to me that after *The Scarlet Letter* New England was a sucked orange and the craftsman was always slipping up on the peel. I never thought anyone could get out of the prosperous, respectable, modern New England with its mitigated puritanism and more tolerable virtue any points of high action or any thrilling morbid growths on which to found an appeal to the dull, dry mind of the average reader like myself. But you have found it this time. I wait for the divorce (which seems to me inevitable),"—he was reading the book as a magazine serial,—"with the same painful apathy I would if it were my own case." He added, "Your art is riper even if a little more Novembery than of late."

Howells, who had thought of Clarence King as one of the

recent California school, had met him in Washington a few years earlier when King was seeking some sort of scientific appointment and Howells had introduced him to President Hayes. Now, at the time of this London meeting, King had just returned from a visit to Spain in search of "Mambrino's helmet," for he shared Howells's passion for *Don Quixote,*— he had dressed for the journey in green velvet, with knee breeches cut like Oscar Wilde's; and he had stopped in Paris on the way back and bought several Fortuny water-colours. At that time Fortuny was admired by the same people who, years later, would have admired El Greco, a painter who could have been bought then far more cheaply, and when Howells exclaimed, "What a lucky man to own Fortunys!" the princely King said, "I will give you one." Sure enough, the next morning the picture appeared at Howells's lodgings. It must have been at about this time that Ruskin at Brantwood gave King a Turner water-colour. King is supposed to have said, "One good Turner deserves another," whereupon Ruskin gave him two. Giving and taking to King were much the same.

The time was coming, but not yet, when for Howells also New England became the "sucked orange" that it was for King; but meanwhile *A Modern Instance* was the cause of a curious break between Robert Louis Stevenson and Howells. Stevenson was for Howells "inevitably a charming and sympathetic writer" (although he confessed in *Heroines of Fiction* that he had never read any of Stevenson's novels), and Stevenson had written to Howells in 1880, "Ever since *The Lady of the Aroostook* I have held you in the best literary esteem." Again, he had written from Edinburgh, *"The Un-discovered Country . . .* more than fulfilled my expectations." On the other hand, in *A Humble Remonstrance,* he expressed his disagreement with this "poet," this "finished artist," this "cunning reader of the mind." Howells, he said, was "a man in love with the appearance of life," but "he has other passions and aspirations than those he loves to draw," for, "while he holds all the poor little orthodoxies of the day," —the belief in science, realism and evolution,—"his work largely contradicts them . . . A man, as I read him, of an originally strong romantic bent, a certain glow of romance still resides in many of his books, and lends them their distinction." So spoke the romantic Stevenson of the realist Howells.

But, shrewd as this was, it only stated Stevenson's dissent from the doctrines of the school of which Howells was a "zealot" who "dreams of an advance in art like what there is in science." (Howells did so mistakenly dream when he said the world would never return to the prolixity of Richardson or the coarseness of Smollett.) There was nothing personal in these animadversions, and in this respect they were unlike the remarks of other English critics who attacked Howells bitterly at this time. What he said of the new technique in novel-writing, of the shapelessness of Scott, Thackeray and Dickens, and of Henry James as the great living master,—all this was met, said Andrew Lang, by "yells and catcalls" in the British press and by various rude remarks about this author. Lang treated him good-naturedly to what he called a "little chaff," in behalf of "inartistic Thackeray" and "clean clumsy Scott," and Edmund Gosse wrote, "So you have demolished poor old Dickens and Thackeray, have you?" ending with this "motto for the American critic":

> Ho! the old school! Thackeray, Dickens!
> Throw them out to feed the chickens.
> Ho! the new school! James and ——
> Lay the flattery on with trowels.

But others went beyond this "doggerel by a candid friend." According to one critic, Howells had written to prove that he himself was a very much finer artist than the best in England. Yet, as Henry James remarked, he had really only said that the confidential manner of Thackeray, for instance, could not be tolerated nowadays.

Then, suddenly Howells received a letter from Robert Louis Stevenson abruptly breaking off relations between them, assuming that *A Modern Instance* generally condemned divorce at a moment when Stevenson was marrying a divorced woman. Obviously Howells meant nothing of the kind, as he showed in *The Rise of Silas Lapham,* in which Silas advises Zerrilla to get a divorce from her good-for-nothing drunken sailor husband, and no doubt a few years later Stevenson perceived this when a common friend brought the two together. Then Stevenson wrote, "Let me apologize for all offences I have ever been guilty of, and assure you I have quite forgotten any offences I may ever have imagined from yourself. And if you can be at the pains, and will be so magnanimous, the circle of Samoa would be glad and flattered to hear from you again." Earlier or later, Howells wrote, "Mrs. Fairchild gives me the chance to take your hand at last, and I give you mine with all my heart."

XII

RETURN TO ITALY

Howells retreated from London to Villeneuve in Switzerland, where he spent three months in this corner of the Canton Vaud, a scene and time that he described in *A Little Swiss Sojourn*, a book that was not published until ten years later.

Homesick for Italy, he presently turned southward, but he found the Swiss republic much to his liking, and he said, "If I must ever be banished, I hope it may be to Switzerland." It was rumoured for a while that he had been appointed minister to "this wise, good little country." Geneva impressed him as a small moralized Bostonian Paris, and what struck him principally in Montreux was its extreme suitability to the purposes of the international novelist, for it was "full of sites for veiled incidents, for tacit tragedies, for subdued flirtations and arrested improprieties." Then he found another occasion to disparage Byron in the story of the Prisoner of Chillon. Howells's propensity to make a character of everybody, even a hotel clerk briefly encountered, appeared in his own account of Bonnivard as gifted with a happy dash, lenient and a gentle scholar, prompt in repartee. Byron's melodramatic prisoner was an artist, he said, and a kind of poet, a lonely yet cheerful sceptic, pacing the path he wore in the stone, while he composed essays and verses.

Howells was to spend a few weeks in Venice before he went home again, but he found it now "benumbing and silencing"; and it gave him the feeling of the Wandering Jew or "the ghost of the Cardiff giant." He felt, in short, as he was to feel about Boston later, that going back was always a mistake; and perhaps he shared a little of the feeling of the American doctor in his *Ragged Lady* for whom Venice, however beautiful, was somehow unreal. To live there would be like spending all one's days at the opera, although it was true that, as a consul, he had been concerned with practical affairs, even at times the affairs of the Venetians. He had been asked for information about the estates of Italians who had emigrated to Buenos Aires decades before, and why certain persons in Brazil and Mexico and parts of Peru had not written home to their families and friends. For the rest, he went to Florence with the intention of writing about it, not as it had been but as it was, for his heart warmed to the famous town more because of its present than because of its past. He had small sympathy with the romantic dreamers who regretted the good old days of the bravo and the footpad. The rags of sentimentality, he said, fluttered from every crag and from every orange-tree and olive-tree in Italy, but he was attracted to real scenes of his own time just as he had formerly been in Venice.

He could have written a book about the Piazza Santa Maria Novella, where he lodged,[1] like Henry James before him, and he was amused by the pensive donkeys, abounding

[1] "It was their lovely ways, far more than their monuments of history and art, that made return to the Florentines delightful. I would rather have had a perpetuity of the *cameriere's* smile, when he came up with our coffee in the morning, than Donatello's San Giorgio, if either were purchasable; and the face of the old chambermaid Maria, full of motherly affection, was better than the face of Santa Maria Novella."—Howells, *Tuscan Cities.*

there, with their fringed and tasselled harness blazing with
burnished brass. Then there was the man who traversed the
square with a wide wicker tray on his head piled with Chianti
wine-flasks like a heap of great bubbles. Howells went to the
hospital for paupers to which everyone was sent who was
found begging in the streets, and he attended a wedding in
the office of the syndic, while he compared the police-court
with Boston's, which he remembered as shabbier and dirtier.
He observed that the people in the streets were on the whole
better dressed than the people one generally saw in Boston;
and it pleased him to see the wash strung over the rear of
Dante's house,—though how could there be so much linen
washed and so little clean in Italy? It seemed to be perpetually washing-day there, and that was the mystery of it. He
enjoyed, in three different theatres, the plays about Stento-
rello, the type who survived from the older comedy destroyed
by Goldoni, and he liked the open-all-day churches where the
Italians were at ease in any rags they happened to have on.
Very unlike the dressed-up church-goers one saw at home
were these entirely natural human beings of this land of
human nature unabashed; and meanwhile he found, as he
remembered, that "in quality of courtesy" the Italians were
"still easily the first of all men." They had not yet learned
bad manners "from the rest of us."

As for most of the works of art, he had long owned to himself that the emotions of others in their presence were beyond
him, and he was rather envious of the seventeenth-century
travellers who had no trouble of mind about the old masters.
They expressed themselves with a tranquil brevity, a beautiful succinctness, wholly without concern for motives or mean-
ings: they would call a cathedral a "neat structure" and say
it was "curiously painted" and there an end. They did not

even vex themselves to speak their Italian correctly. But Howells found Benozzo Gozzoli's frescoed chapel perhaps the loveliest little space that ever four walls enclosed, and, disliking the allegories in Santa Croce, "strutting and mincing" on the tombs, rendering death ridiculous in the manner of Bernini, he delighted in the boys, at Epiphany, in the streets, blowing long slender trumpets of glass. Some of the angels blew these trumpets in the drawings of *A Little Girl Among the Old Masters*, sketches of Howells's ten-year-old daughter who was enchanted with the poetry of mediæval art. She had read Mrs. Jameson's *Sacred and Legendary Art*, and she had drawn the martyrs and saints after Fra Angelico and presently in the manner of Filippo Lippi. She had adhered to all the proper attributions, drawing the tower for St. Barbara and the lily for St. Catherine, who became her favourite saint when she was taken to Siena, the city of saints as Florence was the city of statesmen. There for the first time, she said, she knew what the stigmata was: she had only heard of it before. Howells wrote nothing more sensitive and charming than the notes he published with these drawings.

Naturally, "Francesca" was pleased by this little girl's sketches when the Howellses brought their children to call upon her, when their oldest daughter sang to her and Ruskin's "mouse pet," who was famous now, showed them some of her own primitive drawings. The old consul in Rome, William J. Stillman, the adventurous painter and writer, the former editor of *The Crayon*, was also in Florence, with his Greek wife, the well-known beauty, at whose Pre-Raphaelite parties Howells, once at least, must have been present. Constance Fenimore Woolson, the shrewd and realistic, was amused by the bluestockings in pale yellows and greens, who, having nothing to say about ordinary matters, gazed into space, mysterious and wan. They drifted through the rooms past the pictures of Burne-Jones and Rossetti that hung on the walls. Miss Woolson had written Howells from Rome asking about Venice, where she was to meet in time a violent death, saying that she considered a gondola the next thing to a Beethoven symphony—but was Venice healthy, and where could she find lodgings? She had written to him earlier from the South, from Charleston, Asheville and St. Augustine, saying, "You may be amused to know that my three models, whose style I study and admire, are George Eliot, Bret Harte and Howells,—they are my classics." She too had appeared in *The Atlantic,* and she added in a letter, "Paul Hayne says you are the most fastidious and difficult critic in America." Howells agreed with her about the Duomo in Florence. She found it bleak, and to him it was a "drab vacuity . . . a temple to dampen the spirit with its stony bareness."

Howells was oppressed by the social life in Florence. He was "fatally well known" there, he wrote to his father, and he felt like Frank Duveneck who was also eager to work and hurried off to Venice, half killed with kindness. The irony was that Henry James, who had gone to America, found too little while Howells found too much, and he wrote to his old friend in Florence, "I am surrounded by the social desolation of Boston." The "one feature" there was "Mrs. Jack Gardner's flirtation with Frank Crawford, the American novelist of the future . . . Have you read *Mr. Isaacs,"* he continued, "and do you see a future in it? The Crawford appears to act his novels as well as write them." Howells, Joseph Pennell said, was a "howling swell" in Florence, "very impressive and also jolly when you can get him alone," and, besieged as Howells was, he was no doubt besieged by some of the ladies who later appeared in his novels. For there were Florentine characters in several books that he was to write as well as in *Indian Summer*, which was all about Florence. Some actual person or persons must have suggested Madame Uccelli, inalienably American but also Italianized in her manners and customs, one who had grown eccentric with the passage of time. Then there was Miss Millray, the head of the American colony, who liked bright people even when they were very poor, "if they had something that decently buttoned over the frayed places." It was she who thought Clementina not rustic but sylvan and who rescued her from the vulgar Mrs. Lander.[2] There was Dr. Olney who had been quite willing to live in Italy as long as he had the means to do so, but who became patriotic and felt that he ought to go home to live the moment he had the means no longer.[3] There might have been a Mr. Waters, the old Unitarian minister from Haddam East Village whose motto was "It will all come right in time." (That, he said, was the true American gospel: "There is no other gospel, that *is* the gospel.") He dreamed of the roads and hills of home with the snow falling still and the black wavering lines of the walls in the fields sinking into the drifts that were banked round the houses, but with the aid of his congregation, he lingered in Florence year after year, examining every aspect of Savonarola.[4]

Joseph Pennell had come to Florence commissioned to make etchings, inspired three years before by Whistler in Venice, and he was planning to travel with Howells and illustrate his essays on Pisa, Lucca and other Tuscan cities. He was slow and shy in developing a friendship with Howells who, he was convinced, did not like him. He had written to say that he

[2] In *Ragged Lady*.
[3] In *An Imperative Duty*.
[4] In *Indian Summer*.

was "six feet and somethin' over, thin in proportion, and not an Adonis, ain't married," adding, in this dialect that was rather like Ezra Pound's, "I will join you in Italy if you can stand me." He tried to persuade Howells to write about his own Quaker aunts whom he saw as black-and-whites in real life with white kerchiefs crossed on their breasts, grey gowns and black aprons, sitting all day against white walls and white marble mantel-pieces, sewing in their plain dresses, or reading or knitting. With Howells he sometimes dined at a *trattoria* in the Via Guelpha with Stillman, William Sharp and Arnold Boecklin, the Swiss painter who liked to make soap-bubbles in a salad bowl, blowing them out through a straw. In these, Pennell thought, Boecklin found his iridescent dreams of great blue seas and islands of the dead. On the walls there were sketches and caricatures, and the "Duveneck boys," as they were called, were often there also, pupils of Duveneck in his art school at Munich. They jabbered about Botticelli, about old Piloty's things, about the dishes they were eating and the Chianti, the delicacy of Mino da Fiesole, the over-rated colouring of some of the Venetians and the merits of Italian and German tobacco. They flung their praise and blame about, and no doubt they treated Howells, as they treated Colville in *Indian Summer,* on "the old-boy theory, joking with him, laughing to scorn his antiquated notions of art, condoning them because he was good-natured." Perhaps they also placed on the walls a caricature of Howells. It was they who appeared as the "Inglehart boys" who walked up to sketch in Fiesole in *Indian Summer.*

Like his own Colville, Howells haunted the studies of the old American painters and sculptors in Florence, among them Mrs. Howells's brother, Larkin G. Mead, who was now a professor of sculpture in the Florentine Academy. He was on friendly terms with many who were not in every case quite so friendly with one another, and some of them he had known twenty years before at the time of their hopeful and ardent beginnings. They had gone forward to age and hard work, and they said that people who came abroad no longer gave orders for statues and pictures but spent their money on old chests, chairs and carpets. The vogue had passed for the genre sculptors of earlier days and the marble groups that might once have been called "Westward the Star of Empire" (a female figure advancing over a stretch of prairie with a bison, a bear and an antelope fleeing before her). The old artists had kept up with their country only through the newspapers, and they were dim and vague about it, often talking the American slang of pre-Civil War days with odd Italian idioms inter-mixed. But, simple and innocent, often happy, they were all fervent Americans, with patches of something foreign over-laid, and, while some of them had lost the desire to go back, others thought they were returning very soon. Howells observed that the Europeanized American was always apolo-getic,—he was convinced that America was best and that he ought to go and live there,—while the continentalized English-man had no intention of returning to an England that one of them even called "beastly." On behalf of a certain sculptor, no doubt his brother-in-law, some of whose medallions were being cast at a bronze foundry in Pistoia, Howells ran out there, and he followed a flowering garden path into a group of low roofs that were enclosed in a hedge of myrtle. The master met him with the air of a host: it was very unlike the no-admittance-except-on-business atmosphere that he had encountered in similar places at home. He came away sighing for the day when American foundries would be enclosed in myrtle hedges and reached through garden gates.

In the spring Howells set out with Pennell, who travelled with his etching-plate under his arm and who would begin an etching as others started a pencil sketch the moment you turned your head away. He etched illustrations for Henry James's *Italian Hours* as he did for Howells's *Tuscan Cities,* the series that soon appeared in *The Century Magazine,* in which Howells had begun to serialize his novels. Together he and Howells drove from Pisa to Lucca, whirling past enchanting villas, grey castles and wayside towers that were hoary out of all remembrance. They drove through stone villages in every one of which artist and writer would have been glad to spend a day or a week. It had struck Howells in Pisa that the "Four Fabrics" gained distinction by being set apart from the streets and the shops but that they lost the character of friendly domesticity of all the other Italian religious buildings. At the cathedral in Siena, where all the Howellses spent a month, he felt there was more authority for holding his peace than before Giotto's tower or St. Mark's in Venice, or the curve of the Arno at Pisa, or Niagara, for he liked in this ecstasy of Gothic invention all the "false beauties and affected ornaments" that Addison had despised in favour of the "noble and majestic." In its mighty front of rock, in its mediævalism, in the narrow darkling streets and the old stone houses, Siena recalled to him Quebec, the old-world city of his youth in which every dwelling had told him a story. He was charmed by the exquisite Gothic arches walled up in the house-fronts that had once been the portals and windows of palaces, and especially by the delicate carved red brick that warmed in so many streets the cold grey stone of Siena. He did not see how an architect could better use his eyes than in perusing this brick-work of certain small houses; and presently Seymour, the Boston architect in *The Rise of Silas*

Lapham, showed that he had himself actually done so. There was no such façade on the whole of Beacon Street, as even the untutored Silas was able to see in the new house that Seymour had built for him there. "It appealed to him as an exquisite bit of harmony appeals to the unlearned ear and he recognized the difference between this fine work and the obstreperous pretentiousness of the many over-loaded house-fronts which Seymour had made him notice for his instruction elsewhere on the Back Bay. Now . . . he tried to think what Italian city it was where Seymour said he had first got the notion of treating brick-work in that way."

Meanwhile, Howells found many a story in hotel-registers in this city or that,—for instance, in the comments of the French baronial couple one of whom had visited Pisa before, "But how much more beautiful it is now when I see it on my bridal tour!" The young baroness had written above this, "Life is a journey which we should always make in pairs," a reflection that must have carried Howells back to the days of his own *Their Wedding Journey.* In Siena, he was at work on another novel,—for he worked in hotel bedrooms as on ships and trains,—with his back placed well into the fire-place blazing with the little logs of the country. He was fenced about,—it was February,—with mattresses and pillows, completing his current fiction at the risk of freezing. But, as he wrote to Lowell, "all snap and sharpness" had gone out of the mild old sky, as "out of the mood of a man too much experienced to be eager about anything." The old charm was no longer intimate and constant; and he felt this especially in Florence where "certain sensations" he had known of old "failed to repeat themselves to him." It was Colville to whom this referred in the novel *Indian Summer;* but who was Colville if not Howells whom Florence, "superficially so well known . . . affected somewhat like a collection of views of itself"? One had examined these views before and was disposed to be critical of them. "There was the wonted warmth in the sunny squares, and the old familiar damp and stench in the deep narrow streets. But some charm had gone out of all this . . . A hundred characteristic traits and facts still found a response in the consciousness where they were once a rapture of novelty, but the response was faint and thin: he could not warm over the old mood in which he once treasured them all away as of equal preciousness."

It was this note of disillusion that gave the novel its air of repose,[5] affording many a reader that "exquisite delight" to which William James testified in a letter to the author. *Indian Summer* was "the one *I* like best," Howells himself wrote in a copy of the book, the one that suggested Turgenev most in its little group of characters, in its organization and unity and perfection of style. Howells discovered in this novel his own middle-aged self in an Italy where he had once been rapturously young, and he well sustained this character in Colville, the Middle Western editor who had once been a young American architect in Florence: he might have been Howells himself if the author of the book had remained in the West as editor of his old paper in Columbus. Colville had had a vague purpose of studying the past life of the Florentines in their own architecture, following Ruskin, full of scorn for every modern motive, turning this project over in his mind "with the mounting joy in its capabilities which attends the contemplation of any sort of artistic endeavour." But in Florence, at loose ends, he falls in with Mrs. Bowen, the charm-

---

[5] "It is repose which causes the enduring charm [of a novel], but who can say just what repose is?"—Howells, *Novel-Writing and Novel-Reading*.

ing widow of a Western lawyer whom he had known there twenty years before, and the serious love that develops between them and brings Colville home again to "life, active life, the life of his own day," is the love, precisely, of thirty-eight and forty. On one side is the old minister, on the other Imogene, the radiant young girl who falls in love with Colville, or thinks she falls in love with him and wishes to "defy the world" for him and "atone for the wrong he has suffered" in a previous rejection. She dreams of restoring his youth, retrieving the past for him, avenging him for his unlucky love affair. She binds Colville hand and foot, and a mighty load rolls from his heart when she finds that she does not really love him. He is free to marry Mrs. Bowen, who has been Imogene's chaperon and who has watched this affair with a half-ironical indignation. Howells, who published the novel four years later, in 1886, had then reached the summit of his work as an artist and a writer.

Another fruit of these months in Italy was *Tuscan Cities,* also published as a book in 1886, a collection of papers that reminded him of "bits of *pietra viva* left over from larger mosaics." Howells never lost the feeling for Italy that was to bring him back again, many years later, in 1908, but he felt more than ever implicated now in "the problems of the vast, tumultuous American life." It was Colville who felt this in the novel, and Howells himself said, "After all, *we* have the country of the present and the future." He returned to live in Boston for a few years longer.

XIII

BOSTON OBSERVED

"THERE ARE Bostons and Bostons. The Boston that I belonged to never hears of American books till they are forgotten." So Louise Maxwell says in *The Story of a Play*, a novel that Howells wrote many years later; but even this Boston read Howells in the eighteen-eighties, and he knew this Boston very well. Meanwhile, he had studied all the others. At the moment when Henry James had been exploring London, Howells was exploring and observing the various Bostons.

There were many of them, and Howells had caught the note of one even in the far-away *Suburban Sketches*. There he evoked the Boston of the Italians in Ferry Street with their stuccoed houses, gratings at ground-floor windows and lamps glimmering before pictures of the Madonna. Then there was the Boston of isms in *The Undiscovered Country* and the Boston of the newspaper world in *A Modern Instance*, the commercial money-minded Boston of Washington Street. There was the Boston of boarding-houses and apartment hotels where the tenants dropped in at night from lectures and concerts, and the Boston of swindlers, pickpockets, tramps' lodging-houses and "misfit parlours" that one found also in *The Minister's Charge*. There was the Boston of the police-courts and their free dramatic spectacles with moments of intensity and effects so thrilling that Howells came away with a sense of the highest theatrical illusion. All these Bostons were very remote from the old ideal Boston of which Kitty Ellison had dreamed in *A Chance Acquaintance,* the holy place, the sacred city of the anti-slavery heroes and martyrs and of the Boston authors of the recent past. This was the ideal Boston that had haunted Howells's mind in his own childhood and youth in Ohio. But, in the meantime, Goldoni's picture of the life in Venice had sharpened his realistic eye, and he had accustomed this eye in the years between to see as it really was the life about him.

Coming from the outside, no doubt, Howells saw the various Bostons more keenly than any Bostonian could have seen them, especially as the Boston mind still had an "idealizing tendency," unlike the "realizing tendency" of New York. So Howells, in *April Hopes,* contrasted the two cities. But he was not disillusioned, as Kitty Ellison had been when, thanks to Mr. Arbuton, an image of Boston, unlike the dream of her childhood, rose in her mind, a Boston of mysterious prejudices and lofty reservations that found its social ideal in the old world. It shrank from contact with the reality of this hemisphere, and it seemed to be proud only of the things that were unlike other American things. It was gelidly self-satisfied, fastidious, reluctant, and Howells knew this Boston and presented it very well through the mind of Lord Rainford, for instance, in *A Woman's Reason:* "Very curious, I can't get the people I meet to say a good word for their country. They all seem ashamed of it, and abuse it no end . . . I can't think that a country where I've met so many nice people, and seen scarcely anything but order and comfort even in these very bad times, can be going to the dogs; but I can't get anyone here to agree with me—that is, in society

. . . I find your people—your best people, I suppose they are—very nice, very intelligent, very pleasant—only talk about Europe. They talk about London, and about Paris, and about Rome; there seems to be quite a passion for Italy; but they don't seem interested in their own country. I can't make it out. They all seem to have been reading *The Fortnightly* and *The Saturday Review,* and *The Spectator* and the *Revue des Deux Mondes,* and the last French and English books. It's very odd!"

This was the Boston of which Henry Adams said that it was "very well up in all things European" but that it was "no place for Americanism," and Howells described it not only in the visiting Lord Rainford's words but in the words of the journalist Ford as well.[1] It was, however, as he knew, no more the real Boston than any of the several others of which he was aware, the Boston that went to Nahant or the Boston that went to Nantasket or the Boston of the girl art-students like Miss Carver. There was still another that Kitty Ellison herself had known, the sympathetic easy Boston of Mr. and Mrs. Basil March, or, for that matter, of Clara Kingsbury or Miss Vane or the supremely Bostonian Bromfield Coreys; or that of the "demi-semi literary ladies" who cultivated alike the muses and the modes. Howells presented at great length certain of these Bostons, especially when he contrasted the urban folk with the country folk or those who

---

[1] "If I went to this lady's house, to be like her other friends and acquaintance I should have to be just arrived from Europe, or just going; my talk should be of London and Paris and Rome . . . of English politics and society; my own country should exist for me on sufferance through a compassionate curiosity, half repulsion; I ought to have recently dined at Newport with poor Lord and Lady Scamperton, who are finding the climate so terrible; and I should be expected to speak of persons of the highest social distinction by their first names, or the first syllables of their first names. You see that's quite beyond me."—Howells, *The Undiscovered Country.*

were still of the country though they lived in town. "We are nearly all country people," he said in *An Open-Eyed Conspiracy;* he also said, "We are village people far more than we are country people," and it pleased him to confront the Laphams and the Hallecks with well-bred Boston people like the Bellinghams and Coreys. Or the Maverings, the rich mill-owning family who lived in the country, with Europeanized Bostonians like the Pasmers, or farm-boys like Lemuel Barker with the minister Sewell, the Unitarian pastor of cultivated Boston. The Hallecks, who were country souls, had remained simple and good in their old-fashioned house at the South End with its hideous carpets and chandeliers, a discord of crude colours, dark, heavy with the ugly magnificence of the Civil War time. The rich old leather-manufacturer's family were "outside of everything" and happy in their quiet way to remain outside, while the Laphams, rising in wealth and wishing to advance their children, built their new house on the Back Bay. Both these families became entangled, in a way that threw light on all of them, with Boston society, if only through Atherton, the lawyer, or Miss Kingsbury, who married him, the good-hearted busybody who had shared all the great Boston interests. Among these were the Symphony concerts and George Eliot's novels, John Fiske's lectures on the cosmic philosophy and the classes of William Morris Hunt.

Howells carried on from one novel to another many of his characters, resembling in this Anthony Trollope,—noting that a character he had once developed could not appear as important on a second appearance.[2] So Bromfield Corey and James

---

[2] "If you have first given it a leading part, you have exhausted its possibilities, but if it has been at first subordinated, then you may develop it into something important in the second handling."—Howells, *Novel-Writing and Novel-Reading.*

Bellingham appeared in book after book, importantly once
and earlier or later as secondary characters, and so did Bartley
Hubbard, Clara Kingsbury, Miss Cotton, Sewell, Evans, the
journalist and editor, Miss Vane and others. So did Louise
Maxwell of *The Story of a Play* who appeared as Louise
Hilary in *The Quality of Mercy*, subordinate in the second
novel, important in the first, as Bromfield Corey appeared in
The Rise of Silas Lapham, reappearing elsewhere as a sort
of criterion of Boston. Nor did Howells play favourites in any
of these types. The "effete posterity," as Bromfield Corey
called himself and Bellingham, his cousin, were all the same
to the novelist's imagination as the "ancestors," like Lemuel,
the farm-boy;[3] and it could not be said, though Henry Adams
said it, that Howells could not "deal with gentlemen and
ladies. He always slips up," Adams added, adding further that
Henry James "knows nothing of women but the outside; he
never had a wife."[4] Adams was writing to John Hay, the
author of *The Breadwinners,* to say that Hay "not only
knows women, but knows *ladies,* the rarest of literary gifts";
and he "also knows men and even gentlemen, something least
to be expected from an unknown Western writer." (For
Adams was keeping up the elaborate play of make-believe
that John Hay had not written this anonymous novel.) But
he wrote this in 1883, and he might have thought differently
after the appearance of *The Rise of Silas Lapham.* Francis
Parkman, who knew gentlemen, especially Boston gentlemen,
well, had written to Howells in 1879, apropos of *The Lady
of the Aroostook,* "It paints a gentleman realistically, a thing

[3] But many must have agreed with Robert Louis Stevenson when, in *A
Humble Remonstrance,* he wonders why Howells should have "suppressed"
his natural tastes to "do reverence to the Lemuel Barkers."

[4] Compare with this the remark in Henry James's *Notebook* that Howells
had "never known at all any woman *but* his wife."

so rare in American fiction as to be a conspicuous distinction in itself." Parkman was later enthusiastic also about the "portrait-painting" in *Silas Lapham* that presented the well-known character of Bromfield Corey.[5]

Of this charge, so often brought against Dickens, Howells was not guilty, although another Boston novelist, Frederick J. Stimson, remarked that the name "Corey" belied the type. Tall and slim, with a white moustache, a slight stoop and an Italianate air, together with a certain light cordial frankness, Bromfield Corey was a perfect example of the upper-class Bostonian, originally from Salem, with a house at Nahant. So was Mrs. Hilary, especially perhaps in "looking upon aesthetic honours of any sort as in questionable taste." (This was after her daughter Louise had married the playwright Maxwell and, for her, "it went far to redeem the drama that it should be related to the Hilarys by marriage.") Bromfield Corey had lived as a young man in Italy and for a while he had been a portrait painter, but as "it was absurd for him to paint portraits for pay and ridiculous to paint them for nothing," he had ceased to paint them at all. As a Bostonian of the time when manners and culture went together, he had his own theory of Titian's method, and he had a conception of the architect that might have expressed the mind of Howells himself: "You architects and the musicians," he said to the architect Seymour, "are the true and only artistic creators.

[5] Parkman wrote to Howells, in 1885, about *The Rise of Silas Lapham,* "I think I have never admired your genius more than in this capital book." But, walking out to Cambridge, following the regimen that more or less restored his health,—as Howells relates in *Literary Friends and Acquaintance,* —Parkman expressed a certain troubled uncertainty about the book. He interpreted Silas Lapham's "rise" as the achievement of social recognition, never guessing, said Howells, "that I had supposed the rise to be a moral one."

It goes without saying that Parkman disapproved of Howells's attacks on romanticism.

All the rest of us, sculptors, painters, novelists and tailors, deal with forms that we have before us; we try to imitate, we try to represent. But you two sorts of artists create form. If you represent, you fail. Somehow or other, you do evolve the camel out of your inner consciousness." It was, incidentally, Seymour, Silas Lapham's architect, who educated Lapham away from the craze for black walnut. He suggested white paint with a little gold in it here and there, and, by so doing, there was reason to think, Seymour,—or Howells,—educated a generation in architecture.[6]

Bromfield Corey was not least an example of his type in employing the country boy Lemuel to read aloud to him, though he could not repress a few twinges at Lemuel's accent. In brief phrases Howells touched off many characters, the witty old maid, Miss Vane, for one, who had also employed as a house-boy this "best and most faithful creature in the world." Then there was Sewell, the minister, who stressed rather duties than beliefs, and whose wife was a good woman who liked to "make her husband feel this keenly." Sewell's psychological sermons were always exposing false rationalizations, but he was "frequently at the disadvantage men of cloistered lives must be, in having his theories in advance of his facts." There was Miss Cotton who had a little knot of conscience between her eyebrows, "tied there by the unremitting effort of half a century to do and say exactly the truth": she was like Grace Breen, the serious girl, "in the helpless subjection to the truth in which so many New Eng-

[6] The architect Cass Gilbert wrote, at the time of Howells's eightieth birthday, that he had done more than any of the American architects to cultivate good taste in architecture. "A single sentence in *Silas Lapham* about black walnut," Cass Gilbert wrote, "changed the entire trend of thought and made it possible for the architects of the time to stem the turbid tide of brownstone and black walnut then so dear to the heart of the American millionaire."

land women pass their lives." There were the Pasmers,[7] not least, who had lived for many years abroad "upon the edges and surfaces of things, as Americans must in Europe everywhere. . . . They had to ask themselves, the mother definitely and the father formlessly, whether they wished their daughter to marry an Englishman, and their hearts answered them, like true Republican hearts, not an untitled Englishman, while they saw no prospect of her getting any other . . . Like other people who have always been idle, he [Mr. Pasmer] rather plumed himself upon it, for the man who has done nothing all his life naturally looks down upon people who have done or are doing something . . . But in Europe, in the presence of people who had been useless for so many generations that they had almost ceased to have any consciousness of it, Pasmer felt that his uselessness had not the passive elegance which only ancestral uselessness can give; that it was positive, and to that degree vulgar." It might well have been *April Hopes,* the story of the Pasmers and the Maverings—or of the light-hearted Dan and Alice with her "ideals" and "heroics,"—that led Björnstjerne Björnson to praise the psychologist in Howells. One of the subtlest of all his novels, it was one of the most inconclusive. "If he had been different," the final words were, "she would not have asked him to be frank and open; if she had been different, he might have been frank and open. This was the beginning of their married life."

Howells's Boston novels abounded in shrewd observations regarding, for instance, "the willingness Boston men often show to turn one another's good points to the light in com-

[7] Said Mrs. Pasmer, "Don't you think it's well . . . to see somebody besides Boston people sometimes,—if they're nice?" Mrs. Pasmer, "while presenting to the world the outward effect of a butterfly, possessed some of the best qualities of the bee."—Howells, *April Hopes.*

pany."[8] He referred in *The Rise of Silas Lapham* to "those cousinships which form the admiration and terror of the adventurer in Boston society. He finds himself hemmed in and left out at every turn by ramifications that forbid him all hope of safe personality in his comments on people . . . These latent and tacit cousinships open pitfalls at every step around him, in a society where Middlesexes have married Essexes and produced Suffolks for two hundred and fifty years." Then, in *Mrs. Farrell,* he spoke of "those critical spirits, rather commoner in Boston than elsewhere, who analyze and refine and re-refine and shrink from a final impression with a perseverance that leaves one in doubt whether they have any opinion about the matter." This was at the end of the book when Mrs. Farrell has gone on the stage and shown that she is good only for "private theatricals,"—for she cannot dramatize a part but only herself,—the *femme fatale* who is "like a well-millinered wood-nymph not the least afraid of satyrs." She is ready, with her dark still bewildering eyes, her dusky bloom and overshadowing hair, to try "certain effects of posture and drapery and gesture" upon any handsome young man she comes upon, and Gilbert, speaking of her, spoke for Howells, a master of the art of picturing feminine charm: "I don't believe the subtlest effect of a dress is ever lost upon men, and I believe the soul of any man of imagination is as much taken with style in dressing as with beauty." Most of Howells's young girls and women have what he called

[8] "A defect of the Puritan quality, which I have found in many New Englanders, is that, wittingly or unwittingly, they propose themselves to you as an example, or, if not quite this, that they surround themselves with a subtle ether of potential disapprobation, in which, at the first sign of unworthiness in you, they helplessly suffer you to gasp and perish; they have good hearts, and they would probably come to your succour out of humanity, if they knew how, but they do not know how."—Howells, *Literary Friends and Acquaintance.*

the instinct of dress and the "fine positive grace which is
called style and which is so eminently the gift of exquisite
nerves"; and Mrs. Farrell, in the summer, in the country, has
what might be called an excess of this. She plays off one
young man against another, breaking up their friendship and
losing them both.[9] Meanwhile, this daughter of a Maine
sea-captain, a widow of twenty-six, is in her way also a Boston type who recalls the aesthetic craze of the seventies and
eighties.

For that was the day when young girls painted cat-tail
rushes and drew charcoal heads after William Morris Hunt
and when Mrs. Farrell discovered the "Rosa Bonheur of
West Pekin" and asked this farmer's daughter to visit her in
Boston. The spinning-wheel mania was just beginning, with
the revival of handicrafts and the sort of madness that was
called household art when young ladies also painted storks
standing on stone bottles and knotted ribbons round the arms
of chairs. Helen Harkness, of *A Woman's Reason*, who had
kept house for her father and found herself suddenly penni-
less when her father died, casting about for a means of earn-
ing her living, decorated porcelain vases with sea-weeds and
shells. With her "alarmed ideals and metaphysical scruples,"
she had been bred to be of no use, but she was glad to do
aesthetic millinery, while, working at ceramics, a fad of the
moment, she refused to paint the hollywood boxes that were
popular also.[10] This was at a time when, as Henry Adams

9 "Your Mrs. Farrell is terrific—do for pity's sake give her the Small Pox—
she deserves it."—Fanny Kemble to Howells, 1875, when the novel, published later, was appearing as *Private Theatricals* in *The Atlantic*.

10 "All the undertakings of women, [Verrian] mused, were piteous, not
only because women were unequal to the struggle at best, but because they
were hampered always with themselves, with their sex, their femininity,
and the necessity of getting it out of the way before they really could begin
to fight."—Howells, *Fennel and Rue*.

found, there was nothing in Boston for young men to do and they went in for ranching and farming in the West and the South. Howells was concerned about the place of young women in the new society and their attempts to enter the professions, and his helpless Helen Harkness was as ineffectual as Dr. Breen, the woman doctor of whom he had previously written. Her problem was also solved by marriage. It was the decay of the India trade, the stately old traffic of the East, that had left her at her father's death without resources. The old ship-owner's house was virtually a museum of objects brought back by her father as a young super-cargo in the days when gentlemen's sons sailed before the mast,—grotesque bronzes, ivory carvings, Indian idols and shawls, and fantastically subtle webs of silk and cotton. There were also Copleys and Stuarts and large allegorical landscapes after the fashion of Thomas Cole or Poussin. One of Howells's fine scenes in this rather callow novel was the auction in the old house off Beacon Street during which the auctioneer quotes Shakespeare and Goldsmith in the Boston fashion,—and the story of the sibyl and her books,—while he fabricates the bids that are not made.

These Boston novels were of varying merit,—*The Minister's Charge* and *A Woman's Reason* were in one way or another decidedly weak,—but among them, besides *A Modern Instance,* were the fine-grained *April Hopes* and, best of all, *The Rise of Silas Lapham.* No doubt the strongest of Howells's novels, the most completely realized, this also transcended the local and the period interest partly because the principal character was not merely a Boston or an American type but a type of the whole Western world as well. For the "big" new business man was appearing at the time in all the European countries. "Money is the romance, the poetry of our age," says Bromfield Corey. "It's the thing that chiefly strikes the imagination. The Englishmen who come here,"—and he might have been thinking of Matthew Arnold,—"are more curious about the great new millionaires than about any-one else, and they respect them more"; and this first full-length portrait of an American millionaire bore a certain belated resemblance to the work of Balzac.[11] Intensely prosaic in other respects, Silas is a poet whose paint is a sentiment, a passion, even more than a business, and who is drawn to the young Tom Corey, the son of the Boston swell, be-cause he can also feel that "it's a blessing to the world." The "Persis brand," Silas's special brand, is named after his old wife,—she of the unsparing conscience and the rigorous tongue,—and it is this that remains to him when, ruined, he returns to Vermont, where the paint-mine had been discov-ered on his father's farm. He sets to work with this to begin again. Bull-headed in his pride, simple, rude but kind and just, he has been unjust to his first partner, and,—to the satisfaction of his wife who has been his conscience,—it is this partner who causes his own downfall. He shuts down the works, his new house burns,—he has set it on fire himself, by mistake, in the dark,—the house he has built on Beacon Street to advance his daughters socially, while he and his wife keep their country ways. Silas's material fall is his spirit-ual rise.

But around this main theme spreads a panorama of the whole Boston world of 1885, with the crude rich country

11 H. A. Taine had this in mind when, writing of *The Rise of Silas Lapham,* he recommended to his French publisher a translation of the book: "I have read it in English with the greatest pleasure and with much admira-tion; it is the best novel written by an American, the most like Balzac's, the most profound, and the most comprehensive. Silas, his wife and his two daughters are for us new types, very substantial and very complete."

Laphams becoming involved with the Coreys when young Tom Corey goes into Lapham's business. By the skilful device of an interview with Bartley Hubbard of *A Modern Instance*, Silas reveals himself in the opening chapter, and his two daughters, Irene and Penelope, who idolize their mother, are also revealed by a thousand delicate touches. The book abounds in fine scenes, for one, the great dinner party at which Silas, drunk, plays the clown before the tolerant Coreys and their cousins and friends, and the scene in Penelope's bedroom in which Irene gives her sister the little trinkets that she has hidden away. She has discovered that Tom Corey has not been in love with her but has loved Penelope all along, and to her she turns over the withered bouquet, the pin and the pine shaving, tied with a knot of ribbon, that she has kept. The building and the burning of the new house "on the water side of Beacon Street" are symbols of the rise and fall of Silas's fortunes; and the novel itself evoked as nothing else could ever do a whole historic aspect of the culture of the country. It revealed, as Harold Frederic said, "the scrutiny of a master turned for almost the first time upon what is the most distinctive phase of American folk-life."

"Here, to us," wrote Rudyard Kipling, many years later, "was a new world altogether." Soon after he had read *Venetian Life,*—he was growing up in India,—Kipling heard his father read aloud *The Rise of Silas Lapham* and *A Modern Instance*. They gave him, he remembered, "a large undoctored view into lives which did not concern or refer themselves for judgment to any foreign canon or comparison, but moved in their proper national orbit, beneath their own skies and among their own surroundings. Subjected to the severest test,—that of every word being spoken aloud,—the truthful and faithful fabric of his presentments showed neither flaw nor adulteration, pretence nor precocity, and the immense amount of observation and thought that had gone evenly into its texture shot and irradiated, without overloading, each strand of the design . . . [Howells] was concerned, and passionately concerned, with the springs, spiritual and mental, of the life of his own land, at a time when, as I see it, that land, recovering from the upheaval of the Civil War, and not yet subjected to any vast invasion of unrelated aliendom, had developed into the full individuality that he interpreted to its people and all the world without."

Kipling spoke for a multitude of readers, especially in the United States, but more and more also in other countries, for whom Howells was the representative American writer.

XIV

ON THE BRANCH

THIS WAS "our Howells-and-James epoch," as Henry Adams called the years during which these two novelists ruled the national mind almost as much as Dickens and Thackeray had ruled the mind of England twenty or thirty years before. They ruled at least the minds of the small reading public, mainly, in this decade of the eighties, the minds of women whose favour was "the breath of the novelists' nostrils," as the narrator said in *The Shadow of a Dream*.[1] For the men were more immersed than ever in the affairs of the Gilded Age and the problems of this time of economic turmoil. Henry James was explaining to Europe his countrymen and countrywomen, while Howells explained them to themselves; and the novels of both were equally national events. As a Boston novelist later said, the phrase "Howells and James" was "the catchword of culture."

It was true that four of Howells's most important books

---

[1] "The women . . . are the miscellaneous readers in our country: they make or leave unmade most literary reputations; and I believe that it is usually by their advice when their work-worn fathers and husbands turn from their newspapers to the doubtful pleasure of a book."—Howells, *Three Villages*.

"We poor devils of authors would be badly off if it were not for the women. In fact, no author could make a reputation among us without them. American literature exists because American women appreciate it and love it."—Howells, *A Traveler from Altruria*.

were produced between 1880 and 1890,—*A Modern Instance, Indian Summer, The Rise of Silas Lapham* and *A Hazard of New Fortunes*. He had longed in Italy to be at home and quietly at work again, saying, "I find that I can't write while shifting about so much, and there is no happiness for me in anything else"; yet he was restless when he returned to Boston, where he never settled down again to live. He did not indeed yet have that feeling of satiety towards the place which he expressed a few years later; in fact, having rented a house in Louisburg Square for a while, he bought a house in Beacon Street. This was in 1884, and the house was on the "water side," two doors away from Oliver Wendell Holmes's, with windows overlooking the Charles River Basin, the Cambridge flats and the tower of Memorial Hall. It was a glassy sheet in winter, with a few small boats, all smooth and red in the light of the sunset, and one saw the yellow of the meadows and a black outline of naked trees, spires and roofs. But during that very year Howells suggested to Mark Twain that they should both go to live in Washington. It was also at this time that Mark Twain proposed a "circus," consisting of Aldrich, Cable, Howells and himself, who were to tour the country, with their own cook, in a private car, giving public readings four times a week. Those were great days of lecturing, with authors everywhere on the road, and Mark Twain was to be the impresario; yet the plan came to no more than the plan of going to Washington, which Howells said was "running powerfully in my head these days." He was in Boston provisionally, but, after three years in Beacon Street, he was on the wing again, spending a winter in Buffalo, to be near his elder daughter who was at a sanitarium in Dansville. Then, in 1888, he was more or less settled in New York.

The truth was that Howells' was really at home in the superworld of art and was only a sojourner in any other country. He was detached wherever he was, as a writer should be, and he might have said, with Bernard Berenson, "I am a stranger everywhere." He had become, meanwhile, an impressive personage, one whose face was now more familiar in print than any other writer's, except perhaps Longfellow's or Mark Twain's. With his rugged head set strongly on a neck that was uncommonly short, he gave one observer a sense of directness, of a fastidious forcefulness that was in no way constrained but rather entirely ripe and self-assured. He seemed to have fulfilled the prophecy of Elizabeth Stoddard that he would "butt down the American public"; for his great qualities were "a hard intellect, a hard character and a certain patient tact."

During these years, Howells's novels were read aloud in thousands of families, and, as Hamlin Garland said, clubs and gatherings "rang" with arguments especially about the reality of Howells's women. They were all subterfuge and artifice, many readers thought, or, as Howells said, "mentally frank and sentimentally secret"; and there were those who felt that he libelled American womanhood, as Henry James did in *Daisy Miller,*—he shattered the chivalric fiction of woman's helpless nobility, never presenting a woman as altogether perfect. Others delighted in his Lydia, the "lady of the Aroostook," the centre about which the sentiment of the ship revolved, or Mrs. Vervain who didn't object to "a little ease of manner in the gentlemen," or Mrs. Saintsbury who was "awfully fond of formulating people."[2] They liked to hear about Mrs. Northwick, "One of those hen-minded women

[2] "Oh, everybody in Cambridge does that," said Mrs. Pasmer. "They don't gossip; they merely accumulate materials for the formulation of character."—Howells, *April Hopes.*

. . . made up of only one aim at a time and of manifold
anxieties at all times," and of the ladies "who looked most
distinctly descended from ancestors" and not as if they were
"merely the daughters of fathers and mothers." It charmed
them to hear that Louise Hilary "got as lightly to her feet
as if she were a wind-bowed flower tilting back to its per-
pendicular," and they were amused to be told that a "certain
humorous brightness" was "the most natural quality of Americans." Howells's readers followed his novels from instalment
to instalment, eagerly wondering what was to happen in them.
Would Mr. Arbuton finally capture Kitty Ellison? Would
Silas Lapham disgrace himself at the Coreys' dinner? Then
they were happy to think that at last they could count on
a steady "home-supply," for the monthly magazines brought
them, year in and year out, their Howells and their Henry
James and their Marion Crawford.

Howells was the most talked of novelist in America, and
Hamlin Garland, who had come to Boston to study philosophy and literature, set out in the mid-eighties to interview
him. Howells was living at that time in a hotel in Auburn-
dale, and Garland walked twice past the gate before he found
heart to turn and enter. Dressed in his Windsor tie and
broad-brimmed Western hat, he was so stricken with awe
that his knees failed him, but he found in Howells a justifi-
cation of his favourite theory, derived from Taine, that the
writer should reflect his own race, place and moment. For
Howells was full of the belief that fiction should deal with
conditions peculiar to the author's own climate and country
and that he should express the life that he knew best and
cared the most about. Cable, Harris, Bret Harte and Sarah
Orne Jewett were doing this, and Howells urged Garland to
return to his own frontier West. With this interview the cur-

rent of Garland's ambition changed, and, presently returning to the "middle border," he set to work writing *Main-Travelled Roads.*

At that time Howells was planning to write *The Shadow of a Dream,* a novel of quite another type, one that was rather Hawthornesque and so remote from his usual vein that he asked Garland whether he should write it. He had been reading William James and Ribot's *Diseases of Personality,* and he verified in his own experience Ribot's theory that approaching disease can intimate itself in dreams of the disorder impending. In this case a recurrent dream pursued a man in actual life and would have led to insanity if the man had lived, but Faulkner, the great Western lawyer, dies in the old house at Swampscott where he has been under the care of the nerve-specialist Wingate. His recurrent dream has been that his wife is in love with his best friend, the young clergyman Nevil who has been living with them, that they are waiting for him to die and that his funeral is somehow the same ceremony as their wedding. After his death, the doctor tells the wife what the dream was and Nevil's morbid conscience forbids their marriage until, half-convinced that he is foolish, he agrees to marry the wife, only to be killed by a train that is moving from the station.

Actually, when Howells wrote the book, it turned out to be one of his best, a first-rate story of its subtle kind that was rather like one of Henry James's, all bathed in the atmosphere of the ruined Swampscott garden with the hoarse plunge and wash of the surf on the rocks. It recalled some of the nightmares that afflicted Kant's old age and suggested a few of the dreams of Howells's own childhood, in one of which he had been chased by a marble statue with an uplifted arm and had run along the verge of a pond to escape it. That dream had been recurrent while others were inconsequential, like the one he related in *I Talk of Dreams* in which a clown rose through the air in a sitting posture and floated over the house-roof, snapping his fingers. The antennae on his forehead nodded elastically and the figure seemed to the last degree threatening and awful, like the figure of the barber in another dream who removed his customer's head, in treatment for headaches. Howells earned his own living, as he said, by weaving a certain sort of dream into literary form and he remembered a multitude of ordinary dreams. "The dreamer is purely unmoral," he remarked. "Good and bad are the same to his conscience; he has no more to do with right and wrong than the animals; he is reduced to the state of the merely natural man; and perhaps primitive men were really like what we all are now in our dreams." Neither Freud nor Jung would have objected to that.

One real incident in Howells's life that connected itself with a dream interested Björnstjerne Björnson when he was in Cambridge, where he spent the winter of 1881 in the house of Mrs. Ole Bull, the widow of the Norwegian violinist. The child of a neighbour of Howells was coasting down a long hill with a railroad crossing at the bottom, and as he approached the foot of the hill an express train rushed round the curve. The flagman ran forward and shouted to the boy to throw himself off the sled, but he kept on, running into the locomotive, and he was so badly injured that he died. Before this happened, when he was asked why he did not throw himself off, he answered, "I thought it was a dream," and Björnson who was at Howells's house in Belmont, shortly afterward, was struck by the psychological implications of this. The reality had transmuted itself, in that moment of stress, into the substance of dreams; and for Björnson this seemed to mean all sorts of possibilities in the obscure region where it cast a fitful light. Björnson, the blond Norwegian giant whose simple, natural fiction had once so greatly influenced Howells, was in disgrace at home for calling the king a donkey, for he was a republican and one of the hottest. He had been largely responsible for the separation of Norway from Sweden. Howells admired him greatly, and he in turn wrote to Howells from Paris in 1884, "In your way you are one of the greatest psychologists of your own age in my eyes. That will say, that you are perhaps the greatest now living in the sphere where you have your kingdom and realm."

On the branch, in the early eighties, gradually turning from Boston to New York, Howells usually spent the summers in New England villages, whether at Bethlehem in the White Mountains or at Townsend Harbor or in some hotel on the Down East coast. There, everywhere, was the summer girl, alert for young brokers and lawyers, and herself always in pursuit, as Howells perceived before George Bernard Shaw,—the pretty barbarian in a day of flirtation and lounging before young men came to prefer more robust vacations. Or before the chaperon came to stay and before the growth of the cottage life that spoke for a growing love of seclusion and exclusion. There one found also the husbandless wife, the most monumental fact of the American summer. In 1882, Howells had gone to Lexington, whither he had sometimes driven by a rustic road, full of the safe wildness that especially pleased him, and he had the public library to himself on the days when it was closed so that he could write there every morning. Then he went in 1884 to Campobello, already "a fashionable resort, in spite of its remoteness," he wrote to Henry James,—"so far off that I feel as if I had been to Europe." He continued, "I saw many well-dressed and well-read girls there who were all disposed more or less to talk of you, and of your latest story, *A New England Summer.*" While the greater part of Boston society transported itself in summer down the North Shore to Manchester at the furthest, the more detachable spirits ventured into more distant regions, Bar Harbor, for one, or Campobello. There, said Howells in *April Hopes*, they settled in little daring colonies, not refusing the knowledge of other colonies of other stirps and even combining in temporary alliance with them. "But, after all, Boston speaks one language, and New York another, and Washington a third, and though the several dialects have only slight differences of inflection, their moral aspects render each a little difficult for the others. In fact, every society is repellent to strangers in the degree that it is sufficient to itself, and is incurious concerning the rest of the world." But the novelist Howells was more and more curious concerning the rest of the world as he withdrew more and more from Boston.

Campobello was to appear at some length in *April Hopes*, while other novels reflected the farm boarding-houses where Howells had spent summers in earlier years. There he might have encountered Mrs. Farrell, the charming widow who gave her name years later to the novel that was published as *Private Theatricals* in *The Atlantic;* and he might well have known there the professor and his family who appeared in *The Vacation of the Kelwyns.* It was in some such setting that Mr. Sewell of *The Minister's Charge* fell in with Lemuel Barker of Willoughby Pastures, where he lived in a tumbledown unpainted house and where, in those days when country people could still be described as "green," he suggested Lemuel's disillusioning visit to Boston. Howells observed the visitors ravaging the lanes for goldenrod and asters and boughs of coloured leaves later in the season, catching in their water-colours picturesque bits in the clearings and taking their parts in the annual coaching parades. Then arches in the main street were draped with flags and covered with flowers, and mountain wagons were decorated with bunting, and a young girl stood on the highest seat of a coach, garlanded and wreathed as the spirit of summer.

Well Howells knew the silent rural Yankees with their shy ways and weather-beaten faces, and their rusty boots and scarecrow hats, and he studied them not so closely as more expressive or developed types but with a powerful instinct for documentation. He was supposed to have made a study of Brattleboro before he conceived the village of Equity in Maine, and he went out to Indiana to see a divorce case tried there before he described the divorce proceedings in *A Modern Instance.* The Southern poet Maurice Thompson, who had settled as a lawyer in Crawfordsville, promised to drill Howells in the legal details if he would come and visit "our rude little nest," and in fact they watched the progress of a divorce together. Again, Howells visited mills in Lowell that might have been those that appeared in *Annie Kilburn.* Later, in order to document *The Quality of Mercy,* he consulted with the Canadian police in Montreal. He went to the police headquarters to see how they handled a tip that an American embezzler was there under cover, and the chief turned out the detective squad to get a report on the rumour.

Howells visited Hartford often, and still more often Mark Twain wrote to him, saying, for instance, "You are always writing your best story, and as usual this one is also your best." Mark wrote to Howells about the mistakes in the proofs of *Huckleberry Finn* "of a kind to make a man curse his teeth loose" and about how Mrs. Clemens "goes tearing around in an unseemly fury" when he tells her about his own visit to Boston,—and she not with him to have her part in it. He wrote from Elmira in 1884, "Two ladies came up from the Water Cure at eventide, and one of them got to talking about peculiar people in that museum of invalids down there, and finally quoted this remark from a woman patient who sets herself up as a 4000-candle-power intellectual light, 'Waal, I like Shakespeare . . . but as for James and Howells and Walt Whitman and Swinburne, they're all alike. When you've read one, you've read 'em all!' Isn't that uncreateable? —has to come natural, an edifice like that—can't be planned and built by art." Then Mark asked Howells to come to Hartford to see the typesetting machine on which he had spent three thousand a month for forty-four consecutive months: "Come and see the Master do it! Come and see this sublime magician of iron and steel work his enchantments,"—for "shabby poor bunglers" at typesetting like Howells and himself. "Spacing and justifying? Let him show you that for four centuries the very princes of the art have been slovenly and incapable. Come!"

Howells *had* come to join Mark Twain on a visit to New York to call upon General Grant, some years before, when the elder Howells, then consul at Toronto, thought his position was in danger and appealed to his son, who appealed in turn to Clemens. For Clemens was a friend of Grant, and Grant was a friend of President Arthur. Together they went to Grant's business office, and Grant presently settled the question in the old man's favour, meanwhile insisting that Clemens and Howells should stay and lunch with him on the baked beans and coffee that were brought in. Grant talked constantly with the soft rounded Ohio River accent that brought back to Howells his steamboating uncles, and Howells said afterwards, quoting Dante, "How he sits and towers!" A year later, William Cooper Howells, who was then seventy-six, bought a farm in Virginia, on the James River. He had given up his consulship, but, hopeful as ever, he planted a vineyard and orchards of peaches and pears; nor was he daunted when he had to give them all up and go back to Ohio.

As for Howells himself, remembering the day with General Grant, he said the baked beans and coffee were of the railroad-refreshment quality, but eating them with Grant was like sitting down to lunch "with Julius Caesar, or Alexander, or some other great Plutarchian captain." How could he then have said so often, "I don't believe in heroes"?—and was not Robert Louis Stevenson right in saying that he had a romantic bent which he denied? For no one ever revered heroes more than Howells himself revered not only Grant but Lincoln and also Lowell and "the other big literary fish" of Mark Twain's phrase; and there was the emotion that Dante aroused in him, as he recorded this in *Tuscan Cities*, "the emotion that divine genius, majestic sorrow and immortal fame can accumulate within one's average commonplaceness." Howells distrusted the word "genius" as much as the word "hero," for these words seemed to contradict the ideal of equality that he had grown up with in Ohio. His friendship with Mark Twain, meanwhile, kept active, in his Boston life, the happy sense that he was a Westerner there, just as his friendship with Henry James kept active in him too the happy sense of his own European connections.

TOLSTOY

ONE DAY in 1887, in the railway station at Albany, Edward Everett Hale fell in with Howells who was in the breakfast room on his way home again from a visit with his father in Ohio. Howells was deep in Tolstoy and greatly troubled, wondering whether he should not be doing farmwork, whether he should not be ploughing rather than writing; and he and Hale outstayed their welcome with the waitresses, talking for an hour and a quarter. Howells gave Hale his annotated copy of Tolstoy's *My Confession,* and Hale, the University preacher at Harvard, presently founded a Tolstoy Club in Cambridge. Henceforth he counted Tolstoy as "the apostle for this time of just what the time wants," and he set out to engage in social work the minds of the young men of Cambridge and Boston.

It was Thomas Sergeant Perry who led Howells to read Tolstoy, as he had led him to read Turgenev a dozen years before. Perry had also told him about Gogol's *Dead Souls* which, like Tolstoy at first, he read in French. Howells had read *Taras Bulba* aloud to his family, and, henceforth always a Russophile, he read much of Pushkin, while he remembered having seen Tolstoy's *War and Peace* on the table of a certain professor in Cambridge. Moreover, *The Cossacks* of Tolstoy had been on his own shelves for four or five years before he even dipped into the book, and Tolstoy was still virtually a new name to him when Perry brought *Anna Karenina* and asked Howells to read it. The effect, as he wrote later, "was as if I had never read a work of the imagination before." To him this reading was not what it was to Perry, a literary experience like any other; it was, both ethically and aesthetically, like the old-fashioned religious experience of people who are converted at revivals. "Things that were dark or dim before were shone upon by a light so clear and strong that I needed no longer to grope my way to them." So Howells wrote in one of his papers on Tolstoy. "Being and doing had a new meaning and a new motive, and I should be an ingrate unworthy of the help I had if I did not own it, or if I made little of it."

Long before this, it is true, Howells's general view of life had become more "tragical," as he said to his publisher, and at the height of his success, in his new house in Beacon Street, everything seemed suddenly wrong with him. He had felt as Miss Kingsbury felt in *The Rise of Silas Lapham*, "I have often thought of our great cool houses standing useless here, and the thousands of poor creatures stifling in their holes and dens, and the little children dying for wholesome shelter. How cruelly selfish we are!" He had felt twinges of conscience in the slums of London; and the burning of Silas Lapham's house was in a way symbolic of Howells's feeling about his own. He had become aware for good of the riddle of the painful earth and of "the great community of wretchedness which has been pitilessly repeating itself from the foundation of the world." He no longer shared what he had called in *Dr. Breen's Practice* "the optimistic fatalism which is the real religion of our orientalizing West"; and, in short, the "smiling aspects of life" no longer seemed the most characteristic of "our self-satisfied, intolerant and hypocritical provinciality," as he was to write in *My Literary Passions*. In the old days of his dense darkness about anything like social reform, he had felt as Theodore Dreiser was to feel before he saw Pittsburgh, but now, as he said, "the tramps walked the land like the squalid spectres of the labourers who once tilled it." He was in the mood to recall his father's frontier belief that the world was on the eve of a social revolution. He had always written to his father every week, and his father's Utopian aspirations had suddenly become real to him: he underwent "the lapse from the personal to the ancestral which we all undergo in the process of the years." It was Tolstoy, mainly, who had wrought this change in him, Tolstoy of whom he wrote, "Every other novelist shrinks and dwindles beside him." He said in 1887, in a preface to *Sebastopol,* that Tolstoy was "precisely the human being with whom at this moment I find myself in the greatest intimacy; not because I know him, but because I know myself through him; because he has written more faithfully of the life common to all men, the universal life which is the most personal life, than any other author whom I have read . . . Whenever I open a page of Tolstoy's I am aware of the thrill and glow of wonder that filled me when I first began to read him."

Howells's admiration for Tolstoy remained paramount for the rest of his life, and he wrote a magnificent essay about this novelist whose literary rivals were only "defeated rivals." Tolstoy's "heart-searching books," he said, were "worth all the other novels ever written," for in them "you seem to come face to face with human nature for the first time in fiction." Tolstoy had taught him "to see life not as a chance of a forever impossible personal happiness, but as a field for endeavour towards the happiness of the whole human family . . . I recognized this truth with a rapture such as I have known in no other reading," much as he also delighted in Zola, in Hardy, James and Trollope and for all the "great joy" that Stendhal gave him. He said later that Stendhal had some of Tolstoy's "astounding insight into the motives and intentions of men"; and Zola, "the greatest poet of his day," was one of his literary passions, one who was "always most terribly and most pitilessly moral. . . . Not Tolstoy, not Ibsen himself, has more profoundly and indignantly felt the injustice of civilization, or more insistently shown the falsity of its fundamental pretensions," and the so-called immoralities of his books were underlaid with a conscience capable of the austerest puritanism. So Howells was to write in one of his finest essays.[1] But he still felt that Tolstoy was the greatest of all, and he took for his own Tolstoy's motto, "The truth shall be my hero." He had felt Tolstoy to the full depths of his being, and, after reading him, he said, "I need never again look for a theme of fiction; I saw life swarming with themes that filled my imagination and pressed into my hands."[2]

It was in this year, 1887, that Howells became interested in the creed of socialism. He was in Buffalo, near his invalid daughter, when he heard Laurence Gronlund lecture before the Fortnightly Club, and, reading Gronlund's *Coöperative Commonwealth*, he went on to the *Fabian Essays* and a num-

---

[1] "Only those already rotten can scent corruption in Zola, and these, I think, may be deceived by effluvia from within themselves."

[2] He saw, as he said in *Imaginary Interviews,* "a boundless universe thronged with the most available interests, motives, situations, catastrophes and dénouements, and characters eagerly fitting themselves with the most appropriate circumstances."

Tolstoy returned a measure of Howells's admiration. "I feel particularly sympathetic towards Howells, from all I know of him," he wrote in 1898 to his English biographer Aylmer Maude. (Maude, *Life of Tolstoy, II,* 560.) He also told a common friend that he liked Howells's "fine spirit" as well as his manner of writing.

ber of the tracts of William Morris. Morris and Ruskin said
to him, that to "take from the many and leave them no joy in
their work" was as great an error as to "give to the few whom
it can bring no joy in their idleness"; and he was struck especially by Morris's insistence on the importance of the handicrafts in a world of factory-work. Then presently appeared Edward Bellamy's *Looking Backward,* a book that moved the
nation even more than *Uncle Tom's Cabin.* Howells had already reviewed *Dr. Heidenhoff's Process,* seeing in this author
a romantic imagination surpassed only by Hawthorne's, and
he was to regret that Bellamy was cut off "from writing the
one more book with which every author hopes to round his
career." Mark Twain was fascinated by *Looking Backward,* a
vision of organized labour as the only present help for working-
men, but in socialism he never went as far as Howells, nor, for
that matter, did Bellamy either. The word was one "I could
never well stomach," Bellamy wrote to Howells, for it "sug-
gests the red flag and all sorts of sexual novelties, and an abu-
sive tone about God and religion . . . Socialism is not a good
name for a party to succeed with in America." But Howells
himself was a socialist as long as he lived, although he supported Bellamy and his Nationalist Club in Boston, in the
heart of the financial district, in the Merchants' Exchange.
Edward Everett Hale was present at a meeting at which Howells sat, behind a tall stove, on an empty wood-box. He kicked
his heels vigorously against the wood-box by way of applause,
and this, as an eye-witness remembered, "made us all laugh."

Many years before this Howells had published in *The Atlantic* an article that had been refused by the conservative
magazines, Henry Demarest Lloyd's *Story of a Great Monop-
oly,* the first exposure of the Standard Oil Company. This was
the remote beginning of the "muckraking" movement, and

Howells printed it gladly after consulting with Charles Francis Adams to make sure of the reliability of its factual basis. Now he virtually welcomed abuse for his defence of the "immoral" Zola and Tolstoy, the "socialistic crank," as baneful in the popular eye as Whitman on whom his old friend Stedman had written an essay. When Josiah Gilbert Holland objected to this for *Scribner's,* Howells offered to publish it in *The Atlantic.* Then he took up the cause of the "Chicago anarchists" who were convicted after the Haymarket riot. Only one of these men had been present when the bomb was thrown, and he had been present with his wife and children, yet all were hanged, solely for their opinions; and, among the intellectuals, Howells was alone, or virtually alone, in publicly defending them. For weeks, for months, he wrote to a Chicago friend, the case had not been for one hour out of his waking thoughts,— "It is the last thing when I lie down, and the first when I wake up: it blackens my life." Howells had appealed for clemency, and he had written a letter to be read at the service for these men who were "well hanged," as the liberal, but now always conventional, Lowell said. As a result of all this, Howells felt that his horizon had been indefinitely widened. Harold Frederic was only one for whom he was a "big man" henceforth, above all taboos and conventions except in the sphere of sex. It would have been difficult to implicate Howells in what Santayana was to call the "genteel tradition."

From this time on, Howells was to see the writer and artist as a working-man, economically like a mechanic, a day-labourer, a farmer; and, if he continued to live in what socialists called the bourgeois way, it was because in a bourgeois world one could scarcely live otherwise. For he anticipated Bernard Shaw in perceiving that one cannot live socialistically in capitalistic conditions, though it reassured him that equality and fraternity, the ideals that had once moved the world, were reasserting themselves in people's minds. Dickens had constantly urged them, and Howells saw that the ideal of polite society was equality, although it was naturally only a make-believe there. People were treated there as equals for that time and occasion only, though polite society strove for equality among its members and offered the truest visible image of it. Good society was the highest expression of civilization, and Howells could not see why the "dead level" it dreaded should always be "dead."[3] He was, for the rest of his life, hostile to a world in which there were so many millionaires and so many tramps, in which the men had no ideal but to get more and more money and the women had no ideal but to spend more and more. To Henry James he wrote in 1888, "I should hardly like to trust pen and ink with all the audacity of my social ideas; but after fifty years of optimistic content with 'civilization' and its ability to come out right in the end, I now abhor it, and feel that it is coming out all wrong in the end, unless it bases itself anew on a real equality. Meanwhile, I wear a fur-lined overcoat, and live in all the luxury my money can buy."

Presently, in the following year, Howells wrote to Mark Twain, "I have just heated myself up with your righteous wrath about our indifference to the Brazilian Republic. But it seems to me that you ignore the real reason for it which is that there is no longer an American Republic, but an aristocracy-loving oligarchy in place of it. Why should our money-bags rejoice in the explosion of a wind-bag [the Brazilian Empire]? They know at the bottom of the hole where their souls ought to be that if such an event means anything it means their ruin

---

[3] "Good society is, upon the whole, so nobly imagined and so handsomely realized that one longs to have it perfect, and then to impart its perfection to all human society."—Howells, *Equality as the Basis of Good Society,* in *The Century,* for November, 1895.

next; and so they don't rejoice; and as they mostly inspire the people's voice, the press, the press is dumb." So, henceforth, for a number of years, Howells was disposed to see more of the evil than of the good in American civilization. He was aware of the frauds that people practise on themselves, the buying of votes, for instance, that still went on, and two of his fine novels, *The Quality of Mercy* and *The Son of Royal Langbrith,* dealt with the lives of rascally business men. He observed that nearly every day a notorious defaulter crossed the Canadian border and escaped from the police. "The variety of evil in this strangely constituted world of ours is far greater than the variety of good," he was to write in connection with Tolstoy. "The vices outnumber the virtues two to one."

After *The Minister's Charge,*—in which Boston appeared, in the policeman's phrase, as a "bad place" for so many,—Howells published *Annie Kilburn,* a Tolstoyan novel that showed how little moral convictions count for aesthetic righteousness. For, while this was full of happy touches and well-drawn minor characters, the protagonists were decidedly unconvincing. To the mill-town of Hatboro, Annie Kilburn returns from Rome, —where she has been living with her father, an ex-member of Congress who is buried there in the Protestant Cemetery,— feeling that she must do something for the country, for the town, besides giving it an ugly soldiers' monument. A member of one of the old families, with a summer homestead, Annie "had never consented to be an old maid," but "she had become one without great suffering," and she rejoices in Richardson's new railway station, massive and low, with red-tiled spreading roofs. Neither is she displeased by the look of the Episcopal church in its blameless church-warden Gothic, half hidden by ivy. But she finds in this New England village, expanding into an American town, that it will not do for her to play the lady bountiful, since those who do most of the work of the world should share its comforts as a right and not be put off with what the idlers choose to give them. Something in the air has changed for her; one could not live in the old way if one had a grain of humanity or conscience, though the summer sojourners continue to rest from their fatigues, the labours of afternoon teas and the giving of dinners. (And the suppers of evening receptions, the drain of play-going and charity-doing, the slavery of amateur art-study, the writing of invitations, the trying on of dresses, the musicales and calls.) Annie Kilburn follows the Tolstoyan minister Mr. Peck, who brings to the town not peace but a sword, who "walks too much with the poor and converses too much with the lowly," as the local magnate, Mr. Gerrish, puts it. Unable to see why there should be inequalities in the world, he objects to the social union that excludes the working-people; and, driven to resign, he sets out for Fall River to work in the mills and teach in the public schools there. Annie is to go there after him, intending to be a mill-worker too, realizing how little she can do with money; and then Mr. Peck is killed, at the station, by a train.

While this novel won the praise of Robertson James in Concord,—the younger brother of William and Henry James, and himself an ardent follower of Henry George,[4]—one could only feel that Howells had undertaken too much for him to carry out. He had lost his detachment in this treatment of a theme that appealed so closely to his heart, and Mr. Peck, with his pale blue eyes, who antagonizes the business men, has not

4 "You cannot know how the reading of *Annie Kilburn* and the *Hazard of New Fortunes* has lifted and purged me and made me feel for a while anyway how deep and vast is the circle of human love and suffering in which we are all knit."—Robertson James to Howells, 1889.

"I hope you will never tire of celebrating these obscure lives [in *Annie Kilburn*] because it is only apparently in these that the great fight of destiny is taking place."—Robertson James to Howells, 1890.

weight enough to support the heavy burden. Nor does Annie sufficiently impress the reader; while in picturing Putney, the alcoholic, condemned by his infirmity to the second-rate position of a small-town lawyer, Howells lost his usually infallible psychological tact. For Putney's perpetual jocularity is really insupportable. Tolstoy, Howells wrote in *My Literary Passions,* "robs himself of half his strength when he becomes impatient of his role of artist and prefers to be directly a teacher"; and this might have been said of himself in *Annie Kilburn.* His own Tolstoyanism was better in small doses, when it appeared in subordinate characters connected with other main themes in *A Hazard of New Fortunes* and *The World of Chance.* There one found Mr. Chapley, the Tolstoyan publisher, an old comrade at Brook Farm of David Hughes whose book, "his dream of a practicable golden age," condemned the whole structure of society as it existed. Then there was the old radical Lindau in *A Hazard of New Fortunes,* like the two previous characters admirably drawn and in all ways endearing and magnetic. It is true that *A Traveler from Altruria* and *Through the Eye of the Needle* were wholly,—if not Tolstoyan,—socialist books; and in them one found Howells almost at his best. But neither of them professed to be realistic novels. In them Howells entered the country of romance, to him virtually a foreign literary country.

The scene of *A Traveler from Altruria* is one of those summer hotels that brought together, for Howells, a variety of types one could not readily assemble anywhere else, a banker, a professor, a minister, a manufacturer and various women who speak from many points of view;[5] and the Altrurian Mr. Homos, is the guest of a novelist, one of the fatuous romantic

[5] Especially Mrs. Makely who, "as a cultivated American woman, was necessarily quite ignorant of her own country, geographically, politically and historically."

sort who serves the traveller as a foil. The novelist stands for all the American abuses, while he undertakes to "explain" the country, whereas Mr. Homos is a kind of spiritual solvent who precipitates whatever sincerity there is in the others. The practical men, who have small use for authors,[6]—think Mr. Homos is lacking in a sense of humour because he takes seriously the American professions which in Altruria are put into practice, —equality and human brotherhood. Since the "Accumulation" has given place there to the "Commonwealth," money has been abolished and everyone works partly in the "obligatories" and partly in the "voluntaries" that enable people to follow their own tastes. The normal man is the artist there who works because he loves the work, and everyone labours in the spirit of the artist in the measure of his ability and calling. It is the reverse of the American system, based on self-seeking, so that great wealth has become the American ideal, as the candid banker notes acutely;[7] and Mr. Homos, with his innocent air of polite mystification, somehow makes a monkey of most of the others.

[6] "I have always been suspicious, in the company of practical men, of an atmosphere of condescension to men of my calling, if nothing worse. I fancy they commonly regard artists of all kinds as a sort of harmless eccentrics, and that literary people they look upon as something droll, as weak and soft, as not quite right."—The novelist, in *A Traveler from Altruria*.

[7] "I should say that within a generation our ideal had changed twice. Before the Civil War, and during the time from the Revolution onward, it was undoubtedly the great politician, the publicist, the statesman. As we grew older, and began to have an intellectual life of our own, I think the literary fellows had a pretty good share of the honours that were going, that is, such a man as Longfellow was popularly considered a type of greatness. When the war came, it brought the soldier to the front, and there was a period of ten or fifteen years when he dominated the national imagination. That period passed, and the great era of national prosperity set in. The big fortunes began to tower up, and heroes of another sort began to appeal to our admiration. I don't think there is any doubt but the millionaire is now the American ideal."—The banker, in *A Traveler from Altruria*.

With its Socratic irony, *A Traveler from Altruria* solidified, as one of the characters said, all the soap-bubble worlds from Plato onward; and, moreover, as fresh as Morris's *News from Nowhere,* it had a special charm of style and tone. So did the sequel, *Through the Eye of the Needle,* that Howells published later, letters of Mr. Homos and of the woman he met and married who presently returned to Altruria with him. One learned there about the squalid struggle of a plutocratic world in its golden age,—or "age on a gold basis," as the editor puts it,—where "people live *upon* instead of for each other" and "the man who needs a dinner is the man who is never asked to dine." Howells, who had been drawn to the Shakers, was drawn to the Altrurians, like the Shakers a family of equals but aesthetically minded, with costumes of lovely colours designed by artists, and cities built like Bologna with shaded arcades. From there one looked back on American conditions as a nightmare from which the Altrurians had happily awakened.

APPROACHING NEW YORK

THERE WAS no doubt about the reality of Howells's socialistic views or the depth of conviction and feeling that lay behind them. Howells, as Brooks Adams said, was "genuine to the backbone," and Tolstoy and the social reformers of the time irresistibly appealed to his compassionate, liberal and generous nature. He was to retain their stamp to the end of his life. But, for a novelist, after all, the world is a spectacle in which, just as it is, he takes delight; and lovers continue to fall in love, without harm to any man, while justice is only one of the touchstones of existence. So there was nothing inconsistent in Howells's remaining a "theoretical socialist" and a "practical aristocrat"[1] who went to "two fashionable teas" one afternoon in 1889 and a "socialist meeting" in the evening; for although he blamed himself for it, he delighted in fashion almost as much as Henry James.[2] Hostile to plutocracy, aware

[1] "Mark Twain and his wife and Elinor and I are all of accord in our way of thinking—that is, we are theoretical socialists, and practical aristocrats."—Letter of Howells to his father, 1890.

[2] "Women of fashion always interested him [Colville, who is virtually Howells]; he liked them; it diverted him that they should take themselves seriously. . . . Their resolution, their suffering for their ideal, such as it was, their energy in dressing and adorning themselves, the pains they were at to achieve the trivialities they passed their lives in, were a perpetual delight to him. He often found them people of great simplicity, and sometimes of singularly good sense; their frequent vein of piety was delicious."—Howells, *Indian Summer*.

of evil plutocrats, he could see the head of a trust,—Ralson, for instance, in *Letters Home*,—as in some ways an admirable man. Meanwhile, thinking of New York, he was eager, as he wrote to Hale, "to get intimately at that vast mass of life."

Howells's approach to the city was tentative at first, and he even returned, for two more years, to Boston. To Thomas Sergeant Perry he wrote, in 1888, "I have been trying to catch on to the bigger life of the place. It's immensely interesting, but I don't know whether I shall manage it; I'm now fifty-one, you know. There are lots of interesting young painting and writing fellows, and the place is lordly free, with foreign touches of all kinds all through its abounding Americanism: Boston seems of another planet." But there was no question that, for an all-American writer, New York was the one continental city,—"There's only one city that belongs to the whole country, and that's New York," his Fulkerson said. Moreover, Howells knew as well as O. Henry later that all America was fascinated by it. "Boston belongs to the Bostonians," Basil March remarked, in his reply to Fulkerson in the novel, and Howells had been a "naturalized Bostonian" at best, while for some years already, ever since *A Modern Instance,* his novels had been serialized in New York magazines. Since 1885, he had been in charge of the "Editor's Study" in the monthly *Harper's;* but he had serious doubts whether he could belong to New York, or whether New York could belong to him. Thomas Wentworth Higginson, with true Boston candour, warned him that he was not the fashion there. Higginson had dined in New York, "with some fractions of the Four Hundred," at a cousin's house in 1891, and the talk at table had fallen on Howells's novels. "Nobody," said Higginson, "approved them except Mr. C. and I," and the hostess said that, with many exceptions, it was not the fashion in New York to

admire Howells. "Now in Boston," Higginson said, "I think
it is," adding, "It vexed me to find that just as we are resign-
ing you to New York, you do not seem to stand as strongly
there as here."

Undoubtedly in literary Boston, at least, Howells had been
made much of, and it was symptomatic of this that he had
been asked to write the official biographies of Whittier and
Lowell. Whittier had asked him directly to write his life, and
Norton urged him to write Lowell's, but he had refused in
both cases on the ground that he was not a New England man.
Then he was also asked to go through Longfellow's unprinted
poems and decide which should be published. Boston had
drawn Howells originally for literary reasons when the famous
New England authors acted as a magnet, but, now that these
authors were dead or dying, the town had lost the magnetism
it had once possessed for the imagination. "Young men may
now resort to Boston for culture," the old Bostonian Otis Binning said in *Letters Home,* "but not for the fulfilment of their
dreams of a literary career. We are no longer the literary, as
we are no longer the commercial or the social metropolis, and
the young Ardiths of the land . . . would no more think of
coming up to us than the old Ralsons." (Ardith was the young
Western writer who had come to New York, and Ralson was
the Western head of the Cheese and Churn Trust.)

Howells expressed in several novels his own feeling about
this change, and he had shared Dan Mavering's "sense of
liberation, of expansion" when Dan visited Washington after
living in Boston. He "filled his lungs with the cosmopolitan air
in a sort of intoxication,"—in *April Hopes,*—feeling, "with
the astonishment which must always attend the Bostonian's
perception of the fact, that there is a great social life in
America outside of Boston." That had been Henry Adams's

feeling in the national capital, or the feeling that he attributed to Howells's friend, the younger Holmes; and Howells had shared Colville's enjoyment in Florence, when, in *Indian Summer,* he was introduced to a wider American world. "He found in Mrs. Bowen's house people from Denver, Chicago, St. Louis, Boston, New York and Baltimore, all meeting as of apparently the same civilization." For the rest, Howells wrote in a letter, "At the bottom of our wicked hearts, we all like New York, and I hope to use some of this vast, gay, shapeless life in my fiction. I suppose our home—such as it is—will be there hereafter in the winter, though we expect always to drift back to this good Boston region for the summer." In fact, while New York remained Howells's centre, he agreed with Mrs. March that "the seashore near Boston" was "the only real seashore." One year he bought a house at Far Rockaway, but he sold this after a few months; and he spent one summer at Millbrook,—"like an English landscape, pretty, but with the fatal insincerity of a copy"; and once he wrote, "We are drifting from one place to another this summer, trying to discover some spot within a few hours of New York where we might pitch our ragged tent for the summers that yet remain to us." But, finally settling on York Harbour and Kittery Point in Maine, he spent summers there for the rest of his life. "The neatness and self-respect of New England are more amazing than ever," he wrote, "coming from slipshod New York"; and there, for a part of each year, he felt at home.

Boston, however, was another matter, much as it haunted his mind for a while and much as he may have lamented, with Mrs. March, "the literary peace, the intellectual refinement of the life they had left behind them." (For the Howellses reappeared as the Marches in *A Hazard of New Fortunes,* which told the tale of their hegira.) Only "it was not life—it was death-in-life," in spite of the Boston faces that Howells remembered, "so intense, so full of manly dignity, a subdued yet potent personality, a consciousness as far as could be from self-consciousness." Those faces were sometimes "set and severe, with their look of challenge, of interrogation, almost of reproof"; but they "expressed purity of race, continuity of tradition, fidelity to ideals such as no other group of faces could now express. . . . One sees strong faces elsewhere; I have seen them assembled in England; but I have never seen such faces as those Boston faces . . . I found something finely visionary in it all."[3] But, rereading aloud, years later, James's *The Bostonians,* which appeared in 1886, Howells wrote to the author that the early chapters were "so like Boston that we all shuddered." This was the book of which Mark Twain said that he would "rather be damned to John Bunyan's heaven than read it," but to Howells it was "one of the masterpieces of all fiction . . . such a novel as the like of hasn't been done in our time." To him it was "the greatest blunder and the greatest pity" that James was not including it in his collected edition; and, as he added, "a dear yet terrible time comes back to me in it all." To James it had been a more terrible time, for he felt oppressed in Boston, while he found a kind of happiness in London,—"this big empty wilderness of paving-stones," as he wrote to Howells,—but Howells too had come to feel its limitations as he moved gradually into a larger world. He wished to be the novelist not of American life but of "human life in America," as he preferred to call it, returning to the

---

[3] "We have been in the habit of going to Boston when we wished to refresh our impression that we had a native country; when we wished to find ourselves in the midst of the good old American faces, which were sometimes rather arraigning in their expression, but not too severe for the welfare of a person imaginably demoralized by a New York sojourn."— Howells, *Imaginary Interviews.*

world of his earliest novels, before he had become immersed in Boston, and treating that world on a much larger scale.

This he accomplished in *A Hazard of New Fortunes*—"the most vital of my fictions," he called this book, "through my quickened interest in the life about me,"—an ample undertaking, assembling a great variety of types, with a magazine as the focus that brought them all together. There, as Basil and Isabel March, one found the Howellses once more, living in Stuyvesant Square, facing St. George's, in a world full of novelty and attraction and intensely domesticated there. For Howells was well versed in the problems of apartment-hunting and housekeeping, the price of eggs and of vegetables, game and poultry,—and one soon heard much of the tables d'hôte in which the city abounded and the Italian grocers near Washington Square. It was the quality of foreignness that appealed to the Marches especially, the German, Russian, French and Spanish faces and the touch-and-go character of the New York life which seemed so impersonal after their years in Boston. Through the magazine, *Every Other Week,* and Fulkerson, its manager who had come from the West, they fell in with types from all over the country, the Woodburns, father and daughter, who stood for the old[4] and the new South, the Leightons from New England, Angus Beaton, the painter. There were the Dreyfooses, especially the old father, Pennsylvania Dutch, who had found natural gas and grown suddenly rich, his wife,

[4] Colonel Woodburn has the "rather decorative politeness which men of Southern extraction use toward women" (*The Shadow of a Dream*); and he is writing a book to prove that slavery is the only solution of the labour-problem. "He's got it on the brain that if the South could have been let alone by the commercial spirit and the pseudo-philanthropy of the North, it would have worked out slavery into a perfectly ideal condition for the labourer, in which he would have been insured against want and protected in all his personal rights by the State."—Fulkerson in *A Hazard of New Fortunes.* Does this not rather suggest the thesis of some of the writers of the twentieth century symposium, *I'll Take My Stand?*

as solid a character as Mrs. Silas Lapham, their daughters and their priest-like son, the devoted Conrad. There was Lindau, the old German socialist, with the grand patriarchal head, who explored foreign periodicals for the magazine, translating Dostoievsky and many others, Margaret Vance who entered a religious order, and Kendricks, the lover of Baudelaire and Flaubert, with his dilettantish intention of writing a novel. Howells vivified all these people whom the genial Fulkerson[5] drew together; he caused them to live and endure in the reader's mind, a primary mark of merit in the great age of the novel.

Though the fates of all the characters were still interwoven in this book,—the first fruit of the writer's New York life,— Howells departed altogether here from his earlier method of assembling a small group of people. The figures, minutely particularized, were many and diverse, and Henry James wrote to Howells after he had read the book, "You are less *big* than Zola, but you are ever so much less clumsy and more really various."[6] By means of the great street-car strike, the story rose far above the ordinary love-affairs that abounded in the novel; and, incidentally, Howells, in his eager response to the New York scene, anticipated the painters of the "Ash-

[5] In 1893, Robert Louis Stevenson wrote to Howells, "You will never get me to believe that (in your *Hazard of New Fortunes*) you did not draw from the same life-model as I did in *The Wreckers*. There are speeches in either case that might be transposed, and I think the general lines marvellously coincide; which, in consideration of our different theories and aims, is remarkable and (to my mind) wholly consolatory."
But Stevenson's "Western American with energy and brass" had been studied from Lloyd Osborne, Stevenson's stepson. So, at least, Lloyd Osborne said. Howells's Fulkerson had been suggested by his old picaresque friend Ralph Keeler.

[6] It was of *A Hazard of New Fortunes* that William James wrote to Henry James, "With that work, your *Tragic Muse* and, last but by no means least, my *Psychology,* all appearing in it, the year 1890 will be known as the great epochal year in American literature."

can" school. He, personally, knew Everett Shinn and greatly liked his work, and much of his writing suggested John Sloan and others, the artists who understood, with Basil March, why the poor did not care to live in a respectable quarter. "They would be bored to death," March said, adding, "I think I should prefer Mott Street myself," and he thought of the elevated railway and the wonderful spectacle there, "which in a city full of painters nightly works its miracles unrecorded," —miracles not to be recorded for another dozen years. On the station stairs at Chatham Square he once more had a sense of "the neglected opportunities of painters in that region," the Swiss châlets overhead, the vistas of shabby side streets, the old hip-roofed houses that were still remaining. He preferred the East Side to the West Side lines largely because they "raced into the gay ugliness, the shapeless, graceful, reckless picturesqueness of the Bowery." If the painters had seen Naples, he thought, that frantic panorama, and the life that rejoiced or sorrowed and clattered and crawled around, above, below, in Chatham Square, they would have set it down at once in note-books; but March decided that, if he was going to have his own sketches illustrated, he would have to go and bring the artist there, for the painters were all too busy painting Paris in New York. Basil March delighted in the cockney-ish quality of the ballad-sellers and the "*primo tenore* statue of Garibaldi" that spoke for Italian progress in Washington Square; and Howells himself even found in New York "wild flowers of the asphalt," hepaticas fringing the rails of the cable-cars. He found water-pimpernel there too, where the cable ran with a brooklike gurgle, and cardinal-flowers on Third Avenue in shady stretches, St. John's-wort in the gutters of Wall Street, arrowhead at Dead Man's Curve and golden-rod on the roof of Madison Square Garden.

In at least three other novels Howells presented the great ugly town with its "brute bulks" of architecture[7] and with its note of impersonality, so marked to Otis Binning in *Letters Home* after his "immensely, intensely personal" Boston. One, the weakest, weak indeed,—*The Coast of Bohemia*,—carried on the theme of the painter in New York in a day when studios were often filled with satin banners, tambourines and fish-nets spangled with bits of mirror. Always alert for new types of the moment, Howells introduced here the young painter Ludlow, just back from Paris, and seeing deep purple, indigo blues and rainbow oranges and scarlets with eyes trained by the French impressionist masters. Convinced that the right man could get as much pathos out of farm-folk as Millet got out of his Barbizon peasants and that Americans needed to be shown, moreover, the festive aspects of their common life, he reported on canvas an American county fair. Howells struck there a note of the moment, though the novel itself seemed infantile, surprising after the great stroke of *A Hazard of New Fortunes*, but, as he himself said, "A man who is truly an artist may fail in many efforts and yet at any time vindicate himself by success." At that very moment he was writing *The World of Chance*, followed by *Letters Home*[8] a few years

[7] Howells, always sensitive to architecture, surely expressed his own feeling in the words of David Hughes, in *The World of Chance*, "Take this whole architectural nightmare that we call a city. I hold that the average tasteless man has no right to realize his idea of a house in the presence of a great multitude of his fellow-beings. It is an indecent exposure of his mind, and should not be permitted. All these structural forms about us, which with scarcely an exception are ugly and senseless, I regard as so many immoralities, as deliriums, as imbecilities, which a civilized state would not permit. . . . The city should build the city, and provide every denizen with a fit and beautiful habitation to work in and rest in."

[8] "Dear Howells, You've done it this time and no mistake. I've just read *Letters Home*, which raised me from the dead almost, and which is the most absolutely faultless piece of richness as well as veracity that ever flowed out of human pen. I bar no one and no language. It is nature itself, and

later, two admirable novels with the freshness of first novels
and with a clear image of Howells's own youth. They were
full of the excitement of young writers coming to New York,
as Howells had come from the West in 1861, and later in
1866, and as he had seen so many coming, Stephen Crane,
for one, while he remained young in his own thoughts. For
he was always the Basil March of whom Kendricks said,
"There are very few men of his age who keep in touch with
the times as he does."

For Howells revived in the young writers who appeared in
these two novels,—Ardith of *Letters Home* and Shelley Ray,
the novelist who has come from Midland in *The World of
Chance*,—"that lifting and glowing of the heart which a young
man cannot help feeling if he walks up Broadway on a bright
October morning." That was the feeling of the young man in
Mark Twain's *The Gilded Age* as he walked down Broadway
on a spring morning, past the long line of "palace shops," listening to the roar of the traffic with a sense that the paths to
fortune were all open before him. Howells too had come with
an unpublished manuscript and with a mind swarming with
poems and stories, intending to write New York letters to the
papers at home, struck by the "New Yorky dash" and the thrill
and sparkle of the air, like Ardith, who had come from Wottoma as he came from Columbus. Like Ardith, too, he "didn't
want to go back on the dear old place—or *to* it," as George Ade
said of Indiana. The novelty of New York, with all its noise
and filth, had seemed to him inexhaustibly dramatic, and he
too had seen the world as "a place for making verse and making love and full of beauty of all kinds waiting to be fitted with
phrases." It had been "all copy" for Howells as for Shelley Ray

the wit of it, and the humour of it and the goodness of it! You may go—
that will remain. Your ever thankful William James."—Letter to Howells,
1904.

and Ardith, who hoped to write "the epic of New York," when
people were still talking of "the great American novel,"—and
who found more material there in a minute than one found in
a year at Wottoma or at Midland or Columbus. Howells remembered how he had felt about the young writers in New
York,—Thomas Bailey Aldrich, for example, in the sixties:
their names had a "planetary distinctness" if one came from
the West. So Shelley Ray felt, when he first arrived, listening
to the young men talk, at the French table d'hôte, and eager
to join them.

In this literary aspirant Howells recalled many traits of his
own youth, not only his "young dread of queerness and ir-
regularity," hungry as he was for experience and fond of ad-
venture. No more than Henry James had he shared that
nostalgie de la boue which came in with a later generation, and
he would have disliked the visionaries who gathered about
David Hughes, every Sunday morning, in the tenement-
house, with the trains of the Elevated railway rushing past
the window. He too might have called them "howling der-
vishes," for he had not seen how or why the world was out of
kilter, and Kane, the philosopher, noting how repugnant the
Golden Age is to the heart of youth,—"It likes the nineteenth
century much better,"—might have been thinking of Howells
as a young man. Hughes, the tall gaunt veteran with the
leonine grandeur and the shaggy head who lives in the tene-
ment-house with his two daughters and the son-in-law Ansel
Denton, the wood-engraver, himself an old Brook Farmer,
is working on a book that is much like Howells's own socialistic
writings. For Howells in these later days felt very differently
towards the other Tolstoyans and Henry Georgites, like Mr.
Chapley, the publisher,—David Hughes's old Brook Farm
friend,—who, with his conventional wife, appears in the book.

Howells had not lost the literary passion that saw stories every-where, but once, like Shelley Ray, he might have seen in the notions of Hughes merely good ideas for Christmas stories. He might also have written, moreover, a book like "A Modern Romeo" with that "helpless fidelity to provincial conditions which seemed to come from the author's ignorance of any-thing else." But Howells had already known something of the world before he began to write novels.

The World of Chance brought back a time when old Brook Farmers, such as Charles A. Dana and Curtis, were still liv-ing in New York, although this novel, like *Letters Home,*—which had "all New York in it," as an English correspondent wrote to Howells,—was something much more actual than a period piece. It remained fresh and alive, and *Letters Home,* still more so, pictured the New York of those who "have got too rich to stay at home": they have left their supremacy be-hind in the West, their mansions and their libraries of first editions, accepting seats in New York that are far below the salt, living, like the Ralsons, in the Walhondia,—the Waldorf,—until their new houses on Fifth Avenue have been built and equipped. The book is a novel in letters, with a dozen or more contrasted types, one of whom, the Bostonian Otis Bin-ning, surveys with a benevolent eye the lives of the others, while Ralson, the great business man, regards him as an "intel-lectual" and therefore as "a kind of mental woman." Otis, "very fine-looking in an old family portrait way," combats his Boston sister-in-law's delicate sniffs, and he has the first and last word in the story, absorbed as he is in the love-affair of the young Westerner Ardith and the "large, flowery, sun-flowery" America Ralson.[9] It is her ingenuous social ambition

---

[9] Otis Binning assures his sister that she would understand his absorption if she had met the lovers "in the fine ether of one of James's stories."

that has brought the Ralsons to New York, where "even the rich have to eat humble pie" and where her plain old mother can only talk of the "beautiful home" abandoned in Wottoma. But in the end America marries the young man from the native town who is devoting himself to the writing of fiction; and Miss Holly, who has come from the South "after struggling along at home, putting up lady-like pickles for a reluctant market," takes notes on their affair for her Sunday paper. The book offers Otis Binning a chance to make many wise remarks about the old New Yorkers, for instance, who are "very light, as people of the old Dutch stock are apt to be,"—so different was the Dutch Calvinism from Puritanism. Of the Ralsons, Otis Binning said, "Their manner does not betray the delusion of so many parvenus that aristocrats are refined people, instead of being people who on coming into their social advantages have known how to keep the rude force of their disadvantages, whose cooks, coachmen and lackeys have, generally speaking, always had better manners, because they have been obliged to have them."

PRACTICAL MATTERS

URING THE years 1886-1891, Howells had a contract with Harper and Brothers, agreeing, in exchange for $10,000 a year, to give them all his writings, one novel and the monthly *causerie*, the "Editor's Study." After this the contract lapsed, not to be renewed until 1900, when Howells received the same fixed salary as literary adviser of the publishing house and for his books and for writing the "Easy Chair." Formerly conducted by George William Curtis, this became, Howells said, a "multiple personality," once a month, in which his several selves conversed with one another; and every week he spent three afternoons in the publishing office, discussing the literary side of the company's business. Capital punishment was the only subject that was tabooed in Howells's department in *Harper's Magazine*, and no one ever questioned anything he wrote.[1] To Howells, capital punishment was "the worst form of murder," but he could not believe in punishment of any kind. "I am always glad," he said, "to have sinners get off, for I like to get off from my own sins."

[1] Once, however, Henry M. Alden, the editor of *Harper's Magazine*, is said to have "grieved" over Howells, who praised the tendency of *Robert Elsmere*, by Mrs. Humphry Ward, which seemed to lead people away from the Church. Because they felt it was antagonistic to the teachings of Christ, the Harpers had declined the book, knowing it would be an immense success. Alden foresaw that the newspapers would make much of Howells's approval of the book, and he felt this would injure the magazine.

The arrangement with the Harpers relieved Howells of "all anxiety about marketing my wares," he wrote to his sister, although in the nine intervening years his popularity rose to the point where his income virtually rivalled Mark Twain's. This was the great day of the magazines, *The Atlantic, Harper's, The Century, Scribner's,* when the highest class of readers were magazine readers, Howells said himself in *Literature and Life,* and when writers lived much more by serial publication than by the sale of any of their books. John W. De Forest had written to Howells in 1879, "I fear that I shall be driven to volume publication, which at present is almost without profit," for the magazines were so crowded that he was told he would have to wait two years for serial publication. *Bleak House, The Newcomes, Daniel Deronda* and *Uncle Tom's Cabin* were among the great serials of the recent past, and the novels of both James and Howells had been published in this manner.[2] Howells had said in 1901 that his new novel was to be issued "without serializing, which will be a new thing for me," and yet in 1903 he was able to say, "There is still no falling off of the magazine serials." It was only in 1915 that he wrote to Henry James, "I could not 'serialize' a story of mine now in any American magazine, thousands of them as there are."

When his first contract with Harpers lapsed, Howells became for a few months the editor of the *Cosmopolitan Mag-*

[2] Even the newspapers published literary serials. Howells's novel *The Quality of Mercy* was published in 1891 in the New York *Sun,* the Chicago *Inter-Ocean,* the Philadelphia *Enquirer,* the Cincinnati *Commercial-Gazette,* the Toronto *Globe* and the Boston *Herald.* The Chicago *Inter-Ocean* was obliged to print on the following Monday a second edition of the Sunday edition that contained the first instalment.

Howells's later travel book, *Roman Holidays and Others,* appeared in 1908 through six months of the Sunday edition of the New York *Sun.* Just so, *Venetian Life* had been published forty years earlier in the Boston *Advertiser.*

azine because "it promised me freedom from the anxiety of placing my stories," he wrote to his old friend Charles Eliot Norton. Nothing seemed less in character than this anomalous venture of an author and ex-editor of Howells's standing, and Norton said he would have to exert himself to subdue that noxious atmosphere of "third-rate vulgarity." Did he perhaps think he could make the *Cosmopolitan* "the best thing we have got in a literary way," as Fulkerson had said of *Every Other Week,* a "new departure in magazines," that might give authors and artists a chance and elevate and improve the public taste? However that might have been, he soon resigned from the editorship, partly from a sense of ignominy,—or "hopeless incompatibility," as he put it,—though it left his mornings free for his own writing. But he had certainly hoped to make it a force in American letters, and he had obtained contributions from some of the best writers, Sarah Orne Jewett,[3] Theodore Roosevelt and Frank R. Stockton, an author who had done much to lighten the heart of his generation. Howells enjoyed Stockton's absurdities reduced from logical arguments, together with his wild caprices of the fancy. Theodore Roosevelt, who read Howells's books as they came out and who invited him to dinner to meet Lincoln Steffens, had written to him in 1890 about *A Boy's Town,* published that year, "We have read it once through, and then gone back and reread our favourite pieces. The feelings of the boy in many cases I could thoroughly understand for the excellent reason that I have felt them myself." About this book Roosevelt agreed with Parkman.

Then Henry James sent Howells an essay on Wolcott Balestier, the American writer and publisher who had recently

[3] "Your voice is like a thrush's in the din of all the literary noises that stun us so."—Howells, Letter to Sarah Orne Jewett, 1891.

died, Rudyard Kipling's brother-in-law, who had once stayed with the Howellses at Saratoga. He and Howells had concocted a plan to get Henry James to live there in "a house with a bronze bootblack for a fountain on its lawn" and with a toboggan-slide near by, for they said to one another, "Saratoga is the place for James. It's the only place that would reconcile him to America." Howells added in a letter to his friend, "We thought no other place could be so bad . . . and the whole country would profit by the contrast." The town soon became the setting of *The Day of Their Wedding,* perhaps the weakest of all of Howells's novels, and of *An Open-Eyed Conspiracy,* published the following year, another of scarcely greater moment. Basil March had been vaguely looking for a story in this former "paradise of young people,"—where girls were still "getting acquainted" at the great hotels,—although, beside the ghosts of the past, with their yellow hair and purple moustaches, one really found little of the youth of the present there. Then March fell in with Kendricks, who *became* the story. Meanwhile, he studied the types about him, mostly plain honest Americans of an innocence too inveterate to have grasped the fact that there was no fashion any longer in Saratoga, although, with its charm of ruin, the place was "American down to the ground. No other people could have invented it," as Kendricks said. One saw there the lofty shafts under the roofs peculiar to Saratoga architecture, and one heard those banalities of conversation that had for Howells a piquancy one often found later in Theodore Dreiser. Then, seen from the grandstand, the horses "seemed to lift from the earth as with wings, and to skim over the track like a covey of low-flying birds."

A year before, Wolcott Balestier had been living near Brattleboro, the old home of Mrs. Howells, writing with

Kipling *The Naulahka* which gave its name to Kipling's house, and "hitting it off together smoothly . . . James," Balestier wrote to Howells, "has been reading the first part of it and professes himself delighted with the Western atmosphere. If he could only take one sniff at the real thing! . . . The story is as American as a roller-skating rink and as Indian as Juggernaut"; and then Balestier spoke of Ibsen, whose effect was now apparent in London, even on Pinero and Henry Arthur Jones. "It is at least interesting," he said, "to see realism penetrating to the stage," a fact that meant much to Howells, for whom Ibsen had "looked life squarely in the face" more than any other writer "except perhaps Flaubert or Tolstoy." Balestier himself was projecting a publishing plan which he called "our continental series," saying that he had for this Henry James's approval, and he wished to begin with Howells's *The Shadow of a Dream* and *Tuscan Cities* and then continue with "all of Ruskin." He asked Howells to enlist Mark Twain's interest in the plan. "Mark Twain, you know," he said, "is more valuable on the continent," from the publishing point of view, "than any author English or American . . . He sells in Persia and Samarcand and the Greek archipelago." Would Howells capture him for Balestier's publishing venture?

Howells was well aware of Mark Twain's universal fame, though this was now scarcely greater than his own at a time when Germans and Russians told him that his books were known to all English-speaking Germans and Russians. The Queen of Württemberg bought one of his books at a bazaar in Stuttgart, with one of Mark Twain's and one of Ibsen's, and, presently, with Henry Clay's, John Ruskin's and Robert Burns's, his name and portrait appeared on a cigar-box label. Karl Marx's daughter, writing to him, called him "not only a true artist, and a great writer, but that even rarer thing, a brave and just man." Meanwhile, Stuart Merrill dedicated his French poems to Howells,[4] and Stepniak, the Russian revolutionist, came to see him. "*All* your novels," Stepniak had written to him, "are translated into Russian, and your name is familiar as well as your individuality to many thousands of Russians and all the Russian reading public." He himself had read in London *A Hazard of New Fortunes* "with the absorption of a school-girl until four o'clock in the morning . . . You have heard so many praises in your life and you stand so much above us all as a master in an art in which we have not made even the apprenticeship . . . Your world is not made up. It lives its own life, marvellously concrete and real, and what a splendid ease and naturalness of the dialogue. What variety of types! . . . There is no figure which is not correctly drawn and individualized." The author of *The Career of a Nihilist* said his chief wish in crossing the ocean was to meet this American in whose work he found "the same quality" that he found "in the Russian novelists." A big man in a black ulster who looked like a bear, Howells said, when he slid down the pole at one of the firehouses, Stepniak was lecturing on the Siberian exiles. He wrote again to Howells, "I spent a most delightful day at Mark Twain's and I am exceedingly thankful for the opportunity you gave me of knowing him. I left quite wild with delight at his absolutely unique, wonderfully original personality. I never imagined that in our time of over-civilization

[4] Howells wrote a preface in 1890 to the *Pastels in Prose* that Stuart Merrill translated from French into English. These were "prose poems" of Huysmans, Baudelaire, Théodore de Banville, Mallarmé and others.

At about this time Howells was asked to do books on Venice and Boston for the series called "Historic Towns," and Edward MacDowell set some of his poems to music.

such a man can be found anywhere." But the visit was embarrassing to Mrs. Clemens, for when Stepniak asked Mark Twain what he thought of Balzac and Thackeray he was obliged to confess that he had not read them.

As for Kipling, Howells liked his studies of army life, of which he wrote in the "Editor's Study," and, as he said, this young man who had read him in India "imagined the British Empire for the first time in literature." But, preferring English feeling and thinking to English fighting and ruling, he was not altogether happy about this "laureate of the larger England." He disliked Kipling's jingoism and his knowingness and swagger, and he preferred the tales to the verse, which "always marched," he said, "with the bands playing and the flags flying." But he knew that Kipling held the first place of the day among English poets, and he had happy relations with him. A few years later, Kipling, who was about to leave Vermont, wrote to him, "It's hard to go from where one has raised one's kids and builded a wall and digged a well and planted a tree," adding, "I don't quite think of quitting the land permanently." Then he wrote, "I am going up to Labrador after salmon about the middle of June. Won't you come up here for a week between now and then, bringing your work with you if that seems good? . . . I'd dearly love to have you under my roof ere we leave for the other side in August."

Howells was perhaps as much pleased that Henry George liked his work when they lived near each other in New York, for he greatly admired the short, stout little man who, with his *Progress and Poverty,* had roused the world. It appeared that Henry George's family were fond of several novels of his and George himself was reading *A Hazard of New Fortunes* aloud to his invalid daughter. For the rest, there were certain disadvantages in living in New York that would have pleased a vainer man. One day, passing a butcher's window, he saw an opossum hanging there and stopped to ask who would buy it. The butcher's reply was, "Coloured people." A young woman also stopped to listen and the next day the *Herald* had a long paragraph about it, saying, "Mr. Howells is fond of opossum." If he had not been, he said, unconscious of himself, "I should feel watched," he added, "at every turn."

At David Hughes's Sunday morning meetings in *The World of Chance,* Henry George was often talked about, and Howells himself was as much oppressed by the poverty that led him to say, "Life is mainly sad everywhere." He enjoyed the continuous performance of the streets and the new Fifth Avenue which had risen in marble and limestone from the brownstone and brick he remembered from the old Lincolnian days; and he loved to mount to the upper deck of one of the motor-omnibuses that had replaced the one-horse stages of old. Looking up and down the long vista of blue air, he surveyed the shining black roofs of the cabs, moving like processions of huge turtles up and down the street, and, with a devouring interest in people that was like Walt Whitman's, he studied the multitudinous passers-by. He noted the silly and sordid faces of many women shoppers, expressing emotions roused by the chase of a ribbon or the hope of getting something for less than its worth; and he always liked the cheeriness of the chestnut and peanut ovens, the pleasant smell and smoke at the corners of the streets. But, in the great good-natured town, he was most aware perhaps of "the homelessness," in his phrase, "that prowls the night," and he said, "It is one of my heresies that comfort should be constantly reminded of misery by the sight of it—comfort is so forgetful." On shipboard he always had in mind the men in the furnace-pits creeping out on deck like "bleached phantasms of toil" and the gaunt faces of the steerage passengers who filled him with vaguely reproachful thoughts for all the immediate luxury of his own existence. He thought how once the world had not seemed to have even death in it, and then how, as he had grown older, suffering lurked everywhere and death had come into his world more and more.

Some of Howells's most moving sketches were of East Side rambles and winter walks that led him into the scenes of younger writers, *The Midnight Platoon,* for one, which might have been written by Stephen Crane, a study of the motionless ghosts one saw in the bread-line. Near the East River he met a little girl lugging a pail overflowing with small pieces of coke, and he watched an old woman, hopping about in the wind-swept street, picking up lumps of coal jolted from a wagon. He found another old woman sleeping on a curbstone, "a small dull wad of outworn womanhood," with her withered arms wound in her thin shawl, and he tried to imagine her short and simple annals, the whole round of a woman's life with want through all. Something said to him, in the presence of want, "Give to him that asketh," and he had to give, or else go away with a bad conscience, a thing he hated; and as soon as he had obeyed that voice he heard another reproaching him because he had encouraged beggary in the street. But of two bad consciences, he always chose the least, the one that incensed political economy gave him, for it always made him feel much better; and that was "really my motive for doing it," he said.

XVIII

WHISTLER'S GARDEN

HOWELLS'S SON, John Mead Howells, planned to be an architect. He was a student at the Beaux-Arts in Paris, and Howells ran over in 1894 to visit "the wonderful place, the only real capital of the world," as he called it. He had been married in Paris in 1862, but he had scarcely ever been there since,[1] and the city was virtually all new to him when, calling upon Whistler in the Rue du Bac, he met Henry James's friend Jonathan Sturges. He struck the young man as very sad when, as if brooding, he laid his hand on Sturges's shoulder, saying, "Live all you can. It's a mistake not to. I'm old; it's too late. But you have time; you are young. Live!"

It was the kind of remark that many aging men make, thinking of all they have missed in the lives they have lived, and of all the sorts of lives they might have lived if they had once taken another turning. Henry James made similar remarks, as when he said to Amy Lowell that his whole life had been built on an error; "Don't make my mistake! I have cut myself off from America, where I belonged,"—a remark he repeated to Hamlin Garland still more bitterly, implying that because of this he had been a failure. Howells's own

[1] There were few references to France in Howells's writings. But he said it was "the only country of Europe where such a case as that of Dreyfus would have been reopened, where there was a public imagination generous enough to conceive of undoing an act of immense public cruelty."

remark was no doubt genuine at the time, but was it not more or less casual and of the moment? It could scarcely have been taken to mean that Howells, as certain critics were to say, sat for the portrait of Lambert Strether.

Lambert Strether was the hero of James's *The Ambassadors,* a character far removed in all respects from James's ancient friend, the novelist Howells, and James explained in writing to Howells that the remark which inspired the story had "got away from you, or from anything like you, and become impersonal and independent." It was only the words he had spoken that became the germ of *The Ambassadors,* although it was true that Howells, depressed at the moment and somewhat disillusioned with his own country, might well have wondered if he could have been happier in Europe. Tens of thousands of Americans have wondered about that.[2] A few years later when Mark Twain went to Florence, intending to stay,—for he could not "stand," as Howells said, "the nervous storm and stress here,"—he himself more or less planned to go abroad for the winters too, spending his summers at Kittery Point in Maine; and now, recalled to America by his father's fatal illness, he wrote to his son in Paris, "Perhaps it was as well I was called home. The poison of Europe was getting into my soul. You must look out for that. They live much more fully than we do. Life here is still for the future—it is a land of Emersons—and I like a little present moment in mine. When I think of the Whistler garden!"[3]—stretching behind the house

---

[2] The New York novelist Edgar Fawcett had written to Howells before he left America to live in England, "How piteous is the situation here! How forlorn is the outlook!"

[3] Referring to Whistler's *Gentle Art of Making Enemies,* Howells spoke of those "dazzling fireworks which scale the heavens as stars, and come down javelins on the heads and breasts of his enemies." But he said, "To make enemies is perfectly easy: the difficult thing is to keep them. The first you know they are no longer hating you; they are not even thinking of you."

on the Rue du Bac. He added, "But Saratoga amuses some-what. Here is an image of leisure, if not leisure . . . There are no such intensely American types anywhere, not even in Paris . . . I suppose something will come of it all."

Howells, who had suggested to James the idea of an "in-ternational ghost,"—apparently the one he used in *The Sense of the Past,*—would perhaps have become an international ghost himself if, like so many Americans, he had remained in Europe. What could he have had there in place of the im-mensely effective life he had lived, "tugging away at the old root," in spite of what he wrote to James, from Magnolia, that same year, expressing the disenchantment of the mo-ment, "I don't know what I shall write next, for my love of American life seems to be failing me. For the first time, I got the notion of something denser on the other side. Here every-thing seemed so thin, so thin, when I got back; and, after Paris, what a horror that loathesome New York was!" That was the year when he was writing *A Traveler from Altruria,* in which in a way he rejected American civilization root and branch.

Returning again from Europe three years later, Howells wrote, "We are not yet fully repatriated, in our tastes and feelings. It is so ugly it *hurts,* whichever way I turn." William James, coming back at about the same time, spoke of "the ter-rible grimness and ugliness" he found here, and no doubt Howells would have understood James's way of meeting this: "One must pitch one's whole sensibility first in a different key —then gradually the quantum of personal happiness of which one is susceptible fills the cup." Howells, with his happy dis-position, would surely have known what this meant, but he could never take again an uncritical view of the United States, if in fact he had ever done so; and this was not because of "the impression of the general worsening of things, familiar after middle age to everyone's experience, from the beginning of recorded time." He had written to Henry James in 1888, "I'm not in a very good mood with America myself. It seems to me the most grotesquely illogical thing under the sun; and I suppose I love it less because it won't let me love it more." After the Spanish-American war he could almost have said, with Clarence King, "If being diametrically opposed to the United States is to be Chinese, I am one." What he really said was, "We are as insubordinate as Frenchmen, as vengeful as southern Italians, as treacherous as Sioux, as cruel as Spaniards," and "Our war for humanity has unmasked itself as a war for coaling stations. We are going to keep our booty to punish Spain for putting us to the trouble of using violence in robbing her." Then to his sister he wrote, "After the war will come the piling up of big fortunes again; the craze for wealth will fill all brains, and every good cause will be set back. We shall have an era of blood-bought prosperity, and the chains of capitalism will be welded on the nation more firmly than ever."

Henceforth, at any moment, one might find him speaking of "the inalienably American (I begin to hate this word) quality," discovering errors in "the sort of self-love which calls itself patriotism,"—"seeing America first," for one example. "America is largely a copy of Europe, in things social and civic"; and was not this notion of seeing its cities first like a certain American notion of coming to the great masterpieces of art with a mind prepared by viewing all the copies of them?[4] Howells who, from this time forward, went more and more

[4] "I don't think you'll find a single society rite with us now that had its origin in our peculiar national life. The afternoon tea is English again, with its troops of eager females and stray reluctant males."—Howells, *Through the Eye of the Needle.*

It was Howells's belief that indigenous American "rites" were adapted only to the simpler life of small towns and the country.

abroad, also went on exploratory trips in various parts of the West and South, but he never went West as far as the Rockies, and he never saw the Pacific coast, which even Henry James visited a few years later. He had none of the tourist's piety in Europe or America, and he seemed more and more conscious of the faults of his own country, the cant about individualism,[5] the American "passion for size . . . which above all else marks us the youngest of the peoples." All the arts, he said, are "thankless in a purely commercial civilization like ours."[6] Far from being Altruria, the country was Egoria, Howells remarked in the "Easy Chair," and the Americans "muttering and mumbling over their meat" on shipboard and "trying to be correct and exemplary" also annoyed him. He would almost rather have had the old-style bragging Americans whom one no longer saw in Europe, and of Basil March he said, "He hated to own it, but he had to own that whenever he met the two branches of the Anglo-Saxon race together in Europe, the elder had shone, by a superior chirpiness, to the disadvantage of the younger." Besides, there was the "aching void of our manners . . . That is truly the bottomless pit with us."

Elsewhere Howells said, "It must be owned that in point of manners we are perhaps the least successful people on earth"; and, never a lover of the American accent, he also said, "If I must choose, I should prefer the British gobble to the American snuffle." He spoke of the "flat wooden tones" of American

[5] "If you want to see American individuality, the real, simon-pure article, you ought to go down to one of our big factory towns, and look at the mill-hands, coming home in droves after a day's work, young girls and old women, boys and men, all fluffed over with cotton, and so dead-tired that they can hardly walk. They come shambling along with all the individuality of a flock of sheep."—The young farmer in Howells's *A Traveler from Altruria*.

[6] "The new public estimates the artist's time at the same pecuniary value as the sitting hen's, and the artist usually accepts the estimate."—Howells, *The World of Chance*.

voices and the "catbird twang of so many of our women,"—
the women's voices were worse than the men's, he thought,—
and, at Oxford, he remembered "the slovenlier speech of the
Harvard men . . . for even our oldest university has not yet
taken thought of how her children shall distinguish themselves
from our snuffling mass by the beauty of utterance which
above any other beauty discriminates between us and the
English."[7] He did not seem to like it when one of his characters "spoke with the burr which the Scotch-Irish settlers have
imparted to the whole Middle West," while he said that "the
great American r is destined not to disappear but to overflow
the whole country . . . and return upon the East." Not that
he liked this either: it was one of the provincialisms that
Breckon could not ignore in his Ellen Kenton, her pronuncia-
tion of "the letter r with a hard mid-Western twist" that went
with her "weak, thin" voice and her "momma" and "poppa."
Howells rectified as well as he could these ugly singularities
by causing other characters to reprehend them, Lottie, for instance, Ellen's sister, who would not say "momma" and
"poppa" any more, for "Everybody that knows anything says
father and mother now." Just so, when Cornelia, in *The Coast
of Bohemia,* says, "I don't know as I think," Ludlow "wished
she had said she didn't know *that* instead of *as.*" There were
occasions when Howells himself fell into the abuse of dialect
that had destroyed the fame of Miss Murfree's writings, those

[7] "I suppose one may own to strictly American readers that our speech is
dreadful, that it is very ugly. . . . Who, indeed, can defend the American
accent, which is not so much an accent as a whiffle, a snuffle, a twang?"—
Howells, *Familiar Spanish Travels.*

In an article in *Harper's Bazaar* on "our daily speech," Howells wrote,
"What is it gives the cultivated sojourner, or the transitory stranger among
us the impression that our women are of slovenly and uncouth utterance,
and that the exceptions are so few as not to affect the general impression?"
It will perhaps come to pass, he added, that teachers in our public schools
will have the right to send home a child who speaks through its nose.

fine tales of the Tennessee mountaineers; in one or two cases, Clementina, in *Ragged Lady,* for instance, this lapse of literary tact destroyed for the reader the young girl's credibility as well as her charm. But these occasions in Howells were certainly rare.

Howells, so often benevolent, was sometimes candidly severe or sharp in dealing with other writers directly or in print, in his review, for example, of Max Nordau's *Degeneration,* a case of "the Philistine spirit, besotted with error." Max Nordau had attacked a few really sublime men; he professed to regard as madmen the leaders of their age; and Howells said that he was dishonest and ill-mannered. As an example of degeneration, he added, Max Nordau should have been collected by Lombroso. Then, bored by an author who was fishing for a compliment and who said to him, "I don't seem to *write* as well as I used to do," Howells replied, "Oh, yes, you do. You write as well as you ever did. But your *taste* is improving." To John Jay Chapman, who told the story, this seemed "as good as Voltaire." On the other hand, Howells, as a critic of his country, in *Their Silver Wedding Journey,* made fun of "that arrogant old ass," General Triscoe, who was always complaining of America, its corruption and its crudity and "the futility of our hopes as a people." Beside what he called the veteran duplicities of "histrionic" Europe, Howells liked the sincerity and directness he found at home; and he never lost his belief in "the true state" that America was "destined yet to see established."

*

*   *

There was nothing Howells enjoyed less than writing book reviews, a kind of work that never satisfied him,[8] although he

---

[8] "Eugenio [Howells] had done a vast deal of reviewing . . . and in all this reviewing he had not once satisfied himself with his work. Never once

reviewed, first or last, innumerable books and sometimes, with his reviews, created reputations. It was well known how continuously he reviewed Mark Twain and Henry James, and also, at first in *The Atlantic* and later in *Harper's* and elsewhere, scores of other writers from Bret Harte to Veblen. Among them were Parkman, Turgenev and Taine, Ruskin, Motley, Lafcadio Hearn,[9] George Ade and Archibald Lampman, the Canadian poet. Between 1882 and 1920 he wrote thirty-three prefaces, often establishing the vogue of living authors, while in his fine essays on Zola, Tolstoy, Ibsen and various others, he expressed again his philosophy of fiction. Its function was to enable people to understand one another better, and for this reason Howells, as a reformer of American fiction,—hostile to the sentimental[10] and everything false,— insisted on honesty, reality and absolute truth. He himself

---

had he written a criticism which seemed to him adequate, or more than an approximation to justice, even when he had most carefully, almost prayerfully, examined the work he had reported upon. He was aware of writing from this mood or that, of feeling hampered by editorial conditions, of becoming impatient or jaded, and finally employing the hay-scales when he ought to have used the delicate balances with which one weighs out life-giving elixirs or deadly poisons."—Howells, *Imaginary Interviews*.

"I hate criticism. . . . I never did a piece of it that satisfied me; and to write fiction, on the other hand, is a delight."—Letter to Thomas Bailey Aldrich, 1901.

[9] Reviewing Lafcadio Hearn's *Youma,* Howells spoke of this author's "positive talent that vividly distinguishes itself from all others, and joys in its life and strength."

Hearn said of Howells that he was "a clumsy literary controversialist," but "a great novelist" and the "subtlest and noblest literary mind in this country."

[10] Howells found sentimental some of Augustus Saint-Gaudens's sculpture. He disliked the romantic figure of the Victory, studied from a Southern girl, leading Saint-Gaudens's equestrian figure of Sherman, now standing at the entrance of Central Park, New York.

Saint-Gaudens, in his turn, disliked Howells's realism, as one could see in the dream of which he wrote to Howells on January 9th, 1894: "Sunday night . . . I dreamed that I was with you and some vague personages on

HOWELLS AND HIS DAUGHTER MILDRED

Medallion by Augustus Saint-Gaudens, 1894

could not feel quite sure that he had achieved this aim,[11] but it was his ideal of the realistic method, and he said it was the business of criticism to "break the images of false gods . . . and to take away the poor silly toys that many grown people would still like to play with." For two or three decades, Howells had had his way, more or less, and there were many novelists who followed him still; but in the nineties came a reaction with the "Scott and Dumas people," as Howells's old friend Higginson called these romantics, in favour of the "paper-doll pattern" and the "rag-doll hero." So Howells himself characterized this anti-realistic movement that seemed to have taken possession of the house of fiction.

On the steamship "Norumbia," in *Their Silver Wedding Journey*, a novel that Howells published in 1899, nearly everyone on the deck was reading *The Maiden Knight*, a romance that had just appeared, the book of the season. The story depicted "a heroic girl in every trying circumstance of mediæval life," flattering women "by the celebration of her unintermitted triumphs" and "ending in a preposterous and wholly superfluous sacrifice." That was the moment of *When Knight-*

---

a vague canal boat or barge on the quiet ocean at night, gazing at the sky. You stepped forward with a shotgun to the edge of the awning under which we stood and fired at the planet Venus, bright in the zenith at the time. After you shot it fell with a great sweep across the sky and disappeared below the horizon. This settled the matter of the distance of the stars, as I vehemently assured my vague friends; the astronomers were all wrong and the stars instead of being millions of miles away were within gunshot. The next morning I found your card at the studio."

It was at about this time, in 1894, that Saint-Gaudens made the fine bas-relief of Howells and his daughter Mildred.

[11] "The novelist must endeavour to give exactly the effect of life. I believe he will yet come to do this. I can never do it, for I was bred in a false school whose trammels I have never been quite able to burst; but the novelist who begins where I leave off will yet write the novel which has been my ideal."—Howells, *Novel-Writing and Novel-Reading*.

hood Was in Flower, Graustark and other saccharine romances, a fashion largely brought about by Robert Louis Stevenson's vogue and the vogue of Henryk Sienkiewicz. Serious writers like Mary E. Wilkins and Sarah Orne Jewett, who wrote *The Tory Lover,* fell into this current, and Stephen Crane, after writing *Maggie* and *The Red Badge of Courage,* told Howells he feared the current would overwhelm him. In fact, in a way it did so when he wrote *The O'Ruddy.* Howells was never opposed to the historical novel as such. He delighted in *War and Peace,* Stendhal and Manzoni, but they had embodied real motives and feelings and they represented humanity as it is and therefore as it must have been. But duels and battles were now set forth as the great prevalent human events, and pride and revenge were worshipped as right and fine, while nothing was heard in these romances but the din of arms and "the horrid tumult of the swashbuckler swashing on his buckler." The ideals of the Stone Age triumphed in them, and Howells asked if this was a Pegasus of some new breed or only the old familiar wild ass of the desert, always preferring thistles to any more nourishing diet and having, with a bit between its teeth, the time of its life.[12]

Howells wondered if the new wealth and the Spanish-American war had vulgarized and brutalized the mind of the public, and if perhaps people, ashamed of their blood-lust, were more than ever anxious to escape from looking at themselves. Then he fully realized how gullible the majority of

---

[12] In the "Easy Chair" for May, 1903, Howells suggested the establishment of a Museum of Popular Fiction, with literary properties for the use of intending popular novelists. "As clothes are, in that school of fiction, much more important than characters, costume should be very fully shown in every period. . . . Mechanical dolls of every description should be lavishly supplied, heroes in the act of rescuing heroines or making love to them; heroes that could utter vows, and heroines that could shed tears or emit passionate sighs; villains that could swear strange oaths of all patterns," etc.

people were and how childish was their imagination.[13] Meanwhile, romance, in a profounder sense, was also coming in again, the romance that Howells enjoyed in Shakespeare, or in Hawthorne, or in Henry James, the romance that was not "romanticistic." This true romance appealed to him almost as much as realism.[14] He had perceived long before that his friend Henry James, in practice, if not in theory, had abandoned realism,—"His best efforts seem to me those of romance," Howells had written in 1882; and there was the romance that to Frank Norris "far outshone realism" and was more or less to supplant it in the literary mind. "To romance," Frank Norris said, "belongs the wide world for range, and the unplumbed depths of the human heart, and the mystery of sex, and the problems of life, and the black, unsearched penetralia of the soul of man." It was not in Howells's nature to follow Frank Norris there, much as these two writers admired each other; although he was to mention with great respect Herman Melville in 1919 at a time when few remembered Melville's name.

In the meantime he continued stoutly to follow his own method of the "commonplace,"[15] producing in the nineties

---

[13] "If you wish to darken counsel by asking how it is that these inferior romanticists are still incomparably the most popular novelists, I can only whisper, in strict confidence, that by far the greatest number of people in the world, even the civilized world, are people of weak and childish imagination, pleased with gross fables, fond of prodigies, heroes, heroines, portents and impracticabilities, without self-knowledge and without the wish for it." —Howells, *Novel-Writing and Novel-Reading*.

[14] "There are two kinds of fiction that I like almost equally, a real novel and a fine romance."—Howells, in a review of Mark Twain, 1897.

[15] "Commonplace? The commonplace is just that light, impalpable, aerial essence they've never got into their confounded books yet," says Charles Bellingham in *The Rise of Silas Lapham*.

"Ah, poor Real Life, which I love, can I make others share the delight I find in thy foolish and insipid face?"—Howells, *Their Wedding Journey*. So Howells felt at the beginning, and so he felt to the end.

some of his best work; and he published in 1901 *Heroines of Fiction,* an interesting rambling history of the English novel. Although, as he often said, the American novel was an outgrowth of the Continental novel and he had largely contributed to bring this about with his essays on Björnson, Turgenev, Tolstoy and Zola, he knew quite thoroughly "the most beautiful, the most consoling of all the arts" as it had been practised in England and Scotland. He had even read all of Bulwer at that impressionable time of his life when but to name a woman's name was to conjure up a phantom of delight; and, although he had not read Cooper, he had gone through all of Scott when he was waiting for his passport as consul at Venice. Convinced that a novelist's power is to be tested largely by his success in dealing with feminine nature, Howells, with many acute remarks,[16] noted that fictional heroines have constantly grown more interesting as they have grown more modern. For the rest, a voluntary naturalness and an instructed simplicity were, he said, the chief marks of the modern.

Howells had published in 1892 *The Quality of Mercy,* one of his best, an extraordinary novel, and he followed this in 1897 with *The Landlord at Lion's Head,* not quite masterly perhaps but certainly good. This was the story of a summer hotel in the New England hill-country, or rather of the new landlord, Jeff Durgin, who had gone to Harvard, a young man who was not exactly "bad" but was a "bad mixture," as

[16] "Charles Reade perceived that there is something feline in every woman, but he also divined that in many and perhaps in most cases she wishes to use the arts of the cat for no worse purpose than getting a soft place in a man's soul and sweetly purring there."—Howells, *Heroines of Fiction.*

The two volumes of *Heroines of Fiction* were somewhat marred by the silly illustrations,—animated historical fashion plates,—of Howard Chandler Christy.

WHISTLER'S GARDEN 221

Whitwell, the rustic philosopher, expressed it. In this day of buckboards and picnics in the woods, at which Westover, the landscape painter, read Browning to the ladies, while Whitwell conducted them on "Tramps Home to Nature," there were many intrigues among the guests, as well as much talk about planchette, hypnotism, trance mediums and seances. Westover had come to paint the mountain, which looked like a lion asleep, and eventually he married Cynthia, Whitwell's daughter, with whom Jeff had grown up at Lion's Head but whom Jeff had virtually deserted before he went to Europe to learn how to make the hotel the best in the mountains. The real story was of Jeff's relations with three women, Cynthia, Bessie Lynde in Boston, whose world was so different from his mother's world, and the Nostrand girl who had gone back to live in Florence.

But, good as this was, *The Quality of Mercy* was really a masterpiece, a study of the psychology of an absconding defaulter, written at a moment when the discovery and flight of peculating treasurers and cashiers was a commonplace of every morning paper. But the story transcended the period note, for Northwick, escaping to Canada from his great wooden country palace, was typical in his situation and responses. He is convinced that his life is a precious trust and that he is going to retrieve himself for his daughters, securing his creditors also and clearing his name, and he plans to find a gold-mine or start a paper-mill; but he fails to embark on any of these enterprises. Growing a beard as a disguise in this dreadful exile, he is mentally paralysed in the Quebec village, and the priest, who pities him, is obliged to give him up as a creature of a civilization too arid to be borne. For Northwick had collected pictures merely as investments while his great farm and conservatory were only possessions, and his exile moulds him into a thing of memories and vague hopes alone, without any definite intentions. Overcome with homesickness, he returns to his daughters for a night, then, going back to Canada, he encourages Pinney, the newspaper man, to come and take him home handcuffed at the border. He dies of heart failure on the train. But this is only the central theme of a long and complex novel, one of the half dozen best that Howells wrote.

XIX

APROPOS OF IBSEN

"WE READ eagerly what Mr. William James writes,"
Howells himself wrote in 1903, "because it abounds
in the substance of things hoped for, the evidence of things not
seen." He had resented the scientists who snubbed one's hopes
of a future life, and he welcomed thinkers like James and
Royce with their greater tolerance who scarcely left us "at
peace in our doubts."

With his own will to believe, however, Howells continued
to doubt, although his mind dwelt on the borderland between
experience and illusion as he had known them. He noted that
a whole new order of literature, dealing with life on its mystical
side, and calling itself psychological, had recently arisen, with
Ibsen and Hauptmann among the writers, Maeterlinck and
even Henry James. Howells distrusted mysticism; he was all
for "plain day," but he had had what seemed to him preter-
natural experiences that called, like all the others, for expression. He took to studying psychology and medical books
and magazines, reading case-histories, recording his own
dreams; and this led to his writing two volumes of short
stories about the "filmy shapes that haunt the dusk." These
were *Between the Dark and the Daylight* and *Questionable
Shapes,* and he told Dr. Weir Mitchell that they were all
psychic stories out of his own life.

Some years before, when he was writing *The Shadow of a Dream,* he had a long correspondence with Howard Pyle, a Swedenborgian, like Joseph Jefferson, his old friend, the actor, and like his own father and the father of Henry James.[1] Howard Pyle, the illustrator, who was also a writer, looked up to Howells as "the head of our craft," and he had made line-drawings for Howells's *Stops of Various Quills,* expressing his own view of these gnomic poems. They were pictures of broken columns, setting suns, death's-heads, thorns, the bitter chalice. "What a dreadful valley of shadows it must be through which you are passing!" Pyle wrote, referring to the death of Howells's daughter,—Winifred Howells, who had died in 1889,—referring also to *Heaven and Hell,* the great work of Swedenborg that he had found Howells reading when they first met. Howells, never at home in abstract thought, could not realize, he wrote to Pyle, any clear belief in a future existence,—much as he longed for this belief,—but, with Swedenborg still in mind, he wrote about his dreams, visions that were often hideous and fantastic. "When I wake at night," he said to Howard Pyle, "the room seems dense with spirits." For the rest, he had invented, in *The Shadow of a Dream,* the figure of the nerve-specialist Dr. Wingate. Later, Wanhope, the psychologist, appeared in the psychic stories that he published in 1903 and 1907.

Many of the stories were told in the "Turkish Room," so called for its cushions and hangings of Oriental stuffs, a room in a New York club where four or five friends often met, as in Mark Twain's dreamed-of Human Race Lunch Club. Be-

[1] And like Helen Keller who had written, said Howells, in *The Story of My Life,* "the fairy-tale of her emergence from the darkness and silence of her infancy into the full radiance of such a being as all the senses bring to few of us."

sides Wanhope, there was Rulledge, who spent his whole life in the club, there was "myself, the novelist," and Minver, the painter, and they fell into story-telling over their coffee about occult experiences of some of their friends. They told stories of presentiments, thought-transference, psychomancy, hypnotic suggestion, like *The Eidolons of Brooks Alford* for whom everyone he thought about instantly became visibly present. There was *A Case of Metaphantasmia*, a story of dream-transference in which a sleeper with a nightmare in a sleeping-car communicated his dream to all the other sleepers. *Though One Rose from the Dead*, one of the best, was about the Alderlings, a painter in a sea-faring village and his wife, who was Pre-Raphaelite in type, with a somewhat feline calm, "like some rich blond caryatid off duty." They were so closely bound together that each always knew what the other was thinking, and after her death, though he knew she was dead, he heard her calling from a boat in the fog and, rushing out to find her, never came back.

Another story, *His Apparition*, was about a young man of means who thought he saw a ghost in a summer hotel, and, relating the story, caused the hotel to become a haunted house so that the guests could not be induced to return there. He felt obliged to buy the hotel to save the girl from doing so, she who had also told the story and who was still more stricken by the consequences. Of course they were presently married, and in the meantime they agreed in admiring Hauptmann's plays and especially Ibsen. Miss Hernshaw defended Ibsen's *Ghosts* violently,—it was the "greatest experience" of her life; and Hewson pictured her beating down half-hearted witnesses of the play with her fan, her cobwebby handkerchief and her long limp gloves. "It's astonishing," Hewson said himself, "the effect a play of Ibsen's has with the actors. They can't play false. It turns the merest sticks into men and women . . . They have to be, and not just *seem*."

Howells, who had first written of Ibsen in 1889 in his *causerie* in *Harper's Weekly* called "Life and Letters,"—reviewing plays, books and new art exhibitions,—had placed him more than once with Zola and even Tolstoy as an immeasurable accomplished literary fact. It had been supposed by many at first that his work was insignificant because he depicted a provincial civilization, a small Norwegian town with middle-class people, and there were elderly minded souls who thought Ibsen dreadful for showing us that the house we had lived in so long was full of vermin. But Howells remarked that it was well to know the facts, if the chimney smoked and the roof leaked. The dreadful thing was that the facts were so, not that he showed them to be so,—Ibsen, with his "high propriety and beauty." Just so Howells wrote, in *Heroines of Fiction*, about some of George Eliot's scenes: "These are dreadful things, and so squalid that they must shock the refined reader: but who that knows life can deny that they happen? They happen far oftener than is ever known, and if the veil could be lifted from many marriages that show a fair outside, what hideous things should we not see! It is not ill, but it is very well to be confronted with the ugly realities, the surviving savageries, that the sunny hypocrisy of civilization denies; for until we recognize them, we shall not abate them, or even try to do so." It was true that Ibsen was "one of those masters who are more accepted through those whom they have influenced than in themselves," and Howells, moreover, compared him to "a lonely column climbing to the skies from a pedestal almost as narrow as itself." But he also said, "To my experience, Ibsen is a dramatist of such perfection, he is a poet of such absolute simplicity and veracity, that when I read or see him I feel nothing wanting in the aesthetic scheme. I know that there are graces and beauties abounding in other authors which are absent from him, but I do not miss them. I am sensible of being moved, of being made to think and feel as no other has made me think and feel." Elsewhere he spoke of "the Greek severity of the Ibsenian ideal."[2]

Traces of Ibsen presently appeared in two of Howells's novels, by name in one, *The Story of a Play,* and in the other by implication; for would he ever have written *The Son of Royal Langbrith* if it had not been for Ibsen? The plot of this fine psychological novel, surely among Howells's best, might well have made an Ibsen play, for it showed the tragic results of concealing the truth, of letting "lying dogs sleep," in a New England mill-town. The dead Royal Langbrith had been a scoundrel, though the town knew him as a benefactor, and his son James, to whom he was a religion, lorded it over the mother who shielded the father's memory for his sake. She had never dared to tell him the truth, for she was afraid of her son, while he was insanely jealous of her straying affections. James Langbrith, loyal to the father whom he had never known, opposed the marriage of his mother to the doctor who had known Royal Langbrith for the rascal he was, and meanwhile he compelled the town to pay homage to the "sage and saint" at a ceremony unveiling a tablet in his honour. The

---

[2] In still another paper, Howells spoke of Maeterlinck in connection with Ibsen, "I could not attempt to say just what the strange force is in both Ibsen and Maeterlinck, two widely different modes of motion . . . able to turn nebulous effluxes of the footlights into galaxies of stars. I have seen a little mystical, shadowy situation of Maeterlinck, with no more apparent action in it than a phrase-book, lift a group of dramatic students out of an all but marionette limpness, and endue them with authority to hold a goose-fleshed, gasping audience spellbound."—Howells, in *Literature,* June 16, 1899.

doctor died without marrying the mother, just as the bitter old uncle shattered the son's illusions by telling him the truth, while the "town myth" survived in the minds of the people. Since Royal Langbrith's fair fame was the finest jewel in the history of the town, it was generally agreed that there was a moral necessity not to wake lying dogs that had slept so long.

While this was distinctly a Howells novel, it was unquestionably Ibsenish, too, and Ibsen appeared also in *The Story of a Play,* a novel that was vastly better than any of Howells's own plays but was suggested by his adventures with them. The author of a "rather Ibsenish play" who thinks that a "naturalized Ibsenism wouldn't be so bad" for the American stage, finds himself chiefly appreciated by an "Ibsen crank" in a Western town who turns out to be the young writer in *The World of Chance. The Story of a Play* was also distinctly a Howells novel, abounding in "feminine sinuosity and subtlety," especially in the rivalry of the author's wife and the woman with smouldering eyes who took the feminine part in the production. Beyond a certain point "where the eternal womanly began," Maxwell could make nothing of his wife: "She evaded, and came and went, and returned upon her course, and all with as good a conscience, apparently, as if she were meeting him fairly and squarely on the question they started with." Meanwhile, Maxwell had read all the translations of Ibsen and several of Maeterlinck's plays in French; but, aside from his disillusion with the great actor Godolphin, who treats his work very cavalierly, one saw how much he preferred to be a writer of novels.[3]

[3] "The Portland Boat swam by in the offing [at Magnolia], a glitter of irregular lights, and the lamps on the different points of the Cape blinked as they revolved in their towers. 'This is the kind of thing you can get only in a novel,' said Maxwell, musingly. 'You couldn't possibly give the feeling of it in a play.'

Howells was like Maxwell here again, although there was
no doubt of his continuing desire to succeed as a playwright,
or of his interest in other playwrights and actors, or of his
pleasure in all the lively arts. He loved the circus and the
trapeze, and he loved the vaudeville that he still found so good
when compared with the mechanical drama of the legitimate
stage. In fact, he asked, why was this "legitimate," since there
were vaudeville artists before there were playwrights, whether
in India or in Greece or Rome? He liked acrobats and jug-
glers, and he enjoyed the spectacle of a gifted fellow-creature
swinging himself between two chairs with their outer legs
balanced on the tops of carafes full of water. Howells said,
"How I respected that man!"—who made no more of the feat
than if he were taking a walk in Central Park. But the old
ballet pleased him above all,—"How beatific it always was to
have the minor coryphées subside in nebulous ranks on either
side of the stage, and have the great planetary splendour of
the *prima ballerina* come swiftly down the centre to the very
footlights, beaming right and left!" Was there anything in
life now like that radiant moment?

As for actors, Howells remembered well "the massive
thought and honest amiability of Salvini's face" and "the deep
and spiritualized power of Edwin Booth's," while he questioned Sarah Bernhardt's Hamlet. Seeing this, he could not
escape "the fancy that the Prince of Denmark was a girl of
uncertain age, with crises of mannishness in which she did

"He pointed to a depth of the boscage where it had almost an emerald
quality, it was so vivid, so intense. 'If I were writing a story about two
lovers in such a light, and how it bathed their figures and illuminated their
faces, I could make the reader feel it just as I did. I could make him see it.
But if I were putting them in a play, I should have to trust the carpenter
and the scene-designer for the effect; and you know what broken reeds
they are.' "—Howells, *The Story of a Play*.

not seem quite a lady." As for the American playwrights, he thought Clyde Fitch's work was "gay, brilliant, honest and living," although he could not take this author "without a grain or several grains . . . I dislike," he wrote to a friend, "the sort of hardness which I fancy you feel in him . . . But if he can realize that people like to be touched, and nobly moved, as well as amused and dazzled, he will go far." Howells had attacked the dramatic critics for insisting that American plays should conform to the "Sardou-Scribe tradition," the artificial technique of the "well-made" play, and he had supported from the first the actor-playwright James A. Herne and his realistic honesty of method and freshness of motive. Writing in an "Ibsen climate," Herne had undertaken to represent life truthfully on the American stage, and Howells had been almost the only defender of his play *Margaret Fleming*, which all the regular managers seemed afraid to produce. Howells had urged him to give it anywhere, in a stable or a loft, and he had arranged with a few others to have it privately performed in a hall in Boston. Herne was a forerunner of realism on the American stage.

First or last, Howells himself was connected with many plays, aside from the farces that were produced in London[4] as well as in many cities of the East and the West, and aside from *A Counterfeit Presentment* and *Out of the Question*, comedies that he had written earlier in Boston. *A Foregone Conclusion* was dramatized and played in the United States by Alessandro Salvini, the son of Tommaso, and in England

[4] Ellen Terry and Beerbohm Tree played in *The Mouse-Trap* in 1895. Of another farce, *A Dangerous Ruffian* (called *The Garroters* in the United States), also played in London, Bernard Shaw remarked (*Dramatic Opinions*, I, 265), "The little piece showed, as might have been expected, that with three weeks' practice the American novelist could write the heads off the poor bunglers to whom our managers generally appeal when they want a small bit of work to amuse the people who come at eight."

by the Shakespearean actor Benson, and Howells's dramatization of *The Rise of Silas Lapham* was given in the eighteen-nineties by the Actors' Guild. Then Lawrence Barrett produced his adaptation of the Spanish play that was called *Yorick's Love,* "one of the most beautiful tragedies I ever saw," Howells wrote, "with Spanish passion and Northern conscience in it." He also translated *Sansone* by Ippolito d'Aste in a version that the great Salvini used for all the parts but his own, which he played in Italian. Howells, who had followed, as he said, "troops of Italian dramatists of the militant period of 1860–1865," followed the modern dramatists of Italy and Spain, liking the verisimilitude he found in Spanish plays, just as he found it in Spanish novels; and he continued to watch and review the American stage and the English stage of Barrie, Jones, Pinero and Bernard Shaw, "that comic analogue of the tragic Ibsen." Howells had no objection to plays "with a purpose." Of the plays of Eugene Brieux, he wrote, "They have no scruple in luring you to the theatre and then letting you realize you are as in a church, under a machine-gun fire of homilies from a pulpit that calls itself a stage." Of Ibsen again he said, after seeing four or five Ibsen plays, "He is the master who has more to say to our generation in the theatre than any other, and all must learn his language who would be understood hereafter."

What was the upshot for Howells of his own connection with the stage? He loved the drama but not the theatre, like Henry James and Mark Twain and like his own Bruce Maxwell, the journalist turned playwright in *The Story of a Play.*[5]

---

[5] "Whatever related to the theatre was there [in the theatre magazine], in bizarre solidarity. . . . But he [Maxwell] hated to be mixed up with all that, and he perceived that he must be mixed up with it more and more, if he wrote for the theatre. Whether he liked it or not, he was part of the thing which in its entirety meant high kicking and toe practice, as well as

He had written this novel in the nineties after dramatizing *Silas Lapham* for an actor who wanted it and then did not want it. "What a race!" he wrote to Henry James. "Their obligations are chains of flowers." The book related to Maxwell's adventures with Lawrence Godolphin, the actor, and the lovely creature he had seen on the beach who "seemed to turn the sunlight into limelight as she passed." Maxwell and Godolphin thought that together they might be able "to give the American public a real American drama," and then Godolphin wished to include a skirt-dance. After this he rejected the play, accepted it and rejected it until he at last found an actress who could subordinate her part to his. Maxwell had thought of the drama as "the supreme literary form" because "it stands on its own feet. It doesn't have to be pushed along, or pulled along, as the novel does"; but he finds that "It's a compromise all the way through—a cursed spite from beginning to end." As he says, the actor "imagines the thing perfectly, not as you imagined it, but as you wrote it, and then he is no more able to play it as he imagined it than you were to write it as you imagined it. What the public finally gets is something three times removed from the truth that was first in the dramatist's mind."

"It is strange," Howells wrote to Henry James, "how the stage can keep on fooling us. What the burnt child does *not* dread is the fire, or at least the blue fire of the theatre." He added, "I am glad your evil dream of the stage is lost."

---

the expression of the most mystical passions of the heart. There was an austerity in him which the fact offended. . . . It was the drama and never the theatre that he loved."—Howells, *The Story of a Play*.

XX

GERMANY AND SPAIN

HOWELLS had stood out against lecturing tours until, in 1899, Major Pond persuaded him to undertake one, with fifty engagements beginning at Ypsilanti, Michigan, and leading him through Iowa, Nebraska and Kansas. He saw, as he said, "long-bearded typical hayseeds or Reubs" in the further West and wild-looking men on horseback in Kansas with lariats at their Mexican saddle-bows; but, although the tour was an immense success, his head felt sprained by the nervous wear and tear. "I look back on my lecturing with terror. What a hideous trade!" he wrote when it was all over. He had many a heart-quake and many a sleepless night; and, among the kind people of Indianapolis, "a stately and beautifully livable city," he was struck by the intolerance he felt in the air. "We are *freer* in the East, and say what we think," he wrote. "In the West, I should be first mobbed with praise, and then, if I differed, with rotten eggs. People are freer *from West to East*. In the West, they are all terrible water drinkers—they must be topers or temperance, just as they must be saints or sinners. People are *free* only as they are *rude* here."

But he returned to Ohio often, and he wrote from Jefferson, in 1898, to his friend Brander Matthews, "I wish you might see this little place . . . in the Western Reserve . . .

a bit of New England flattened out along the lake shore . . .
The streets are leafy tunnels of maples, where the white
houses lurk unseen in the perspective. The American thing is
in its way unsurpassed and is hardly discovered." There his
brother Joseph still conducted a rural weekly paper, and Howells had some of his later books electrotyped there before the
plates were sent to New York, to Harper's. With Joseph, in
1902, Howells went for a voyage on the Ohio, like the voyages they had made as boys with their pilot uncles, a thousand
miles on the Tiber-coloured stream from Pittsburgh to Cincinnati, and all the way back. Once later he floated "down
the river on the O-Hi-o," in fulfilment of a long-cherished
dream, and he brought back some old Ohio stories to be used
in one or another of his books. Nothing seemed to have
changed on the stern-wheel steamboat, with the river-folk
from the farms and villages getting on and off and the backwoods surviving into the day of trusts. The tranquil and unhurried life brought back the scenes of his childhood, and he
saw through a veil of coal-smoke the ugly little house in the
little ugly town where he was born. To Norton he wrote,
"The steamboat let me visit a vanished epoch in the life of
the shores where the type of American, for good and for bad,
of fifty years ago, still prevails. . . . I should like to write
a book about it."

Still later he went on a voyage of discovery as far as Du-
luth on the Great Lakes, a continental experience that was
almost on the scale of the voyages that were taking him to
Europe. He might almost have said, with Tennyson's Ulys-
ses, "I cannot rest from travel," and a large part of two of his
novels, *The Kentons* and *Their Silver Wedding Journey*,
dealt in great detail with life on ocean liners. Moreover, he
must have met on shipboard many of the characters in his

essays and stories,—for one, *The Amigo*, the little boy from
Ecuador who was on the way to Paris to join his father. Another was *The Mother-Bird*, whose children were in Dresden
and who, on the ship, fell in with two birds of prey. Then
there was *The Daughter of the Storage*, an excellent story
about a romance in a New York storage-warehouse. For a
generation the Breens and the Forsyths had been going abroad
continually, taking things out and putting them into storage,
and the little girl and the little boy who had played together
in the corridors played to some purpose there when they grew
up. They too had been in and out of storage twenty times,
like countless other Americans in this age of travel, and
Howells's fine essay *Storage* reflected the views of one who
was continually moving. The warehouse contained "the dead
bones of homes, or their ghosts, or their yet living bodies
held in hypnotic trances, destined again in some future time
to animate some house or flat anew"; and the upshot for
Howells was that one should not hoard the mummified image
of the past. Too much household gear! He was rather of the
opinion of John La Farge, who praised the simplicity of
Japanese houses.

"I do not think I can ever write of marriage and mating
again," Howells remarked more than once; but he kept returning to "this stale old love-business,"—never stale as he
wrote of it,—Basil March's phrase in *Their Silver Wedding
Journey*. There Agatha Triscoe pursued Burnaby from the
first moment she set eyes on him, with the settled belief that
she was running away from him, and he imagined that he
had been boldly pursuing her without the least encouragement from her.[1] But this man-and-superman story was only

---

[1] "He never could have imagined how many advances a woman can make
with a man in such an affair and the man never find it out."—Howells, *The
Story of a Play*.

a thread that ran through the book. Howells had returned
to his earlier method of mingling fiction and travel-writing,
taking up the couple who had figured in *Their Wedding
Journey,* "with the changed point of view and the evening
light on everything." The Marches were the Howellses a
generation later as they had felt in 1897, when they had gone
to Carlsbad to be "kneaded and prodded" in the cure there
and when they had travelled through various German cities.
Basil March was on vacation as editor of *Every Other Week,*
the well-known magazine of *A Hazard of New Fortunes;* and
Mrs. March, always a match-maker, constantly forwarded
love-affairs, especially the affair of Burnaby and Miss Triscoe.
Wherever they went they continually met the shipmates they
had crossed with,—as American travellers did in that easy
going epoch when "people never lost sight of each other in
Europe"; and one followed the vicissitudes of these others
also in Carlsbad, Nuremberg, Weimar, Ansbach, Würzburg.
There was the pivotal girl, for one, tilting and turning from
her waist up and slanting her face from this side to that as if
to make sure that everyone saw her smiling, and there was
Mr. Stoller, the buggy-maker, who was shocked to find he
was preaching socialism. There was Kenby who had crossed
twenty times and could not get over the fact that our continent was of no interest, apparently, to Europe, that "they
don't want to know anything about us," and there were the
two elderly ladies from central Massachusetts who were "obviously of a book-club culture that had left no leaf unturned."
Nor should one forget "those autumnal men who were going
seriously and anxiously home, with faces fiercely set for the
coming grapple, or necks meekly bowed for the yoke." March
reserved his irony for his wife's preoccupation with "high-
hotes" of all nationalities,—their word for the *hoheits* (the

Grafs and Gräfins, the Excellenzes and the mere well-borns) that they found more descriptive and therefore adopted. It comforted March's republican pride in the mockery it seemed to pour on the feudal structure of society among the Germans.

But, with its fictional elements, *Their Silver Wedding Journey* was in fact so much a book of travel that *Hither and Thither in Germany,* a book of travel only, was cut from its voluminous pages later. One found there the beds "equipped for nightmare," the immutably preposterous beds of Mark Twain's satire, together with notes on the wonderful German syntax that might almost have been Mark Twain's also. One lost oneself in the labyrinths of this and made one's way perilously out past adjectives and articles blindly seeking their nouns and verbs dancing like swamp-fires in the distance. Then there was the swelling and strutting of the modern German *denkmals,* more boastful than anything else in perennial bronze, though in painting the great soul of Lucas Cranach had sincerity enough to atone for all this noisy sculpture. Howells remembered the streets of New York, "not foul but merely mean," in the dignity and quiet civility of the German cities,[2] and although he did not go in for "the madness of sightseeing, which spoils travel," he somehow felt guilty for his omissions. "It was as if they really had been duties to art and history which must be discharged, like obligations to one's Maker and one's neighbour." But, in the

[2] In Hamburg, the conductor "let them get fairly seated before he started the car, and so lost the fun of seeing them lurch and stagger violently and wildly clutch each other for support. The Germans have so little sense of humour that probably no one in the car would have been amused to see the strangers flung upon the floor. No one apparently found it droll that the conductor should touch his cap to them when he asked for their fare; no one smiled at their efforts to make him understand where they wished to go, and he did not wink at the other passengers in trying to find out."— Howells, *Hither and Thither in Germany.*

way of architecture, he missed little even in Carlsbad ("one of the great marriage marts . . . where mothers brought their daughters . . . and the flower of life was blooming for the hand of love"). In Nuremberg he more or less indulged the passion for the Gothic that he had once imbibed from Ruskin, —in the days of his early Italian travel,—Nuremberg where the roofs of red-brown tiles, drowsily blinking from their low dormers, pressed upon one another in endless succession. But Ruskin's horror of the baroque he had long outlived, albeit, remembering his youth, with a sense of recreancy in his abounding admiration for it. In Ansbach, the little obsolete capital, he rested his sensibilities, bruised and fretted by Gothic fronts and angles, in the neo-classic façades of the streets and houses that recalled Lucca and Mantua in their yellowish cast; and there and in Würzburg he delighted in the perfection of the baroque, architecturally in the cathedral as well as in the sculpture. No one could deny its prodigiously effective keeping.

A few years later, in 1908, Howells returned to Italy for a literary purpose, as ever in his travels. While he was revising *Venetian Life* for a new edition, the old wine, as he wrote, got into his brain and he began to dream again of the subject of *Roman Holidays and Others,* the book that resulted from the journey. Soon he was writing to Norton, "I wished you could have been with me in the Borghese Gardens to creep with me round among the busts of the poets and find our mutual acquaintances. Dante would have said to you, 'Oh, yes,' as Niccolini and Giusti said to me in friendly recognition: they appeared to like having been written about." For among these nineteenth-century poets he had fancied a growing consciousness at this encounter with an old admirer: they, at least, seemed to remember his book. Then Howells, who

had met Guglielmo Ferrero and read his Roman history, finding the point of view very modern, asked Norton if he would
arrange to have Ferrero, who was going to Boston, give the
Lowell lectures when he arrived there. Ferrero, he said, had
seen ancient Rome as "an efflorescence of commercialism
much like our own." For himself, he made an effort to be
honest with antiquity, although not in the manner of the
author of *The Innocents Abroad*. Björnstjerne Björnson, in
Rome at the moment, exclaimed, with both hands out-
stretched, "My dear, dear Howells," when they met in the
street, for the first time since 1881 in Cambridge; and they
saw a great deal of each other there. Howells was received by
the King in private audience. He remembered standing in the
Piazza di Spagna hearing Severn talk of Keats when he had
first visited Rome in 1864, and, finding his old rooms near
the Pantheon, he seemed to see his own young face peering
out of one of the windows as he looked up. Howells thought
of the dull, sad fate of the American exiles who were still
living in Rome, "for somehow," he reflected, "we seem born
in a certain country in order to die in it." The amiable, un-
envious interest of the Italians in the pleasure of others had
struck him when he was there before, and he felt again that
they had only to make a real effort in any direction to go
ahead of everybody else.

In Leghorn, Howells visited the neglected grave of Tobias
Smollett, who had once tried in vain for a consulate there,—
that "meek hope of literary ambition," as he called it; and it
was partly to see another living novelist that he went, in 1911,
to Spain. In London, he had taken lessons in Spanish to
prepare for this journey at seventy-four,—or, at least, to brush
up his knowledge of it,—hiring a young man from Barcelona
to talk Spanish with him for an hour each day; but, finally

meeting Palacio Valdès, his old correspondent, he left the Spanish to Palacio and spoke Italian. At the time of the Spanish-American war he had written, "We Americans are apt to think, because we have banged the Spanish war-ships to pieces, that we are superior to the Spaniards; but here, in the field where there is always peace, they shine our masters. Have we any novelists to compare with theirs at their best? . . . Our money would have been far better spent if we had acquired three Spanish novelists,—Perez Galdós, Palacio Valdès and Emilia Pardo-Bazan, instead of Cuba, Porto Rico and the Philippines." He had read all these novelists, and Juan Valera, too, the author of the fresh *Pepita Ximenez,* and he had introduced with a preface the *Doña Perfecta* of Perez Galdós; but for many years he had been reading Palacio Valdès with the "joy that truthful work always gives." Again and again he had reviewed Palacio Valdès's novels, so graphically faithful in their pictures of life in Spain, and the two novelists had long corresponded, Howells always writing in Italian. They had agreed on aesthetic questions, and a number of years before Palacio Valdès had written to Howells, "I believe that a mysterious current of sympathy joins our hearts and minds across the ocean. The same things impress and disgust us. I believe that we must think alike on many other subjects besides art." They were of one mind, as Palacio Valdès said, that "no literature can live long without joy," because no civilization can live long without it. Palacio Valdès asked Howells to write an introduction to a volume of selections of his work in Spanish, to be prefaced with a brief biography of Howells, and in fact the whole Howells family had long been devoted to Palacio Valdès. Howells's architect son had called upon him in Spain.

While Howells did not go to Spain merely to see this ad-

mired old friend,—he had always longed to visit the land of
Cervantes,—he was eager to meet a writer for whom he cared
so much and whom he saw often in Madrid. He found Palacio Valdès up five flights of stairs, in a shawl,—at the moment
he had a cold,—a blue-eyed, white-haired Asturian, dignified
and sweet, who might almost have come from Brattleboro.
For he struck Howells as a species of Spanish New Englander. There were many visits back and forth between the
two novelists. They went together for long walks and drives,
and Palacio Valdès showed Howells the scenes of his novels
in Madrid, the best way for one to see the city. Howells, for
the rest, had also read many modern Spanish plays, and he
asked a bookseller in Madrid to procure for him whatever
plays he could find that were still more modern. With all
their love of realism, he had a great liking for the verisimilitude of the Spanish writers, and he had shared this taste with
the Cuban writer, José Marti, who had come to see him in
New York. The great Marti, who was later killed in the cause
of Cuban independence, was editing a Spanish newspaper at
the time, and Howells had been drawn to the young man's intellectual spirit and grace as they talked about the Spanish
novelists and playwrights.

But Howells's main reason for travelling in Spain was to
visit the scenes of *Don Quixote* there,—he had brought the
book with him as a sort of guide,—and, having read it at ten
or twelve, he was to publish before he died his own edition
of it with an introduction. The name of Cervantes had en-
deared for him the Spanish name and nature, so that they
had always been his romance, and he had never met a Span-
iard without clothing him in some of the honour he had
lavished on Cervantes. A passion for all things Spanish had
ruled him as a boy, and he felt he had arrived after sixty

years' delay and after so many long visits to other parts of
Europe. Now, in his mid-seventies, in the magical air, he had,
in Madrid and Granada, in Burgos, "the grim old capital of
the Northern uplands," and in Cadiz and Seville and Malaga
with their musically syllabled names, all the fresh feelings
of his first youth. It was as if his sensibility had been kept in
full repair for this "wild, beautiful, ugly, monstrous land," as
he called Spain in a letter to Henry James, feeling that the
Spaniards were "a great race, with a church on its back,
holding it down." He took his curiosity into his own keeping,
—for the book he called *Familiar Spanish Travels*,—and he
looked at nothing that did not interest him. What interested
him most was the life of the streets,—a drama in Madrid, more
tragic and less comic than the life in Italian streets,—the lean,
dark men, the women, white-stuccoed, plaster-pale, the Oriental calm, the national repose of manner. The quiet of the
Spanish face was beautiful to see,—its self-respectful self-
possession,—in a Europe abounding in volcanic Italians, nervous Germans and exasperated Frenchmen.

Howells remembered in Seville the long, sad calls of the
street-hucksters, and he was convinced that those whom we
brutally call tramps were known by quite another name in
Spain. They were doubtless called indigent brethren overtaken
in their wayfaring without a lodging for the night. He delighted in the wine-skins, distended with wine and piled on
vintners' wagons, such as Don Quixote had seen as fell en-
chanters, and although, as he said, "no literary art has ever
reported to me a sense of picture or architecture or sculpture,"
he wrote about all of them in Spain. He remembered how
John Hay, just back from Madrid, had blown into his Cambridge house and said the best Titians in the world were in
the Prado, and Howells, just back from Venice himself, had

questioned this at the time. He could not believe that anything was finer than Titian's "Assumption" in Venice, and despite the "Paradise" he was a partisan of Titian over Ruskin's Tintoretto. Going to the Prado to see if John Hay was right, he was astounded by the pictures of Velasquez, supreme in virtue of that reality which all Spanish art seemed to have striven for and which he found also in Goya. He "wanted Goya, more and more Goya"; and, going to the house of El Greco in Toledo, he found a special charm in the colouring of this painter and his long features. In Valladolid he liked the life-sized wooden sculptures that were painted in the colours of flesh and costume, like the sculptures of John Gibson he had praised in Rome; and the baroque in Burgos, in a convent chapel, pleased him as much as the German baroque in Würzburg and Ansbach. It seemed to him not decadent but sombrely authentic, ripe from a root and not a graft. He wondered how Spaniards, so civil and gentle, had built up such a name for cruelty and perfidy, and he could only say that Americans, by repute good and just, rather often, on mere suspicion, burned Negroes alive.

XXI

ENGLAND AGAIN AND AGAIN

"I WOKE today thinking of the folly of nationalities, and the stupid hypocrisy of patriotism," Howells wrote in 1905 to Charles Eliot Norton.[1] "By night I shall doubtless have changed my mind; but now I ask why James or I, even, should not live forever out of America without self-reproach. The worst is perhaps that he will grow lonelier with age. But we grow lonely with age anywhere!" Howells also said that his wife had just had a letter from Henry James, "who bears a tenderer heart than I should have supposed towards his native exile."

During the previous year James had returned to the United States, where he collected impressions for *The American Scene,*[2] and Howells himself had gone to England to receive at Oxford an honorary degree. He had begun to experience again "the old delight of foreign travel" that was taking him to Europe year after year, and especially to England for three or four visits between 1904 and 1913. "English travel

[1] "Probably nations will go on making themselves cruel and tiresome till humanity at last prevails over nationality."—Howells, *Hither and Thither in Germany*.

[2] Howells had written to James, "I can understand your hunger for New England, in these later years. I feel it myself in New York, even, though it is not my country. It has a strange feminine fascination. It is like a girl, sometimes a young girl, and sometimes an old girl, but wild and shy and womanly sweet, always with a sort of Unitarian optimism in the air."

is pure joy," he wrote,—"there is no travel like it"; and he had outlived the resentment he had felt so keenly in the embittered Civil War time. He was less aware now of the England "that never makes a friend whom injustice and insult can alienate" than of the other England "that never forgets a friend once accepted"; and he had many of these friends there now, like the professor at Edinburgh who wrote, "My fondness for your books is almost a joke in my family. I have read most of them four or five times and am continually looking forward to having forgotten one so that I may renew its acquaintance." James himself, who had returned, he saw "never too often." To his wife, who had remained at home, he wrote that James had grown "very stout, and all over, filled out from head to foot, in a sort of chamfered squareness . . . He must have had terrible Americans to handle here, but I don't think he suffers as keenly as he used. He seems to have grown more and more inward, and to retire to his own interior to ruminate the morsels of his fellow-men which he captures in his consciousness of things outside." Later Howells wrote, "He is older and sadder and sweeter, and we communed of many things, of the past, with one dear long walk through the Park well into Kensington." Howells had continued to review James, book by book, just as he had reviewed Mark Twain, feeling as he had felt thirty years before that "in richness of experience and splendour of performance we may compare him with the greatest and find none greater than he."[3]

[3] Henry James, in his turn, praised Howells continually: "Your literary prowess takes my breath away—you write so much and so well. I seem to myself a small brown snail crawling after a glossy antelope."—Letter of 1888.

"Your nomadic ways give me an overwhelming impression of large, free power and make me feel like a corpulent fireside cat, tied by a pink ribbon to the everlastingly same fender."—Letter of 1891.

"You remain the sole and single novelist of English speech, now produc-

In 1904, Howells had been out-at-nerves with too much work, and he had gone with his daughter Mildred, for the cure, to Bath. Feeling for the first time fairly spent, he expected to get a great deal of radiance into his system from the Bath waters; and then he was eager to look up the places that Jane Austen had made memorable either in a scene or a character or by dwelling there herself. He rather hoped to encounter that "elusive phantom of ironical observance" while he sipped the glasses of lukewarm insipidity. The many ghostly witnesses involved in the spectacle of life at Bath recalled for him the soft afterglow of the decline of Boston, and meanwhile he was amused by "the gloom which Americans achieve when they mean to be very good society in public places." London to him was like nature, "so simple and so vast and unhurried," and in letters to his wife he wrote the impressions he developed in *London Films* and *Certain Delightful English Towns.*[4] (Another book, *Seven English*

---

ing, whom I read—read the more, therefore, with concentrated passion."—Letter of 1902.

"I have read *Letters Home* and *Questionable Shapes* with the same rich response with which I have read you always, from the first immemorial day —reading into you and reading out of you, I make bold to declare, more than all your readers put together are capable of doing, vast though their number and inflamed their spirit. Both books quite hum with your own fine note."—Letter of 1903.

"Your supreme expertness and intimate intelligence or 'technical' insight and general possession of the whole art and mystery make your judgments for me—well, the only ones (to be flatly frank) that raise in my aged breast today the slightest breeze."—Letter of 1908.

4 On one of these travel books, Henry James wrote to Howells, "I have lived in England now more than 33 years (am in my 34th), and should still be unable to warble any one of the twenty tunes of which you catch the note in 33 days. You are verily the most delightful, natural, artful singer and sayer" (1909). In fact, regarding England, though they lack James's poetry of metaphor, these books, in complexity of impression and density of style, are comparable with James's *The American Scene,* written at about the same time.

Cities, followed.) Hoping to seek out the springs and sources of the American nation that might be traced in London and elsewhere, he had developed a new taste, the taste for reading history which had been dormant all through his first and second youth. "I go to sleep reading English history," he wrote to Norton. "I wake to it in the night, and resume it in the morning. What an amazing people they have been. If we had not been English ourselves at the time we could never have dared to stand up against them. In all my thinking and writing, I recall what you said of the thinness of the soil we work, and the depth of theirs. The withered leaves of their tremendous past have enriched their present like the layers of fallen leaves in the forest." Now, following the traces of American origins, Howells recalled his old statement that "everything in England is appreciable to the literary sense, while the sense of the literary worth of things in America is still faint and weak with most people." Naturally ordinary English novels were more comfortable to ordinary Americans than American novels. For the American novels dealt with relatively new motives, and it cost an effort to adjust oneself to these that no ordinary person likes to make.[5]

Looking out on the grey sky, with the chimney-pots mezzo-tinted against it, Howells asked himself what he thought about this England that had more or less troubled his mind; and the final chapter of *Seven English Cities,* perceptive as it was, might have been added to Emerson's *English Traits* ("a book about the English," said Howells, "that makes all

[5] "An English novel, full of titles and rank, is apparently essential to the happiness of such people; their weak and childish imagination is at home in its familiar environment . . . whereas a story of our own life, honestly studied and faithfully presented, troubles them with various misgivings. They are not sure that it is literature; they do not feel that it is good society; its characters, so like their own, strike them as commonplace; they say they do not wish to know such people."—Howells, *Criticism and Fiction.*

other comment seem idle and superfluous palaver"). For the rest, St. Paul's seemed to him "a dispersed and interrupted St. Peter's," while the mighty interior of York minster, with its tree-like clustered pillars and measureless windows, suggested breadths of stained foliage in autumnal woodlands. He marvelled over the soft, swift English trains that "come like shadows, so depart." The expresses whirled in and out of the stations with no more noise than humming-birds, soundless within the vast caravansary where the enchanted traveller changed from them into a world of dreams. But of the "tomfoolery of kings," the "superstition of royalty," Howells shared Mark Twain's bitter disapprobation. "They still have kings and queens," he wrote, "in that romantic island, and lords and ladies who have no more relation to its real life than gnomes and fairies, but must be indulged with the shows and games invented for them in days when people believed in them, and not merely make-believed."

Once, in London, Howells visited the Swedenborgian Society where he found his father's two Swedenborgian tracts, and it pleased him to discover that they were well and clearly written, especially the tract on the origin of evil. They were both highly valued and had had large sales. Meanwhile, his old friend Bret Harte, from whom he had not heard for twenty years, had died in London, a mystery, in 1903; and Aldrich wrote to him, "Wasn't he entertaining company?" —albeit most entertaining "by things in him that were least commendable." Then Mark Twain wrote from Florence, "You have written of Harte most felicitously—most generously too, and yet at the same time truly; for he was *all* you have said, and, although he was more and worse, there is no occasion to remember it, and I am often ashamed of myself for doing so." Henry Harland, who had lived in London, also died in

1905, and he and Howells had seen each other every day three years before when Howells had spent the winter in San Remo. Harland's cousin Stedman had scolded Howells for leading the young man astray, "luring him from the flowery ways of romance into paths strewn with the flints and shards of realism . . . There was not the making of a realist in Harland, and it is pleasant to think how after one try he left the flints and shards, and went back among the blossoms." Stedman was right about the founder of *The Yellow Book,* and Howells had long since accepted this verdict; but he could not forget that Harland had once thanked him for understanding what he called "my innermost and dearest hopes." Harland had been planning then to write about the Jews of the East Side, "an immense and fruitful field," he called this world of which "I have only touched the outer edge," and he had wished to show the interaction of this gifted race with the community round about it. He had heard many people say, "We don't want realism. The truth is dull and monotonous. Give us romance," and he resented the "contemptible flings" at Howells's utterance "in which . . . third-rate literary folk are fond of indulging . . . I tell you, Mr. Howells, my heart feels full when I think of your kindness to me"; and, leaving for London in 1889, he had written "to tell you again how very dear you are to us, and how much good in every way your friendship has done us." Howells had passed Harland on to Henry James.

But in San Remo in 1902, Harland, still full of his American gaiety, was already dying of tuberculosis; and he was obliged to go to bed at sunset every day when the cold of the Alps stole down on the little city. He had mingled there with the Anglo-American-Italianate society that appeared in *My Friend Prospero* and *The Cardinal's Snuff-Box;* and Howells himself set in San Remo one of his own "border-line" stories, —perhaps the best,—*A Sleep and a Forgetting.* A young girl, Miss Gerald, had lost her memory witnessing her mother's sudden death, and, under Dr. Lanfear's care, she recovers her memory when her father is attacked by a madman in the street. In the town that climbed the Alpine foothills, the invaders now were the invalids, no longer the corsairs, and Miss Gerald's dark beauty of eyes and hair and her slender figure and flowing walk captivated the doctor among the palms and the roses. Howells, returning to San Remo later, wrote there a good part of *Certain Delightful English Towns.*

Meanwhile, he had kept in close touch with English writers, many of whom he reviewed in magazines at home, novelists especially but playwrights also, and, above all perhaps, Thomas Hardy. He was a "devoted, not to say doting" reader of that "very great and singular artist," the author of the "tremendous" *Jude the Obscure;* he had come to the love of Hardy "with all the ardour of what seems my perennial literary youth." He had written in the nineties to George Du Maurier when *Trilby* was only half printed to tell him how much he liked the gay, sad story that "won the heart, kindled the fancy and bewitched the reason," and he was glad he had not waited, for the last third was so forced that he could have said nothing good of it. In George Meredith's *Beauchamp's Career* he found a "splendid massiveness of effect," though the narrative was "so often apparently wandering and capricious" and the style was "so wilful"; and he praised the "prodigious veracity" of George Moore's novels, as one found it in *Celibates* and *Esther Waters.* George Moore, he said, had "a very great talent . . . worlds better than anything else English, always excepting Mr. Hardy." Then he said of John Oliver Hobbes that her characters were "none the less real for being artificial: everyone knows plenty of real artificial people." Howells delighted in "the blithe and beautiful inventions of Sir William Gilbert"; and there were English writers who were as grateful as American writers for Howells's special praise of them. For Leonard Merrick it was "the turn of the tide" when Howells wrote an introduction to his collected edition, and Mark Rutherford,—William Hale White,—said that a review of his was "the only one which has much moved me." Of the *Autobiography* Howells had written, "You feel you have witnessed the career of a man as you might have witnessed it in the world, and not in a book."

Howells, moreover, was one of the first to recognize J. M. Barrie's quality, his "endearing kindliness," his "charming domesticity"; and he praised one of "the two Arnold Bennetts,"—the Bennett in whose books "things happen," not the Bennett in whose books things "are made to happen." In turn, Bennett wrote that he had "stolen innumerable ideas" from Howells's novels, and he said that Howells had given him some of his first notions of what subtlety could be in literature. "I can well remember," he said, "how my brother and I agreed, after reading *The Mouse Trap* in *Harper's*, that it had set up a new standard of subtlety for us." Howells took seriously, but not too seriously, the plays of Sir Henry Arthur Jones, the best of which did not give him the ultimate literary satisfaction he had got from *Ghosts*, *Hedda Gabler* or Bernard Shaw. Of *Arms and the Man* he had written in 1895 that it was "fresh, keen and bright" and that this play of the gayest temper transcended for him even the extreme cleverness of Oscar Wilde. Since then Shaw's "incomparably paradoxical dramatizations of human nature" and his bold gaiety and frankness had been, he said, "my daily, my nightly joy."

Later, in a letter to one of his sisters, Howells wrote, "I

have got a famous scheme for a Bacon-Shakespeare story, something seriously fantastic; but I have more schemes than years before me." He had visited Stratford in August for the Shakespeare festival, the pageant, the folk-dancing, the masque and a lecture; and at an earlier performance in Cheltenham of *A Midsummer Night's Dream* he had noticed two gentlemen who were sitting in front of him. They had been dressed in ordinary suits, but these had seemed to change into something else with broad flat collars and doublets of velvet and with an effect of luminous transparency about them. The two apparitional figures had reappeared on the train to Stratford, and there was no doubt that they were Shakespeare and Bacon, Shakespeare who had asked Bacon down for the weekend, for he had himself a tenderness for Stratford. Shakespeare kept dropping in at Howells's hotel and taking him for a walk about the town or along the river where they heard the soft clucking of oars in the rowlocks and the wiry whine of a gramophone in the distance. Or past Anne Hathaway's cottage where the rush bed with the mattress on the rope webbing brought back to Howells the movings of his childhood. (He remembered how the cords had to be trodden and tightened by the paternal foot.) They passed various American men "with a savage, suspensive air, as if, having given Europe a fair trial, they were going to see about it when they got home"; and they were passed by American motorists, "suffering a mental and moral dyspepsia from bolting the beautiful scenery untasted." About Shakespeare, Howells did not agree with his friend Mark Twain, although scarcely a dozen facts were known about him. Who knew anything much about Virgil either, although he was a central figure of Rome at the zenith of her glory, with a fierce light beating on the throne of the great Augustus? When it came to the question of authorship, Howells's Bacon was staunchly Shakespearean, and the colloquies all took place within Howells's brain where Shakespeare had been an idol ever since boyhood; but one half believed in his actual presence when the shade became part of the atmosphere, with the words, "I should like to say good-bye in the open air, in the sun."

XXII

AT KITTERY POINT

WITH ALL this going and coming, and moving in New York, Howells had a fixed base on the coast of Maine, at York Harbour now and then but chiefly at Kittery Point, where he bought a house on the shore in 1902. It was over the water from Portsmouth, at the mouth of the Piscataqua, and the harbour was in full sight, with fishing boats at anchor, all softly tilting with the ground-swell. "In Europe everything is permanent," he wrote, while everything is "provisional" here; but this seemed less true at "the Maine stay," Mrs. Howells's name for the place,[1] in the country of Sarah Orne Jewett. The people lived where their forefathers had lived for two hundred and fifty years, and they had the freer and easier manner of men who had known other coasts and were in some sort citizens of the world. Their speech was very unlike the clipped nasals of the hill-country, and their lounging native walk had, as Howells said, the lurch and the sway of the deck in it.

The house was "almost as ugly as the first edition of *Their Wedding Journey*," Howells wrote soon after to the elder Trevelyan, the historian of the American Revolution who

---

[1] Howells suggested naming it "Cold Cholderton," in reference to Mrs. Howells's "lack of general hospitality, she being an invalid," as their daughter said. One of Mrs. Howells's forebears had been the rector of Cholderton in England.

had once lent his copy of the book to Matthew Arnold and had never got it back. Trevelyan said he had "lived a second life for many years past" in Howells's books, most of which he had read several times; and Howells, who was touched by this, rescued the old dies from the printer and had a new cover stamped for a new copy of the book. He sent this "in its pristine ugliness" to Trevelyan. The cottage had a mansard roof, but, ugly as it was, he had a big study made out of an old stable; and there he worked away "like a pretty blonde in the employ of an appreciative broker." The yachts, coasters and coal barges, with their riding lights, made the harbour gay at night.

There, sitting under his ash-trees, or digging in the garden, when he was not working at the round table in the study, he spent in this refuge from New York many a summer "in full sound of a very emotional bellbuoy and a very pessimistic foghorn." There was also "a thing they call a syren, which has the voice of a psychological novelist of the syren sex." Howells did not care for games but he loved gardening, and he planted a nectarine, peaches and grapes as well as Japanese lilies, white stock, marigolds and phlox. One year he planted fifty trees and bushes, the prettiest a Japanese maple shrub that turned, he said, a lovelier colour than any native leaf. He knew all the nurserymen round about, and every seed-store charmed him, though once his melons turned out to be cucumbers and some egg-plants he set out flourished and then suddenly blossomed as petunias. So much for the so-called vegetable kingdom which, as he remarked, "We should prefer to call republic." He liked to wield axe and scythe in the groves and meadows.

During his first summer there, Mark Twain rented a wide, low cottage overlooking the York River, not far away, and he had a room in a fisherman's house with a table where he could write and a bed where he could lie and read. There was also a veranda where the friends could read to one another. "But how sad old men are," Howells wrote to Charles Eliot Norton about his "mainstay for talk," his old friend Clemens. "We meet and strike fire and flicker up, and I come away a heap of cold ashes. And on what evil times we are fallen! Now I understand how the Puritans felt after the Restoration." He was referring to the triumph of plutocracy that followed the Spanish-American war, a war they all agreed in deploring,—especially the conquest of the Philippines,—and that meant to William James, who wrote to Howells from Rome, "simply the death of the old American soul." To Howells this war meant the close of the mission of America to mankind, for the country could hardly again be the sun of the morning towards which the struggling peoples turned their eyes. "Wealth and power can sympathize only with wealth and power, and freedom, so far as it remains ours, will never again 'shriek when Kosciusko' falls." Howells visited the Spanish prisoners of war, hapless conscripts, wretched fishermen and peasants, who were kept behind barbed wire near Portsmouth. But he delighted in "the joyous trolley car that bounded and pirouetted" to York Harbour, the "tamest of the electric tribe, cousin still to the bolts of heaven" that carried him to Mark Twain in forty minutes. He felt the charm of its course past village houses, over the trestles of the shining inlets and through the pine woods with their deep reaches of shade and sun.

For a memorial meeting at Portsmouth in honour of Thomas Bailey Aldrich, Mark Twain came up again a few years later, and he and Howells sat on the stage, along with the governor and his staff, side by side on a short willow sofa.

Howells said to Mark Twain that it looked like an old-time minstrel show,—"if we were blacked and had long sharp-pointed collars," and that Aldrich would have said, if he had been there, "How is you tonight, Brer Bones? How's your symptoms seem to segashuate?" Howells spoke briefly and read a poem, and he came back to his seat looking, Mark Twain said, like a pardoned convict. That was still the day of croquet and hammocks that suggested Aldrich's Marjorie Daw "swaying like a pond lily in the golden afternoon." In that year, 1908, Mark Twain moved into the house that John Mead Howells had built for him at Redding, hoping that Howells himself would also build a house, near his own Stormfield and on his land. He had thought of calling it Autobiography House because it was built from the proceeds of his autobiography. It was an Italianate villa with an avenue of cypress-like cedars, designed perhaps in memory of his life in Florence.

To Kittery Point came other visitors. There Brand Whitlock spent a week, the sober political novelist of *The Thirteenth District*, one of the many younger writers who idolized Howells as the great reformer of American fiction. Whitlock said he came away with feelings "like those with which Moses came down out of Mount Horeb." Howells himself had outlived his earlier propagandist mood, though he still fought "our appetite for gross fable," disliking the "unreal," the "romanticistic," and he had never ceased to follow American fiction closely, always putting in his word for realism. It had been his policy to "bring the whole territory of the United States under cultivation in fiction," and how many novelists he had encouraged since he had urged Mark Twain to write for him *Life on the Mississippi*. Now, besides Henry B. Fuller, Frank Norris and Stephen Crane, important writers with whom he was closely connected, there were many like Brand Whitlock who turned to him in gratitude as E. W. Howe had turned to him years before.[2] Along with *The Story of a Country Town,* he had signalized in reviews Edward Eggleston and Joseph Kirkland's *Zury,* Harold Frederic's *Seth's Brother's Wife,* Hamlin Garland, Robert Herrick, Booth Tarkington and the Georgia "localist," Will N. Harben (who sometimes went in for an "abnormal activity of plot"). He had spoken of Robert Herrick's Chicago and "the sense he conveys of a rich society wholly of women trying to be intellectual and artistic, while their men-kind look on in ironical and stupefied detachment," saying that Herrick's work was "much more broadly based than that of any other American novelist of his generation." This was virtually, as Herrick said, the first authoritative criticism he had ever received. For a full generation, Henry B. Fuller wrote to him, "the dominant influence has been yours."

Nor could Howells have had any doubt about his "European reputation . . . however little I sell in America," when Count Witte seemed greatly excited at the prospect of meeting him at the dinner in Portsmouth celebrating the end of the Russo-Japanese war. Count Witte had not seemed interested at all in Pierpont Morgan, who was also there, but it appeared that, like Stepniak, he had read all of Howells's books. Not long after this, when the "supply" failed to appear, one Sunday morning, in the pulpit at Kittery Point, and when the crowd begged him to speak, Howells raced home and came back with a copy of *A Traveler from Al-*

[2] "I shall always believe that your notice in *The Century* sold 2,500 copies of *The Story.* . . . There are so many contemptible and mean men in the world that it is a real satisfaction to meet one who is not only great but good. . . . I have always admired W. D. Howells and Mark Twain. I will admire them more than ever now that I know what splendid fellows they are."—E. W. Howe to Howells, 1884.

truria. "I gave 'em a good dose of socialism," he wrote to his wife. "Mentally and morally a Russophile," as he also said once, he was to write in the "Easy Chair" a paper describing two Martians who came to lecture about their civilization. This was entirely socialistic, and chairs and benches were broken in protest at the lecture, while the two Martians were presently deported. On the theory that they were Bolshevists, they were sent to Russia. It was obvious that Howells was all on the side of the Martians, and this amusing skit, as lively as anything he wrote, was published in *Harper's* when he was dying at eighty-three. Many years before, in Maine or Boston, he had lunched with Sarah Orne Jewett and Mrs. Jack Gardner who was building Fenway Court and who boasted of having bluffed the workmen out of a threatened strike and beaten them down in the matter of wages. Howells denounced, after she had left, the arrogance of this woman and her hard-hearted grinding of the faces of the poor. They were Italian workmen, and this made it all the worse from the point of view of Howells.

At Kittery Point he had time to read, sometimes in bed "to fight away from the awful thinking that living comes to when it lasts long, or too long";[3] and now and then he counselled younger writers. He wrote to Garland, "You have got some newspaper diction on your pen-point and you must shake it out. Be plain as you please; there is nothing better than homespun, but the clothing-store is no place for your thoughts to dress themselves." Before that he had written to W. H. Bishop, the consul at Palermo and the author of *The House*

---

[3] Just so, in *Their Silver Wedding Journey*, Basil March,—Howells,—on shipboard, spent many hours reading in bed, "safe from the acquaintances which constantly formed themselves only to fall into disintegration, and cling to him afterwards as inorganic particles of salutation, weather-guessing and smoking-room gossip about the ship's run."

of the Merchant Prince, "For heaven's sake, don't be sprightly.
I am now striking all the witty things out of my work; it
bolts the manuscript fearfully, but it is the right thing to
do. There oughtn't to be a quotable passage in a novel, unless it is dialogue." Then, reading Wilbur Cross's life of
Laurence Sterne, he was reminded of Sterne's naturalness of
language,—"he puts the preposition last where it belongs." In
the evenings he read aloud to his wife Thomas Hardy's
novels, and, by an open fire, the life of Richard Edgeworth.
This gave him "a sense of the larger peace in that admirable
eighteenth century, which the philosophic mind could enjoy.
Was it the fact, or is it only a fancy? This time is so rude, so
loud, so fast, and that is like our eternal old Cambridge of
the later 60's. The Edgeworths were distinctly old Cambridge
people. How was it that I never met them at the Miss Ash-
burners'?"

He had found much of Henry James in the town library
at Kittery Point and read him over again also to his wife. "Do
you know *The Reverberator?*" he wrote to a friend. "Really
a masterpiece . . . and of a delicate patriotism lost upon the
brute beast of a public that knows not Joseph." To James
himself he wrote, "We read you with a touching constancy
. . . and adore your art, with violent exceptions . . . Your
things seem to be always and evermore finer and better. I
cannot tell you what a delight I read you with . . . I must
own to you a constantly mounting wonder in myself at your
'way,' and at the fullness, the closeness, the density of your
work." Of James he also wrote, "I like to read his novels when
they are new, and read them over and over again when they
are old . . . I cannot bear to lose the least pulse of the play
of character"; and he spoke of *The Sacred Fount* "of which
I do not hesitate to say that I have mastered the secret, though

for the present I am not going to divulge it."[4] Then Howells enjoyed George Borrow and especially George Crabbe, "a poet who saw so much beauty in simple and common life that he could not help painting it." Crabbe was "a dear delightful poet, altogether neglected in these days, who deserves to be known wherever reality is prized. His tales," Howells continued, "blink nothing of the sordid, the mean, the vicious, the wicked in that life, from which they rarely rise in some rare glimpse of the state of the neighbouring gentry, and yet they abound in beauty that consoles and encourages. They are full of keen analysis, sly wit, kindly humour, and of a satire too conscientious to bear the name; of pathos, of compassion, of reverence, while in unaffected singleness of ideal they are unsurpassed."

Howells wrote to Norton that he had had great difficulty in finding a complete edition of Crabbe; but this poet had shaken into form a vague purpose he had had of writing in verse about the Ohio village where he had spent his later boyhood. "I used to hate it," he said, "so that for many years after my escape from it I trembled to think my dead body might be brought back prisoner and buried there. But I have long since forgiven it and I see it now in a tender retrospect which seems friendly to a treatment in heroic couplets." The poem or poems might have been a more genial *Spoon River Anthology*, for in his later work Howells often anticipated

[4] There was a certain ambivalence in Howells's feeling about Henry James, as there was in James's feeling about Howells. Bliss Perry, in *And Gladly Teach*, describes an evening at Norton's in Cambridge during which Howells read aloud some passages from James's *The American Scene*. Perry did not like the much-discussed "third manner." Norton disliked it also, and so did Arthur Sedgwick, but Howells would not admit that there was anything amiss with it. Two or three days later, however, Perry met Norton, who said, "I think I may tell you that Mr. Howells agreed with you entirely about *The American Scene*, but he wouldn't admit it."

the work of many of the younger novelists and poets. He was to describe in prose that period of his early life in *Years of My Youth* and other writings; but Norton had predicted that the thinness and poverty of the American background would have kept him from following the poetic realism of Crabbe.

Meanwhile, Howells sent to Norton a copy of George Ade's *Doc Horne* and told him about this young writer he had met in Chicago, "a nice young fellow, with a regular smooth-shaven face, calm and shrewd." Of George Ade's *Fables in Slang* he said, "His humour is not only a far advance upon the earlier Western humour, but it is a reversion to the still earlier humour of the East in refinement of form." George Ade wrote to Howells, "I am now submerged in the vernacular. . . . Don't cease to hope for me, as I shall get around to the work I like and swear off on Capital Letters sooner or later." Howells noted that town life in America interested our writers very little beside country life or village life,—a condition that changed greatly in another generation,—and he said the people of George Ade's *Artie* were as much native to our soil and air as the New Englanders of Mary E. Wilkins. "Their civilization," he added, "is as ignorant of Europe as Europe could possibly be of them."

Since Howells had broken with Boston and Cambridge and saw Norton less, his letters to this loyal old friend had become more frequent, and on his way down from Kittery Point he sometimes stopped off at "the house of treasure," Shady Hill,—"where there seems more love for me than anywhere outside of my own." After one such visit he said, "My pleasant day with you has already taken on the mist of dreams that overhangs all my Cambridge past"; and he spoke of the bluebirds "plaintively piping the same notes that I heard in your woods forty years ago where once I walked away from your door in a first transport with the friendship which has never failed." He thanked Norton for his translation of Dante, "which I have been looking through this afternoon for my favourite passages, and comparing your English with the Italian which I have in my heart," finding it all "clarity, grace and conscience"; and he wrote asking Norton if he had Giusti's *Proverbi Toscani,* for he was writing a grimmish story he wanted to call by a proverb, "God does not pay Saturdays," which he seemed to remember in that pleasant book. "Does it afflict you," he added, "to find your books wearing out? . . . Just now I went to my old Baretti to see whether *Sabato* was spelt with one *b* or two, and it almost came apart in my hand. It was as if I had found an old friend dying. The mortality of all inanimate things is terrible to me, and that of books most of all, and my library is turning into a cemetery."

Again he wrote, "An English friend has precipitated on me a terrible question, which you alone can answer. Why are the four lions in Niccola Pisano's pulpit [in Siena] gnawing the heads of four horses? In all your delightful account of the Siena cathedral you do not say. Is there no symbolic meaning in the fact, or is it merely a caprice of the sculptor? That hardly seems possible." Of Norton's printing of Ruskin's letters to him, Howells wrote, "The letters are, like most things in these days, immensely pathetic, with their voluntary insolences and involuntary sweetness and affection. They form a terrible picture of the literary temperament, crossed with strange Puritanic misgivings and restraints, and finally bursting through these into madness . . . After that continual tempesting in a teapot, your voice comes clear and cool, like a sound of water flowing and falling." And again, "I copied your praise of Mrs. Wharton's book [*The Valley of*

Decision] into a note I was writing her, and she was greatly pleased and told me of your gift of a doge's letter. I have not read the book yet, dreading somewhat to find Stendhal in it as I find James in her stories. She is a great creature, and I wish she used her own voice solely."

Then, in 1908, Norton wrote to Howells, "I am sliding down hill at rather an accelerated pace, but with no objection to finding myself at the bottom." That year, in fact, Norton died, almost the oldest of Howells's friends in those Boston days that meant youth, "with the shadows westward instead of eastward."

XXIII

OVERLOOKING CENTRAL PARK

IN NEW YORK, Howells and his wife moved uptown, and, before settling for good at 130 West Fifty-Seventh Street, they lived on the south side of Central Park. They often went for drives in a shabby old victoria,—"with our unknown friends, the millionaires,"—and the other drivers knew them as the property of Mr. Broderick, who took a fond interest in them. In the afternoon, Howells usually went for a long walk in the park, sometimes sitting on a bench where squirrels, foraging for nuts, climbed on his knees as if to explore his pockets: they were of a tameness flattering to human pride. He liked to mount the steps to the bust of Schiller where the young writer Ardith watched the young lovers in *Letters Home,* and sometimes he sat in the Mall, unmolested under the trees by the company of some of the worst statues in the world (of which he had known the sculptors in Italy, no doubt). It pleased him to see the art students setting up their easels on the edges of the lawns. Occasionally he sat near the "Indian Hunter" of his old friend J. Q. A. Ward or where the figure of Daniel Webster looked down on the confluence of two driveways. At night, from his windows in winter, he observed the skaters on the pond in the limelight that deepened their flying shadows.

Howells delighted in the careless good nature and friendly

indifference, as he called it, of the vast, sprawling, ungainly city, and he was excited and pleased by all kinds of people. One morning before breakfast he went out to buy some rolls, and the bright little black-eyed German woman at the bakery said to him, "It is not officially *vinter*."—"No," said Howells, "but it is practically . . ." and then, he continued, writing to his sister, "we had some conversation worthy of those cultivated and accurate expressions. How charming and interesting people are! I wish I could live a thousand years, and see more and more of them." He was right in saying that he was a friend of human nature, personally outside all social classes,[1] and that he liked it all the better because it had suffered so much unjust reproach. He called now and then upon Mark Twain when he was living on the Hudson, at Riverdale, where he could see the steamboats passing, a sight that recalled to both Clemens and Howells their early days on rivers in the West.[2] Mark Twain "is the only tie that binds me here to the old times," Howells wrote to one of their common friends, and they could meet there on the old terms. But Howells was once turned away by the gardener, who told Mark Twain he was a stranger, "a stumpy little grey man with

[1] "Yes, I suppose it is well to make some sort of exclusion,
    Well to put up the bars, under whatever pretence;
  Only be careful, be very careful, lest in the confusion
    You should shut yourself on the wrong side of the fence."
          —Howells, *Stops of Various Quills*.

[2] As well as the night-boat to Albany in Howells's first novel, *Their Wedding Journey*: "There is no other travel like river travel: it is the perfection of movement, and one might well desire never to arrive at one's destination. The abundance of room, the free, pure air, the constant delight of the eyes in the changing landscape, the soft tremor of the boat, so steady upon her keel, the variety of the little world on board. . . . There is for the moment nothing more satisfying in life than to have bought your ticket on the night-boat of the Hudson and secured your state-room key an hour or two before departure."

furtive ways and an evil face," who "called me a quadrilateral, incandescent son of a bitch."—"Oh, that was Howells," Mark Twain said to the gardener. "Is that what annoyed you? What's the matter with it? Is that a thing to distort into an offence?" So Mark Twain ran on in his comic letter of apology. Once, when Howells was ill in a hotel, Mark came in his white suit, and the bellboys were so impressed that he was ushered to Howells's room between two rows of them bowing to the floor.

With Mark Twain and several others, among them John Burroughs and Carl Schurz, he once went to dinner at Andrew Carnegie's. It was supposed to be a literary dinner in honour of an English Shakespeare scholar, and Howells found Carnegie rather pathetic, like the young man in the gospel who had great possessions. With his idea of buying off a war by paying the debts of a nation, he was a dreamer, Howells thought, and a kind of poet. When Howells congratulated John Burroughs on going to the Yellowstone to hold bears for the President to kill, this writer seemed to him to have latent misgivings. Howells could say that he agreed with Theodore Roosevelt on the subject of spelling reform, simplified spelling. He wrote an article on "our impudently false orthography . . . our dictionary spelling," and he also agreed with the President about the malefactors of great wealth; but Roosevelt might not have agreed with him about Thorstein Veblen. Howells had reviewed in 1899, more sympathetically than anyone else, Veblen's *The Theory of the Leisure Class*. Believing that everyone should work, he liked this analysis of "conspicuous leisure," the "pecuniary" standard of living and canons of taste that rejected beautiful things if they were not costly. Veblen seemed to him all the more effective because of his passionless calm, and Howells felt that he

opened a new field for novelists, who could present the in-
adequately rendered American life of leisure, translating
Veblen into dramatic terms.

Howells had often been the first to recognize new talents,
beginning with Mark Twain and Henry James, and following with the novelists who were his disciples and with Henry
B. Fuller, Frank Norris and Stephen Crane. He was the
"lookout on the watch-tower," as Theodore Dreiser called him
in an article in *Ainslee's Magazine,* "straining for a first
glimpse of approaching genius"; and he had hopes in New
York of the Jewish writers who might have sprung out of
Harland's early books. He felt that "these children of the
race chosen to attest the creative power in spite of all hardships of condition" might, when they "burst from their pa-
rental Yiddish . . . slake our drouth of imaginative literature."
There was Abraham Cahan, the socialist editor, a "Mary E.
Wilkins of the East Side," whose *Yekl* was followed by *The
Rise of David Levinsky;* and there was Morris Rosenfeld's
Songs of the Ghetto. This, to Howells, was the Song of the
Shirt from one who made the shirt, and not merely the pity-
ing witness who looked on while it was making."[3] It grieved
him to hear that young people were taking up literature as a
business—"the thing that all my life I have fondly dreamed
was an art, dear and almost holy! Are they going into it for the
money there is in it?" But there were others whom he could
admire with a whole heart, and among these was Henry B.
Fuller. Howells had wondered if the "Chicago school" was

[3] "With us the popular taste is so bad, so ignorant, so vulgar, that it sug-
gests the painful doubt whether literacy is a true test of intelligence and a
rightful ground of citizenship. . . . We will go a little further and say
that the literary taste of the Russian Jews on the East Side is superior to that
of the average native American free-library public."—Howells, *Editor's Easy
Chair* in *Harper's,* 1915.

not an outcome of the intense public spirit of the town, which focussed the minds of writers on it,—Robert Herrick, Garland, Dunne, Henry B. Fuller and George Ade with his pictures of "our good, kind, droll, ridiculous American life." Fuller, he thought, had drawn Chicago "with an epic, a panoramic largeness," though Fuller himself said, writing to Howells, "Who wants to read about this repellent town, my allotted field?"

Fuller had read Howells and James when, in 1880, he had first come back from Europe, and these two novelists had weaned him away from Dickens. Now he was writing about Chicago "on the chance of being able to take off the edge of the world's scorn for my birthplace," for he hoped, as he wrote again to Howells, "to raise this dirt pile to some dignity and credit . . . by annexing it to the principality of literature." Howells, who was later momentarily tired of writing his own novels, said, "Can't you see it as your duty to write, hereafter, my novels for me?"—for there was a Howellsian quality in *With the Procession;* and he had praised in *The Cliff Dwellers* "an art that nowhere falters or begs the question." He also said, "Don't forget this old Harlot-by-the-Sea," —New York—"in your virgin metropolis of the prairie!" There was small danger of this in Chicago where, as Charles Whibley wrote to Howells, "They had never heard of H. B. Fuller."

The two young writers whom Howells undoubtedly admired most were Frank Norris and Stephen Crane, whose *Maggie* had been sent to him in 1893 when it had been first privately printed. Howells reviewed it, praising the "grim, not to say the grimy truth" of this tale of a girl of the streets who had become a prostitute and finally committed suicide. It had "that quality of fatal necessity which dominates Greek tragedy," he said, and the note of artistic beauty was "as present in the working out of this poor girl's squalid romance as in any classic fable." Howells went to several bookstores and tried to interest them in the book, and he introduced Crane to other writers, saying, "He can do things that Clemens can't" and "He is a writer who has sprung into life fully armed." He invited Crane to dinner and read to him Emily Dickinson's poems, which he had reviewed in 1890 when virtually nobody had ever heard of her.[4] Shortly afterward, in consequence of this, Crane wrote *Black Riders,*—"the most striking thing of the year," Howells called this book,—poems that Emily Dickinson had largely suggested.

Howells, who liked *George's Mother,* too, said of *Maggie* later, "I shall never understand what was found offensive in the little tragedy," for he had been escaping from what he called, in an essay on Ibsen, "the puritanic narrowness" that "cramps all our race."[5] Still later he said that *Casuals of the Sea,* William McFee's first novel, would be shocking if one viewed it "in the old-fashioned way . . ." but, he added, "why look at it that way?" He said that sexual relations were an important ground "through which the pioneer must break his way," and "it may be it is time that way were broken"; and he who had found Flaubert's *Madame Bovary* "one impassioned cry of the austerest morality" might well have been moved by Dreiser's *Sister Carrie.* But every critic's imagination has a time-limit, and Howells, who had recognized all the

[4] In his review in the "Editor's Study" for December, 1890, Howells had called Emily Dickinson "this most singular and authentic spirit . . . a distinctive addition to the literature of the world." There was "no doubt," he said, "a radiant happiness in the twilight of her hidden, silent life," and her "strange poems will form something like an intrinsic experience with the understanding reader of them."

[5] In an article in 1902, on what young girls should read, Howells said they should read anything they like, except the Woman's Page.

new talents for forty years, may well have had to draw the line at this. Meanwhile, he gave a men's lunch for Stephen Crane at Delmonico's, as he gave one for H. G. Wells, whom he had met in London. After this, Crane, who had scarcely spoken, fell asleep on a sofa in Howells's study. He was at the time twenty-seven years old, and Howells was amused when he spoke of "my youth" and "when I was young."

Stephen Crane, who, as Howells said, found New York "his inspiration, the New York of suffering and baffled and beaten life," admired Howells in his turn[6] as Frank Norris also did,[7] though Norris preferred "the true Romance that far outshines Realism." Howells regarded these two writers as his successors, but on the whole he preferred Norris to Crane, who could only put forth his energy "in nervous spurts, in impulses vivid and keen, but wanting in breadth and bulk of effort." Norris, he said, "heard nothing or seemed to hear nothing, but the full music of his own aspiration, the rich diapason of purposes securely shaping themselves in performance" with his "most conscientious and instructed art." He was, said Howells, after Norris's death, "in the divine secret of the supreme artists" and only lacked, with his master Zola, "the spiritual light and air which the larger art of Tolstoy

[6] "I always thank God that I can have the strongest admiration for the work of a man who has been so much to me personally, for I can imagine the terrors of being indelibly indebted to the Chump in Art or even to the Semi-Chump in Art."—Stephen Crane in an undated letter to Howells.

Stephen Crane dedicated one of his books to Howells as "a token of veneration and gratitude."

[7] "Mr. Howells alone is left . . . after the elimination is complete. Of all producers of American fiction he has had the broadest vision. . . . But one swallow does not make a summer, nor one writer constitute a 'school.' . . . Just as we had with *Lapham* and the *Modern Instance* laid the foundation of a fine, hardy literature that promised to be our very, very own . . . we commenced to build upon it a whole confused congeries of borrowed, faked, pilfered romanticisms."—Frank Norris, *The Responsibilities of the Novelist.*

gives." From Norris, Howells received the impression of strength and courage that would hold out to all lengths, and perhaps it pleased him that Norris had come from "the quarter of the world to which all things are still possible." For so Howells spoke of the West, anticipating Ford Madox Ford. Norris "lived to give us in *McTeague* and the *Octopus* two novels of such signal mastery, so robust, so compact, so vital, and yet so graced with the beauty of an art which came to its consciousness in full maturity, as to merit that comparison which they need not fear with the best of our time." Norris had written to Howells about his review of *McTeague*, "It has encouraged me more than anything that has ever been said of my work."[8]

In one of their meetings Frank Norris outlined to Howells the "continental" plan that could only be carried out after years of study, the story of the wheat that was for him the allegory of "the industrial and financial America which is the real America." To this America Howells himself, like Henry James, felt "very unequal";[9] it was a task that belonged to another generation, and especially to Theodore Dreiser, whose novels were still to appear when he interviewed Howells.

[8] In Frank Norris's *A Lost Story*, Howells appears as Trevor, "the great novelist and critic. . . . The short, rotund, elderly man of letters . . . above the influence of fads." Trevor had seen "a dozen schools . . . rise and fall," and he was "infallible in his judgments of the younger writers . . . all the stages of their evolution were known to him—all their mistakes, all their successes. He understood: and a story by one of them, a poem, a novel, that bore the stamp of his authority was 'sterling.'"

In Frank Norris's *The Pit*, the Chicago capitalist, Curtis Jadwin, who corners the wheat market, likes Howells because he "knows all the Howells people." He loves Silas Lapham as a brother, and he has encountered fifty Bartley Hubbards in La Salle Street.

[9] "Eugenio"—Howells,—"felt very unequal to the whole mighty spectacle of Western Industrial development . . . the giant forms of the Trusts and Distrusts which threaten our peace."—Howells, *The Editor's Easy Chair*, in *Harper's*, 1908.

Dreiser had found him "truly generous and humane . . . one of the noblemen of literature . . . a wholly honest man" with "a wonder at life" that was "fresh and unsatisfied." Howells possessed, moreover, he said, "a deeply religious nature unanchored to any religious belief," and it was this that appealed to Dreiser in some of Howells's later poems, *The Bewildered Guest, Company* and *Friends and Foes.* Dreiser had been keeping a commonplace book for the last five years, and he wished to convey to Howells his "spiritual affection" and "offer my little tribute and acknowledge the benefit I have received from your work." The poems, he wrote, were "a source of never-failing delight to me, and I have often turned to them. The very uncertainty of hope in them seemed to answer some need of fellowship when I can no longer feign to believe that life has either a purpose or a plan . . . Thomas Hardy has provided some of this spiritual fellowship. Count Tolstoy yet some more. Of you three, however, I should not be able to choose, the spirit in each seeming to be the same, and the large tender kindliness in each covering all the ills of life and voicing the wonder and yearning of this fitful dream in what, to me, seems a perfect way . . . The beauty of your mental attitude is enough for me. If the common ground is to be credited with the flowering out of such minds as yours, I shall not be disturbed to return to the dust."[10]

For Howells had been writing poems again, no doubt the best of all his poems, in *Stops of Various Quills* and elsewhere, better than any he had produced since, with *In Earliest Spring,* he commemorated a blustering March day in Cambridge,—

[10] Theodore Dreiser, Letter to Howells, May 14th, 1902.
The poems Dreiser mentioned had all appeared in *Stops of Various Quills.*

Tossing his mane of snows in wildest eddies and tangles,
   Lion-like, March cometh in, hoarse, with tempestuous breath;

and he published in 1903, in London, the fine poem, *Black Cross Farm,* that suggested a rhyming Robert Frost. It was three times longer than any other poem *The Spectator* had ever printed, the editor, J. St. Loe Strachey, wrote to Howells, and it described a long drive on a spring morning through half-lost wood-roads in the New England hills. Amid wild scenery the two companions were looking for an old deserted farm, and, finding it, they discovered a cross painted in black nailed to the door,—no one knew why,—of the vast grey barn. This was not Howells's only work that reminded one of Robert Frost, to whose "very distinctive power" he later paid tribute, for *The Mother and the Father,* dramatic passages based on his own early life, were much in the vein of the author of *North of Boston.* He had written this in 1900 when, as he said, "The shadows acquire a curious density in their eastward slope, and the substances lose flesh, so that I wonder they can cast the shadows."

Nor was Frost the only younger writer of whom one found in Howells precursory notes and touches here and there, in *The Pacific Express,* for instance, a little tale for children that might have been one of Carl Sandburg's *Rootabaga Stories.* It was about a Pony engine that played round the Fitchburg station on the side-tracks and that slept in the car-house among the big locomotives, one of them being its mother, in point of fact. Later, in St. Augustine, Howells found a pathetic interest in the "home-towners" on the Plaza, reading their "home-town" papers and exchanging their personal histories, sitting on the benches near the band-stand; and he began to write a novel to be called *The Home-Towners* that would surely have had much of Ring Lardner in it. He was prepared to think, as he wrote in the "Easy Chair," that "the new Bohemianism of Greenwich Village may have in store such splendour of achievement as shall dim and diminish those glories of the past in New England," and he who had discovered and written about almost every American talent of his time regretted that he could not keep up with the new writers. "I used to hear of every new author," he wrote to Fuller, "but one gets hard of hearing with age."

With the new poets, however, Howells kept up very well. "There is now a great wash of young poetry on these shores," he wrote betimes to Henry James; and, when the so-called Renascence of poetry was in full flood, he said, "There is much more beauty in the new poetry than there was in the old, or, if not that, then in the middle-aged," of the time after Tennyson, Longfellow and Browning. He spoke of Robinson's *Captain Craig* and its "fine manly *go*," of Lindsay's *General Booth* that "makes the heart leap," of the music and colour of Conrad Aiken's *Earth Triumphant*,— with its "somewhat solicited associations,"—and the "extraordinary worth" of the work of Masters. Much as he liked the poems of Stephen Crane, he called the new free verse "shredded prose, with the bark and splinters clinging to it," and he was drawn to Robert Frost all the more because he was "faithful to the lineage of poetry that danced before it walked." Frost, he said, had "always the skill of the artist born and artist trained . . . at play, or call it work, for our delight." Then he signalized, among short stories, Dreiser's *The Lost Phoebe* and Ambrose Bierce's *An Occurrence at Owl Creek Bridge*. The first he called unique in its "plain poetry," while Ambrose Bierce carried further the sort of postmortem consciousness that Tolstoy and Turgenev had been the first to imagine.

XXIV

1920: BEFORE AND AFTER

"Youth lurks about in holes and corners of us as long as we live." So Howells was to remark in *Eighty Years and After,* and he himself continued to feel that he was breaking new ground in each of his later novels and essays of travel. He refused to "keep on doing what's been done already"; and, eager always to study new types, he seemed fresh mentally to the end and never showed any sclerosis of the imagination. The first things we get stiff in are our tastes, not our joints, one of his "recurrent selves" noted in the "Easy Chair,"—Eugenio or the "Higher Journalist" or some other,— and his tastes had never been more tolerant or supple than when they were expected by others to contract and harden. In his mid-seventies, it is true, he lost the physical resiliency of youth, as he realized when he struck the ground, jumping from a carriage, with all the springiness of an iron casting; but he found also that he had no tendency to reject new persons or places or books. At moments the youthful emotions came back, like certain birds in winter, and the heart chirped and twittered as if it had been young.

There were ever-besetting dangers in old age, as Howells observed, indolence, weakening conscience and slovenly performance, that required every atom of one's force to keep one going. Then age was not slow, he found, in its mental motions; it was, on the contrary, hurried and anxious, with that awful mystical apprehension of the swift-coming moment when only eternity would be left and no more time. In the intervals between one book and another, when his friends supposed that he was purposely letting his mind lie fallow, he was really in an anguish of enquiry for something on which to employ his powers, and the incessant agitation of the atoms in the physical world was a faint image of the excruciating state that he was in. His apparent repose was the mask of violent vibrations and volcanic emotions that required, to clear themselves, months of labour. One had lost then, besides, the prevailing censure of earlier years that came from the rivalry, the envy, the emulation of those who had witnessed one's endeavours, their love, hate, approval, disapproval, when no slip or slight defect was lost upon this censure, sympathetic or antipathetic, and always useful. But with age came a relaxing, a withdrawal of this censure; a compassionate toleration followed, or the contempt of indifference; it no longer mattered to the world whether one worked well or ill, and then came the most perilous days of one's years. Then one felt tempted not so much to slight one's work as to spare one's nerves, in which the stored electricity was lower and scanter. One felt tempted to let a feeble performance blight the fame of more strenuous achievements in the past.

To Howells, who continued to love his work, it mattered more and more whether he did this well or ill, and to his last day the "old, great, high affair of literature," as he had once called it, filled his horizon. "We know, being elderly . . . where we are at," his Basil March had said. "We have got all sorts of perspectives and points of view"; and Howells continued to pour out books, good and less good but genuine all, looking towards the future or the past or reflecting the present.

Through the Eye of the Needle concerned the future, *The Kentons* concerned the present, and various others presented scenes of the past,—*Literary Friends and Acquaintance, New Leaf Mills, The Leatherwood God, Years of My Youth*. "In these days I seem to be all autobiography," he had written in 1900, when he was writing *The Father and the Mother;* and he had never ceased to be interested in old Ohio stories and characters from Ohio whom he had imagined or met. One was "the rare American who had never been to Europe," Major Eltwin of *Their Silver Wedding Journey,* in whose talk Basil March "lived back . . . into his own younger days," though he knew he would never return to his native section. It amused and touched him "to find how much the Mid-Western life still seemed the same as he had known." Another was Judge Kenton who lived in Tuskingum in one of those big square brick houses that Howells recollected from his youth in Columbus. The Kentons, all honourable innocence, knew just enough about the world to know that they knew nothing whatever about it.

Years before, Howells had written an essay an Gnaden-hütten and the eighteenth-century massacre of the Moravians there, and he liked to remember the quiet Ohio folk who had lived when he was a boy on the borders of the forest. In those days the great statesmen, not the great millionaires, had been the American ideal, but religion had been the chief interest of the people in their rustic remoteness from the political centres of the still youthful republic. Howells had known some of the families who appeared in *The Leatherwood God,* a story his father had told him about the impostor Dylks, and he evoked the superstition that ran from mind to mind, catch-ing like fire in dry grass. That was the day of camp-meetings in the woods, and Howells might have recalled himself the "jerks" and the mourners' bench as well as the linsey-woolsey and the butternut trousers. He knew all the types he wrote about, Squire Braile, the village infidel, the Reverdys, Laban Billings, the leader of the Hounds, as he knew the benevolent Owen Powell, his own father, in *New Leaf Mills*, who had hoped to "turn over a new leaf" in this backwoods venture. His dream was to establish a sort of Brook Farm there.

From this father Howells had inherited a slowly growing sympathy with socialists, Utopians and the visionary Shakers who reappeared in another novel of these later years which he had thought of calling *The Children of the Summer*. Finally entitled *The Vacation of the Kelwyns*, it was an idyll of the eighteen-seventies, a story of the golden age, as it seemed to Howells, the years when he had first explored New England. Professor Kelwyn, the Harvard sociologist, rented for the summer, with his family, a big house of the Shakers, a community already in decay, and a romance arose between the niece Parthenope and the "experimental" Emerance who kept reappearing. It was the day of Eastlake furniture and Morris wall-paper, when Ruskin was the authority over architecture and much was still expected of the Gothic, though "cities and suburbs were filled with empirical guesses in brick and wood that were to remain the wonder of posterity." Parthenope had inherited a wilding quality from her artist father and mother; she was a sculptor's daughter, born in Naples, who was left "mostly to her own inspirations and conduct," and there was a mysterious note in Emerance's nature that "seemed to turn the prose of every day into the poetry of every other day." He and Parthenope wandered about in the pleasant countryside where the hills were lighted up with the stems of birches and the mill-ponds were starred with yellow lilies that looked like flights of canary birds

stooping on the water. It all somehow recalled *The Undiscovered Country*. An Irish linen-pedlar appeared, a bear with
a leader from the mountains near Toulouse, an organ-grinder
from Genoa and a van of Gypsies. The book had the dream-
like atmosphere of *The Blithedale Romance*: it was altogether
very Hawthornesque.

Howells was looking backward here to the first summers in
New England which he sometimes spent in farm boarding-
houses; and he was thinking much of the Cambridge of that
time, of which he wrote in 1903 (he had been reading some
old letters): "The old Cambridge returned with all its bright
ghosts. The midsummer air . . . was hushed and tense with
the past; and I realized once more what a grand passion the
place used to be with me. I doubt if anyone born to it could
have loved it as I did." Then Boston had been "frosty at the
edges but genuinely cordial at heart," he said, feeling that
Henry Adams had been rather unjust in the *Education*;[1] and
one winter he returned to spend some months on Beacon
Hill, "now largely inhabited by ghosts . . . a ghost myself."
There was "too much past" in Boston, he wrote to a friend,
although "the past is everywhere for such a vagabond as I
have been"; and he was "almost ready to say . . . that one
had better never go back anywhere," for "you are not on
terms with those old selves" whom you encounter as "old
ghosts." In earlier days he had held all *Atlantic* readers at his
mercy; he had given them to read whatever he chose; and
at that time even society veterans like Bromfield Corey had
been obliged to be intellectual men. But now Boston seemed

[1] When the American Academy of Arts and Letters was being formed,
Howells wrote to the secretary in 1904, "First, and all the time, I vote for
Henry Adams." Howells was elected the first President of the Academy in
1908 and was continually reëlected until his death in 1920.

to him a society that neither idealized nor read nor thought. It was true that one felt in Boston the old authors whom one no longer saw, while, in New York, "the immense slattern mother," one never felt the character of her great children. But, as a "conditional New Yorker of long sojourn," in his phrase, he liked its lighter-minded civilization.

Howells thought that, after a real country circus, there were not many things in life that were better than the New York Hippodrome, and one day in 1912 he took Thomas Sergeant Perry there,—the "poor dear consistently pessimistic Tom Perry." So Henry James called this very old common friend, who wrote in turn to him that Howells, "the tenderest and most amiable of men," was "revelling in anarchy and social upheaval and all modern improvements." For Howells at seventy-five was as radical as ever, and he was pleased when, after the beginning of the first world-war,[2] the government took over public facilities as a war measure. He hoped that "the people's management of their own affairs" might be continued in the future. Meanwhile, he carried on with Perry a notable conversation on "Recent Russian Fiction" that was presently published.[3] Perry, who had introduced both Howells and James to Turgenev, had visited Russia himself in 1908, and he had found that Chekhov's plays seemed not to be constructed, not built up, yet hung together beautifully without any apparent architecture. Perry thought that the

[2] "The German war on mankind," as Howells called it. He felt obliged, in 1916, to write a letter to the New York *Evening Post* protesting against "the cruel folly of the English government in putting its Irish prisoners to death. . . . What an infinite pity! She has left us who loved her cause in the war against despotism without another word to say for her until we have first spoken our abhorrence of her inexorable legality in dealing with her Irish prisoners."

[3] In the *North American Review* for July, 1912.

simplicity of the Russian novelists was possible because of their want of a literary past, that they had "simply grown up," as he felt in reading the French translations; for, while Tolstoy wrote as if he was writing a letter to his aunt, the French always introduced "old faded flowers of rhetoric." Now he pointed out to Howells how Artzybashev described with almost absolute nakedness, with the utmost simplicity, but also with spiritual feeling; and Howells, who felt that the novelist's business was merely "to see and record," supposed that if he was an artist he would not have "much philosophy."— "I don't think he has any," Perry said. "He is like the cinematograph." He was, in short, a camera eye. Howells, who had written his tribute for Tolstoy's eightieth birthday, saying that he had awakened the conscience of mankind, noted how, from first to last, from Gogol to Gorky and Artzybashev, "the same ideal was continuous in that wonderful Slavic race."

That was the year, 1912, of the seventy-fifth birthday dinner that Howells's publishers gave for him at Sherry's, a dinner at which there were four hundred guests and among them President Taft who had come up from Washington for the occasion. Letters of praise were written for this by Thomas Hardy, H. G. Wells, Henry James and others in America and England, and Howells said again that "our fiction so far as it really exists is of the European and not the English make." Then he surveyed the lifetime during which he had seen a whole literature grow up and flourish into national proportions. A year before, at the suggestion of Edith Wharton and Edmund Gosse, he had written to the secretary of the Swedish Academy to recommend Henry James for the Nobel prize. "He is mortified and subdued," wrote Gosse, "by a poverty which makes us disregard all the civilities in other cases," and, appealing to Howells as "manifestly the leader of American literature," he added that the English committee already backed Henry James. But James did not receive the prize and Howells continued to puzzle over his "baffling failure of immediate acceptance." The last paper he was ever to write, after his last letter, was to be on Henry James, and even in their death they were not divided; for Howells and James were both to be buried in the Cambridge cemetery, scarcely more than a hundred yards apart. "You have greatly and nobly lived for brave as well as beautiful things," Howells had written to James a few years before, adding, "On the whole I should say your worship was spreading among us. You are he on whom the aspiring eyes are bent of those who hope to do something themselves."

Mark Twain had died in 1910 and, three weeks later, Mrs. Howells, after a marriage of forty-eight years that spanned the whole of Howells's literary life. They had met first in Columbus, and no doubt it was of her he had thought when he said that Isabel March "tenderly begrudged his having existed before she knew him and longed to ally herself retrospectively with his past." After her death he discovered in himself what he called the dual life that Bartley Hubbard found in *A Modern Instance,* the strange separation of the intellectual activity from the part that suffers, "by which the mind toils on in a sort of ironical indifference to the pangs that wring the heart." He was, he said, as happy as ever in his work. Then, soon thinking of his old friend Clemens, "a man nearer and dearer to his generation than any other author," he wrote the little book, *My Mark Twain,* celebrating Mark Twain's "great burly fancy," together with the magnificence of his imagination. He might have said, with John

Hay, his thick-and-thin admirer who had written to him in 1903, "The solitude deepens around me year by year."[4]

As ever a nomad, Howells, in his later years, began going South, usually with his daughter, in the winter, whether to St. Augustine, Charleston or Savannah, or to Bermuda, which reminded him of Venice. With its lagoon-like expanses, it wanted only a few gondolas to complete the coming and going illusion and there the trees simply dropped their leaves when they were tired of keeping them on and put out others when they felt like it. Twice he went to Savannah, with its wooded and gardened squares full of the milky streaming of the dogwood blossoms, and he loved St. Augustine, with the wooden balconies drooping from the walls of time-stained coquina. The air, the sky, the live-oaks there with the mocking-birds lyrically nesting in them, and the old city gates from which Charles McKim borrowed the design for his gates at Harvard, brought back, with the architecture of the seventies and eighties, the time when St. Augustine had chiefly flourished. The names of Constance Fenimore Woolson and her *East Angels* were cherished then, and the city promised to remain the permanent winter resort of the whole sneezing and coughing North. Then the American girl prevailed in the excess of fashion that she still exploited everywhere but with a mother distractedly struggling to keep up with her and a helpless father fettered to her high-heeled shoes.

Howells noted that the manner and tone that were still called *fin de siècle* were more akin to the *fin de siècle* of a

---

[4] "I wish I might see you oftener. I have no gossip left but Henry Adams and we quarrel like cat and dog. It is wholesome, I know, to be told what an ass I am, and what ignoble company I keep, and Adams deals faithfully with me. But it's only for a month or two each year. Then he scuttles away to Paris and lives in the Thirteenth Century. The solitude deepens around me year by year."—John Hay, Letter to Howells, 1903.

hundred years before than they were to the temper of the
world that he had known, and when *Harper's* refused one
of his articles he realized that his vogue had passed after his
"inevitable acceptance" for more than half a century. He had
written to one of his friends, in the vein of Heine, "I am
comparatively a dead cult with my statues cut down and the
grass growing over them in the pale moonlight." Readers no
longer asked themselves what was to happen in his books;
they seldom talked about them or even bought them; and the
so-called Library Edition of his work that was to fill thirty
volumes or more was suspended after six volumes were published. The most eminent American man of letters was not
half as well known to the new generation as any one of a
dozen English writers. "When I was young many praised me,"
Howells had written in 1912; "then came scornings and
buffetings from every side," even before Ambrose Bierce said
that Howells's readers were mostly "oleaginous clergymen"
and "fibrous virgins." Then Mencken called Howells "a
placid conformist,"—albeit the creator of a "pungent and admirable style,"—a chronicler of small beer, trivial, monotonous
and superficial, as Trollope, after his death, was said to have
been. Howells, like Zola, was obliged to swallow his toad
every day, and he said to a fellow-novelist, referring to critics,
"You'll find they can still hurt you long after their power to
please you is gone." He even received one day from a "home
correspondence school" an invitation to take lessons in story-
writing, with small regard for the vanity of the aged author
of a hundred books whose name appeared in all the encyclo-
pædias. He did not indulge in what he called "the morbid
desire authors have to press their bosoms against a thorn if
they can find one in print"; but he remarked somewhere

that history was "an unwilling guest in our unmemoried land."

In short, Howells came to be treated as a valley of humiliation between two mountains of pride,—like North Carolina, —the mountains being Mark Twain and Henry James; and, although he had been scarcely more fecund than these others, he had without any doubt written too much. Two out of every three of his novels had been inferior to the best; and he had perhaps a defect of virility, as Walt Whitman said of him, "fine, cute, subtle" as he was. He may have been too sane to seem exciting, and this might have explained why he could not command the homage of a time that was wholly submissive to the "power of blackness." But there were ten or a dozen novels of this more poetic American Trollope that were destined to be read in a long future,[5] and he was "to remain embedded," in Henry B. Fuller's words, "as a definite, integral and respected figure in the national literature." He had "swept the whole horizon of his time," one friendly critic said, so that other American novelists seemed local beside him, or, if not local, episodic; and, if his picture of the "Howells age" was necessarily fragmentary, it was because of the decentralized nature of the country. No one ever registered as Howells did its customs, traditions and thoughts, but American society was too scattered and too thin for anyone to record it with a massive effect. When so many wrote with their foot on the loud pedal, so to speak, Howells's scarcely heard melodies were not always even audible; but he had a secret in what Kipling called "the charm by which he wrought upon men in remote countries." Then he was

[5] *The Undiscovered Country, A Modern Instance, Indian Summer, The Rise of Silas Lapham, The Shadow of a Dream, A Hazard of New Fortunes, The Quality of Mercy, The Landlord at Lion's Head, April Hopes, The Son of Royal Langbrith, The World of Chance, Letters Home.*

"the father of a multitude of heirs who have inherited his treasures but forgotten the paternity. Time will prove it so," Kipling continued, "and your land's literature will acknowledge it." For the rest, "He had the natural kindness of the good and the utter simplicity of a great man."

INDEX

INDEX